CHURCH GROWTH IN BRITAIN

There has been substantial church growth in Britain between 1980 and 2010. This is the controversial conclusion from the international team of scholars, who have drawn on interdisciplinary studies and the latest research from across the UK. Such church growth is seen to be on a large scale, is multi-ethnic and can be found across a wide range of social and geographical contexts. It is happening inside mainline denominations but especially in specific regions such as London, in newer churches and amongst ethnic minorities.

Church Growth in Britain provides a forceful critique of the notion of secularisation which dominates much of academia and the media – and which conditions the thinking of many churches and church leaders. This book demonstrates that, whilst decline is happening in some parts of the church, this needs to be balanced by recognition of the vitality of large swathes of the Christian church in Britain. Rebalancing the debate in this way requires wholesale change in our understanding of contemporary British Christianity.

D0145795

Ashgate Contemporary Ecclesiology

Series Editors
Martyn Percy, Ripon College Cuddesdon, Oxford, UK
D. Thomas Hughson, Marquette University, USA
Bruce Kaye, Charles Sturt University, Australia

Series Advisory Board
James Nieman; Sathi Clarke; Gemma Simmonds CJ; Gerald West;
Philip Vickeri; Helen Cameron; Tina Beattie; Nigel Wright; Simon Coleman

The field of ecclesiology has grown remarkably in the last decade, and most especially in relation to the study of the contemporary church. Recently, theological attention has turned once more to the nature of the church, its practices and proclivities, and to interpretative readings and understandings on its role, function and ethos in contemporary society.

This new series draws from a range of disciplines and established scholars to further the study of contemporary ecclesiology and publish an important cluster of landmark titles in this field. The Series Editors represent a range of Christian traditions and disciplines, and this reflects the breadth and depth of books developing in the Series. This Ashgate series presents a clear focus on the contemporary situation of churches worldwide, offering an invaluable resource for students, researchers, ministers and other interested readers around the world working or interested in the diverse areas of contemporary ecclesiology and the important changing shape of the church worldwide.

Church Growth in Britain

1980 to the Present

Edited by

DAVID GOODHEW
Cranmer Hall, Durham, UK

ASHGATE

© David Goodhew 2012

Published by
Ashgate Publishing Limited
Wey Court East
Union Road
Farnham
Surrey, GU9 7PT
England

Ashgate Publishing Company
Suite 420
101 Cherry Street
Burlington
VT 05401-4405
USA

www.ashgate.com

British Library Cataloguing in Publication Data
Church growth in Britain : 1980 to the present. -- (Ashgate
 contemporary ecclesiology)
 1. Church growth--Great Britain--History--20th century.
 2. Church growth--Great Britain--History--21st century.
 3. Great Britain--Church history--20th century. 4. Great
 Britain--Church history--21st century.
 I. Series II. Goodhew, David, 1965-
 274.1'082-dc23

Library of Congress Cataloging-in-Publication Data
Church growth in Britain : 1980 to the present / edited by David Goodhew.
      p. cm. -- (Ashgate contemporary ecclesiology)
  Includes bibliographical references (p.   ) and index.
  ISBN 978-1-4094-2577-9 (hardcover) -- ISBN 978-1-4094-2576-2
(pbk) -- ISBN 978-1-4094-2578-6 (ebook) 1. Church
growth--Great Britain. 2. Christianity--Great Britain--History. I.
Goodhew, David, 1965-
 BR759.C458 2012
 274.1'0828--dc23

2011050167

9781409425779 (hbk)
9781409425762 (pbk)
9781409425786 (ebk)

Printed and bound in Great Britain by the
MPG Books Group, UK.

Church decline is neither inevitable in prospect nor accurate in retrospect. This book reviews the reality of what is happening in Christian religious practice in the UK. As such it comes at a crucial time, when the Church of England appears to be gathering the will to change, and when an accurate and reasoned understanding of what is really happening, and has done so since 1980, is essential.

The Rt Revd Justin Welby, Bishop of Durham

Church Growth in Britain *is a welcome and well researched challenge to the widespread assumption that Christianity in Britain is suffering terminal decline. Without pretending that there is no significant demise in some areas or that its findings will not provoke robust debate, the "mosaic of micro-studies" in this book illustrates the vitality, depth and breath of Christianity within the United Kingdom. Its central thesis certainly reflects what I witness when visiting the parishes of the Archdiocese of Westminster. For there I see people's faith shaping their everyday lives such that Christ is truly present in the streets of our land.*

Archbishop Vincent Nichols, Archbishop of Westminster
and President of the Catholic Bishops' Conference of England and Wales

Church Growth in Britain *is a timely book with a polemic point. Contrary to received wisdom, David Goodhew and his associates argue that Christianity is thriving in Britain-but Christianity of sorts that fall under conventional radar screens. The book will draw cheers from the minority of like-minded observers, serious critical attention from a broad middle, and no doubt counterattacks from the sociological and religious establishments whose standpoints are attacked. Yet the book's most telling observations are made only partly through pointed argument and mostly through calm and informative case studies of overlooked churches.*

R. Stephen Warner, University of Illinois at Chicago, USA

What I particularly liked about this book was the way it brought out, in serious historical perspective, the very different situations in which churches find themselves according to particular environments and the kinds of strategies that revive growth. The divinity lies in the detail and there is much genuine divinity in this volume.

David Martin, Emeritus Professor, and Fellow of the British Academy

We have needed a wide-ranging academic book on church growth for a long time - and now we have one. Church growth is not just a subject for "how to" books, and here we have careful, evidenced work to encourage further reflection and action. This is a wise and timely study.

The Rt Revd John Pritchard, The Bishop of Oxford, UK

During the last 30 years we have all become familiar with shrinking congregations and churches closing. But few people realise that the same period has seen the opening of several thousand new churches across the UK. And while the larger denominations have all lost members, other smaller denominations, as well as many independent congregations have grown. This fascinating collection of case-studies shows how and where this has happened, and suggests why. It also provides a convincing account of how the nature of religion in our country has changed as a result.

Hugh McLeod, Emeritus Professor, University of Birmingham, UK

An excellent collection. It is commonly supposed that the Christian church in Britain is moribund, but the essays in this volume all demonstrate, from different angles, that in the recent past there are signs of vitality and growth. Nor is the vigour confined to new churches, for mainstream bodies have also partipated in the upward trend here depicted with scholarly care.

David Bebbington, Professor of History, University of Stirling, UK

I have been waiting for someone to write this book!

Rodney Stark, Distinguished Professor of the Social Sciences and co-director of the Institute for Studies of Religion, Baylor University, USA

This book tells us the untold story of church growth in this country over the last thirty years. It's scholarly, easy to read, and full of hope and optimism ... I thoroughly recommend it to you.

Revd Canon Roger Simpson, Archbishop's Evangelist to the North

Contents

List of Figures and Tables

Figures

Tables

List of Contributors

The Revd Lynda Barley was Head of Research and Statistics for the Archbishops' Council of the Church of England, prior to her recent appointment as Truro Diocesan Secretary and Canon Pastor at Truro Cathedral.

Dr Richard Burgess is Research Fellow in the School of Philosophy, Theology and Religion, University of Birmingham.

Dr Rebecca Catto is Research Associate for the AHRC/ESRC Religion and Society Programme, based at the University of Lancaster.

Dr Paul Chambers is Senior Lecturer in Sociology and Subject Group Leader for Social Policy in the Faculty of Business and Society, University of Glamorgan.

Amy Duffuor has recently completed an M.Phil in Migration Studies at the University of Oxford.

The Revd Dr David Goodhew is Director of Ministerial Practice at Cranmer Hall, St John's College, Durham.

Dr Alana Harris is Darby Fellow in History, Lincoln College, Oxford.

The Ven Bob Jackson is lecturer at St John's College, Nottingham, a Visiting Fellow of St John's College, Durham, a church growth consultant and the former Archdeacon of Walsall.

The Revd Canon Dr. George Lings is Director of the Sheffield Centre, the Research Unit for the Church Army.

Dr Claire Mitchell is a freelance researcher, formerly a senior lecturer at the Department of Sociology, Queens University, Belfast.

The Revd Dr Colin Marsh is Ecumenical Development Officer for Birmingham Churches Together.

The Revd Dr Hugh Osgood is the Senior Minister of Cornerstone Christian Centre, Bromley, London and the founding President of Churches in Communities International.

The Revd Dr Ian Randall is Senior Research Fellow, Spurgeon's College, London and International Baptist Theological Seminary, Prague.

Professor Ken Roxburgh is St Louis and Ann W. Armstrong Professor of Religion and Chair of the Department of Religion, Samford, Alabama.

Professor John Wolffe is Professor of Religious History at the Open University.

Acknowledgements

There are a number of people who richly deserve thanks for their help in bringing the project to fruition.

First and foremost, the contributors have shown commendable patience with all that has been asked of them and considerable juggling skills in ensuring that the project was finished on time.

Michael Thate acted as my research assistant in the final stages of production. His assiduous hunting down of material, careful editing and stimulating comments have been extremely helpful in bringing the book into being.

The staff and students of Cranmer Hall and the Wesley Study Centre constitute a highly stimulating environment in which to work through the ideas propounded in this book. David Wilkinson, as Principal of St John's College, Durham provided crucial support which ensured the project could be finished. Michael Volland and Joanildo Burity provided perceptive sounding boards towards the end of the writing. David Bebbington, Grace Davie, Rodney Stark and Stephen Warner provided wise comments and encouragement at the outset of the project.

Sarah Lloyd has been the primary link with Ashgate and has been unfailingly thoughtful, encouraging and wise. Sophie Lumley, Barbara Spender and David Shervington provided crucial help in preparing the manuscript for publication.

A wide range of libraries, churches and individuals have given generously of their time in enabling the research of this volume to be drawn together. On behalf of myself and all the contributors, we wish to express our gratitude both for that help and for all that you have taught us.

My wife, Lindsey, and our children Aidan and Benjamin have shown commendable patience with a distracted husband and dad during the preparation of *Church Growth*. I am immensely grateful to them for this – and much more besides.

David Goodhew
Cranmer Hall
Durham

PART I
Introduction

Chapter 1

Church Growth in Britain, 1980 to the Present Day

David Goodhew

It is a truth almost universally acknowledged that Christianity in Britain is in decline.[1] However, not all universally acknowledged truths are actually true. *Some* churches in *some* regions are declining, but this volume shows that substantial and sustained church growth has *also* taken place across Britain over the last 30 years. This growth is large-scale; it is occurring across a wide geographical range; it is highly multi-cultural in its social reach; and it shows no sign of slowing down. The current consensus, by focusing almost exclusively on decline, is seriously mistaken. The thesis of this book is sustained by the work of an international team of scholars, working across a spectrum of disciplines, coming from a variety of theoretical and ideological perspectives.

Thus, for example, there are now 500,000 Christians in black majority churches in Britain. Sixty years ago there were hardly any. Across the 30 years since 1980 new congregations have been founded at an average of one per year in a single medium-sized northern city, the city of York. Even the contemporary Church of England is not immune from church growth. The membership of the Anglican diocese of London, the largest Anglican diocese in the country, has grown by over 70% since 1990.[2]

Such developments are no cause for ecclesiastical triumphalism, given the extent of church decline elsewhere. But this narrative of *Church Growth in Britain* subverts the dominant narrative in much of academia and the media, a narrative which heavily influences many church leaders as well as wider society. The dominant narrative assumes that there has been wholesale church decline in recent decades and that such decline is the primary reality of British Christianity. The dominant narrative, called by some the 'secularization thesis', is, in part,

---

[1]   The dominant studies of contemporary British Christianity all assume decline, the only difference being whether decline is seen as gradual or cataclysmic: see works by Callum Brown, Steve Bruce, Robin Gill, Grace Davie, Linda Woodhead and Paul Heelas. These, along with the wider literature on church decline, are discussed on pp. 10–17.

[2]   See Chapter 9, A. Duffuor, 'Moving Up and Moving Out'; Chapter 11, D. Goodhew, 'From the Margins to the Mainstream' and Chapter 2, J. Wolffe and B. Jackson, 'Anglican Resurgence'. See also R. Warner, *Secularisation and its Discontents* (London: Continuum, 2010), p. 161.

correct. Most 'mainline' denominations have seen large falls in support.[3] The aim of *Church Growth in Britain* is not to airbrush out such decline but to highlight the sides of the story which have been hitherto marginalized. Since church decline is widely publicized and church growth is almost totally ignored in wider debate, the focus of this volume is on church growth. Such growth is a matter of deep significance both for the churches and for wider society.

Is Christianity in Britain, overall, declining or growing? One of the key findings of this volume is that overall statistics regarding Christian churches in Britain need to be treated with considerable caution. Some attempt at an overall assessment will be offered in the conclusion, but all national figures concerning churches need to be taken with a pinch of salt. An example of the problematic nature of national statistics is provided by initial data for the 2011 British Census, which shows that, whilst only 47% of 18 to 34 year olds declared themselves to have any religious affiliation, 67% (or more) of the same age group also declared that they occasionally or regularly pray.[4] The philosopher Alasdair MacIntyre once stated that whilst the English do not believe in God, they do like to pray to Him from time to time. MacIntyre's diagnosis is well illustrated by the contradictory data of the 2011 Census.

This volume starts in a different place. *Church Growth in Britain* is contemporary church history written 'from below'. The focus is not on national statistics, nor on national leadership via bishops, synods or conferences, but on local congregations and particular neighbourhoods. This volume is a mosaic of micro-studies; from Catholics in Canning Town to Brazilian Pentecostals in York to new churches in Edinburgh. But mosaics are more than random arrangements and can portray complex realities. This mosaic of micro-studies is assembled so that it includes the global backdrop of belief. *Church Growth in Britain* offers a 'glocalized' picture, in which the local and global are interwoven. The volume focuses on congregational life and particular regions, rather than national statistics or measures of the national significance of Christianity, not because the wider picture is unimportant, but because national observations often miss local dynamics, because congregational life is at the core of Christian identity and because the argument for the secularization of Britain rests heavily on the presumption that local congregations are in deep decline.[5] The ultimate test for secularization is not what opinion polls say but what is happening out on the street.

---

[3]   See P. Brierley, *Pulling out of the Nosedive: A Contemporary Picture of Churchgoing* (London: Christian Research, 2006) pp. 21–49.

[4]   www.yougov.polis.cam.ac.uk/archive, accessed on 21 September 2011. Regarding prayer, 67% of those aged 18 to 34 said they prayed regularly or occasionally, 26% said they never prayed and 7% said they didn't know whether they prayed or not. The religious census shows that attitudes to belief are highly contradictory and that the type of question asked heavily determines the kind of result given. Any conclusions based on such data should be accompanied with an ideological health warning.

[5]   The continuing influence of a more diffuse Christian Britain has been well charted in J. Garnett (et al), *Redefining Christian Britain: Post 1945 Perspectives* (London: SCM, 2006).

This introductory chapter has four sections: first it summarizes the findings of the volume; second, it compares those findings with the secularization thesis and other theoretical perspectives; third, it offers a chronological overview, situating British church growth historically; fourth, it explores the theoretical implications of church growth for theology and for other disciplines.

Section One: Church Growth in Britain since 1980

The volume is divided into four parts: the first part (this chapter) introduces the debates about church growth and decline and summarizes this volume's contribution; the second part (Chapters 2 to 6) surveys the older, 'mainline' churches; the third part (Chapters 7 to 12) surveys new churches (where 'new' means founded within the last century); the fourth part looks at Northern Ireland, Wales and Scotland. This is followed by a brief conclusion in which the arguments are tied together and an agenda for further work is sketched.

The key findings of *Church Growth in Britain* can be summarized under the following headings.

Church Growth in London

Chapters 2 and 3 focus on London. John Wolffe and Bob Jackson explore the large-scale growth of the Anglican diocese of London during the last 20 years in which church membership has expanded by over 70%. Whilst many Anglican dioceses outside London are shrinking – some rapidly – London offers a very different trajectory. Alana Harris looks at a single Roman Catholic parish in the East End of London, showing how the latter's traditional role as a haven for immigrants is leading to dramatic (and hugely diverse) church growth in Catholic London. A number of other chapters, particularly those concerning black majority churches, point to major growth in the capital.[6] The Christian church in London is growing both in absolute terms and as a proportion of the population.[7] London, in its burgeoning Christianity, is becoming more like American cities such as New York or Chicago which are very far from being 'secular cities' (this is especially the case if we add in the growth of other faith communities).[8] Steve Bruce says of the secularization thesis, that 'what would threaten the paradigm is sustained

---

[6]   See Chapter 2, J. Wolffe and B. Jackson, 'Anglican Resurgence'; Chapter 7, H. Osgood, 'Rise of Black Churches'; B. Burgess, 'African Pentecostal Growth', Chapter 9, A. Duffuor, 'Moving up and Moving Out'. and P. Brierley, *Pulling out of the Nosedive*, pp. 44–46.

[7]   J. Wolffe and B. Jackson, 'Anglican Resurgence', p. 23.

[8]   T. Carnes and A. Karpathakis, *New York Glory: Religions in the City* (New York: New York University Press, 2001); L. Livesey, *Public Religion and Urban Transformation: Faith in the City* (New York: New York University Press, 2000).

and widespread growth in places that were previously secular'.[9] Leaving aside the experience of nations such as Russia and China, something like this is happening in contemporary London.

Growth in Mainline Churches

Examination of London indicates that, whilst across the whole of Britain there is much evidence of decline amongst the long-established, 'mainline' denominations,[10] mainline churches have the capacity to grow in some contexts. Chapters 4 and 5 explore this phenomenon by looking at signs of life in very different sections of the mainline churches. Ian Randall explores the robust performance of the Baptist denomination across the last three decades; it is a performance which raises uncomfortable questions for the other mainline churches as to why they declined but the Baptists did not. Lynda Barley shows the continuing vitality of English cathedral congregations. Sunday worship has remained stable over recent years, but weekday worship has mushroomed. This raises the question of why traditional forms of Christian worship in cathedrals are growing when, for the most part, they are declining elsewhere.[11] More broadly, evidence of mainline growth could be extended by examination of growing networks such as New Wine, which are backed primarily by mainline congregations.[12]

In Chapter 6, Rebecca Catto explores the notion of 'reverse mission' in mainline denominations – where Christians from outside Britain are invited to boost worshipping life here. What is striking is its limited impact on mainline churches, especially compared to the huge growth of black majority churches across the same decades, as shown in later chapters of this volume. This suggests that mainline churches continue to fail to release the energies of black, asian and minority ethnic Christians within their ranks.

Church Growth and Minority Ethnic Communities

Discussion of London leads onto a recurring and central theme of the book: the very substantial growth of black and other ethnic minority churches in Britain in recent decades. This is the heart of Chapters 7, 8 and 9 but this thread runs throughout this volume. Until the 1950s, there were hardly any black majority churches in Britain. Hugh Osgood's overview in Chapter 6 shows the way this stream of Christianity began, deepened and widened as the black, asian and minority ethnic communities have grown. Richard Burgess' chapter on the Nigerian Redeemed Christian Church of God shows the same process with regard to a specific new

---

[9]   S. Bruce, *God is Dead: Secularisation in the West* (Oxford: Blackwell, 2002), p. 173.

[10]   P. Brierley, *Pulling out of the Nosedive*, pp. 21–49.

[11]   Ibid., pp. 52–53.

[12]   B. Jackson, *The Road to Growth: Towards a Thriving Church* (London: Church House Publishing, 2005), pp. 106–10.

denomination which has shown startling energy in church planting in the last three decades. In a superb, fresh piece of research, Amy Duffuor explores a single, rapidly expanding, congregation of Ghanaian Pentecostals in Peckham as they plant a new church in the suburbs of London, facing the question of whether the social upliftment that church membership offers to members will blunt the edge of their discipleship in the long run. Black, asian and minority ethnic church growth brings challenges as well as possibilities.

Church Growth and New Churches

A further theme of *Church Growth in Britain* is the substantial growth of new churches and of new forms of church. Chapter 11 explores the city of York, showing the extraordinary shift within a single city. One congregation per year has been founded across the last three decades and the rate of foundation has accelerated since 2000. George Lings gives a history of what has been termed 'fresh expressions' of church, 'church plants' and 'emerging church' within the Church of England, showing how they have moved from being rare in the early 1980s to numbering well over a thousand and being attended by tens of thousands in the present day. He writes as a participant in this story and his chapter has something of the quality of oral history. Lings' chapter shows how Anglican churches are, in part, borrowing models conceived either outside the UK or by new, non-mainstream UK churches. He concludes that these 'fresh expressions' and church plants have great potential, but also that some are fragile. Colin Marsh closes the section on new churches by looking at the city of Birmingham, showing that those strands of Christianity which were on the margins a few decades ago – such as black majority churches and new churches – are beginning to overtake the 'mainline' churches in one major British city. This chimes with other chapters to indicate the significance of newer denominations in contemporary Britain.

The number of new churches, from all denominations, that have started up since 1980 is startling. One detailed study by Peter Brierley calculated that 2,950 new churches were started between 1989 and 2005.[13] Chapters from this book – notably those in Part 2 – reinforce Brierley's figures and suggest that this momentum was in place prior to 1989 and has been sustained after 2005.[14] Calculating the precise number of churches started in Britain between 1980 and the present is difficult; those who are the most dynamic in their ecclesiastical entrepreneurship are also the least interested in the statistical record. Based on a range of studies, it is likely that over 5,000 new churches have been started in Britain in the 30 years since 1980

---

[13] P. Brierley, *Pulling out of the Nosedive*, p. 10.

[14] See Chapter 7, H. Osgood, 'Rise of Black Churches'; Chapter 8, R. Burgess, 'African Pentecostal Growth'; Chapter 11, D. Goodhew, 'From the Margins to the Mainstream' and Chapter 10, G. Lings, 'A History of Fresh Expressions'.

– probably significantly more.[15] However, until further research is undertaken, the number of new churches in Britain cannot be estimated with precision. To put these numbers into some kind of scale, the number of new churches started since 1980 is substantially greater than the total number of Roman Catholic churches in England and equivalent to one third of all Church of England churches. It is likely that as many churches have opened as have closed in Britain during the last three decades – although within any given region the balance may tilt in the direction of decline or growth. Newspaper headlines and book covers which presuppose vast numbers of church closures are misleading in their failure to note the similarly substantial number of new churches which are opening.[16] The sheer number of churches opening and closing vividly illustrates the extent of growth *and* decline in recent British Christianity.

Church Growth, Demography and Economics

A key finding of this volume is the way that church growth in contemporary Britain is most common in areas of migration, population growth and economic dynamism. Corridors of church growth have developed alongside major economic arteries such as the A1 and the east coast mainline and the growing cities to be found on those arteries – as the chapters on London, York and Edinburgh show.[17] Paul Chambers' chapter on Wales shows how church growth can happen outside of these zones, but is significantly harder.[18] That church growth is more pronounced in areas of population growth and economic dynamism does *not* mean that growing churches are populated by the well-off. As the various chapters show, church growth connects with a wide social spectrum. Moreover, there are proven connections between societal affluence and secularity.[19] Just as the early church

---

[15]   If new churches in England had been founded at the same rate prior to 1989 and after 2005, as for the period covered by Brierley's study, then the total number founded between 1980 and 2010 would be around 5,500. This volume has shown how even detailed academic studies tend to undercount the number of new churches and that there is evidence to suggest that the rate of new church start-ups has increased during the last decade. Taken together the evidence suggests that the figure of 5,000 is probably a substantial underestimate of the number of new churches founded between 1980 and 2010. See Chapter 7, H. Osgood, 'The Rise of Black Churches'; Chapter 8, R. Burgess, 'African Pentecostal Growth' and Chapter 11, D. Goodhew, 'From the Margins to the Mainstream'.

[16]   This is the author's considered judgement, based on Brierley, *Pulling out of the Nosedive*, p. 10 and the other studies in this volume. However, much greater research is needed to achieve certainty in this area.

[17]   See Chapter 3, A. Harris, 'Devout East Enders'; Chapter 2, J. Wolffe and B. Jackson, 'Anglican Resurgence'; Chapter 11, D. Goodhew, From the Margins to the Mainstream'; and K. Roxburgh, 'Growth amidst Decline'.

[18]   See Chapter 14, P. Chambers, 'Economic Growth'.

[19]   P. Norris and R. Inglehart, *Sacred and Secular: Religion and Politics Worldwide*, (Cambridge: CUP, 2004); H. McLeod, *The Religious Crisis of the 1960s* (Oxford: OUP,

grew most strongly along trade routes, so, *mutatis mutandis*, something similar is happening in modern Britain. This is far from an automatic correlation – as the many declining churches along the 'trade routes' of Britain testify. Yet there is a connection between economic dynamism, the consequent attraction of migrants (internal and external), population growth and the growth of churches.

Church Growth as a Regional Phenomenon

Following on from the link between church growth and economic dynamism is the need to understand church growth and decline regionally. It is a crude, but correct, generalization to say that church growth diminishes the further away you get from London. Thus, the best data to support the secularization thesis is to be found in parts of the north of England, Wales and Scotland. Yet even in areas some distance from the metropolis, there are signs of growth. Chapter 11 shows the religious dynamism present in one northern city and points to similar patterns elsewhere in the north of England. Three chapters look at the special religious ecologies of Scotland, Wales and Northern Ireland. Claire Mitchell shows how Northern Irish Christianity continues to buck the secularization thesis and is showing both adaptability and vigour. Ken Roxburgh and Paul Chambers look at Scottish and Welsh churches – areas which illustrate the secularization thesis better than anywhere in Britain. Yet Wales and Scotland, by their comparative lack of population growth, limited experience of immigration and limited economic dynamism are also different from most of the UK. Even after saying all this, Chambers shows that there is significant resilience amongst Welsh churches, and Roxburgh shows significant signs of Scottish church growth in the city of Edinburgh.

Church Growth and Gender

The churches which are growing vary markedly in their attitudes towards gender, some being more conservative, some less so. But these churches also undermine preconceptions about gender roles. Harris shows in Chapter 3 how the vibrant spirituality of multicultural catholic London is, to a large degree, driven by women. Likewise, Chapter 11 shows that the new churches of York, though mainly led by men, are heavily affected by the agency of women. There is statistical evidence to suggest that churches led by women are as likely or more likely to grow than those which are not.[20] Here, as in many other parts of this volume, is an agenda for further research.

2007), p. 257; J. Hirschle, 'From Religious to Consumption-Related Routine Activities? Analysing Ireland's Economic Boom and the Decline in Church Attendance', *Journal for the Scientific Study of Religion*, 49.4 (2010).

[20]   B. Jackson, *The Road to Growth*, p. 44.

Section Two: Church Growth in Britain and the Secularization Thesis

There are a variety of academic approaches to the subject but academic agreement as to the fact of church decline is close to unanimous. Printed and electronic media and many church leaders echo these assumptions.[21] The division between contemporary academic writers on modern British religion lies in the greater or lesser degree of their pessimism, not in whether or not to be pessimistic.[22]

Secularization, as a concept, can be defined in a variety of ways. In an influential typology, Dobbelaere suggests three; the secularization of a whole society, secularization in terms of the organizational decline of churches or secularization in terms of the decline of individual subscription to Christian faith.[23] With such a division it is possible for a society to be growing more secular in terms of one measure but not in terms of another. Thus the USA is highly secular in terms of the separation of church and state yet highly religious in terms of organizational or individual activity. Conversely, many countries in northern Europe retain state-funded churches alongside profound organisational decline and widespread individual antipathy or apathy towards Christian faith. This study will focus on organizational and individual Christianity, rather than discussions of societal secularization, which has been well covered elsewhere.[24] It is perfectly possible for Britain to grow more secular by some measures and more religious by others.

Steve Bruce, Callum Brown, David Voas and other writers offer substantial arguments for why recent decades in British history represent the profound secularization of Britain, including large-scale shrinkage of the churches organizationally and in terms of individual ascription to Christian belief. Whilst Brown stresses that his *Death of Christian Britain* points not to the complete demise of Christianity but to its removal as a core narrative in British life and whilst he and Bruce disagree as to the chronology of decline, they are at one in

---

[21]   Thus, for instance, the influential Church of England report, *Mission-Shaped Church*, is predicated on C. Brown's analysis in *The Death of Christian Britain* (London: Routledge, 2001). See, The Archbishops Council, *Mission-Shaped Church* (London: Church House, 2004), p. 11.

[22]   Attempts to rebut secularization theory do exist but such rebuttals come from outside the UK: see R. Warner, *Secularisation and its Discontents*, pp. 68ff. The volume *Redefining Christian Britain* (J. Garnett et al) challenges the secularization theory by asserting that Christianity remains a key force in British life – but makes no attempt to challenge the view that churches *per se* are shrinking. The subversive writing of Bob Jackson, which has for some years pointed to areas of growth in parts of British Anglicanism, remains largely ignored by academic discourse: B. Jackson, *Hope for the Church* and *Road to Growth*.

[23]   K. Dobbelaere, *Secularisation: an Analysis at Three Levels* (Frankfurt am Main: Peter Lang, 2002). Different, but overlapping breakdowns of what secularization entails can be found in J. Casanova, *Public Religions in the Modern World* (Chicago: University of Chicago Press, 1994); and H. McLeod, *The Religious Crisis of the 1960s* (Oxford: OUP, 2007), p. 21.

[24]   J. Garnett et al, *Redefining Christian Britain*.

stressing its profundity. 'Britain is showing the world how religion as we have known it can die.'[25]

Other leading writers offer a view which is not quite as pessimistic – but hardly upbeat. Grace Davie coined the influential term 'believing without belonging' as a way of described a Britain in which the bulk of people claimed nominal Christianity but did not worship at a Christian church. In later work, Davie has preferred to speak of 'vicarious religion' as a more dilute description of the same process, whereby a majority of the British people are content that a minority practice religion for them. Davie's analysis assumes a highly secular nation. Church decline is a given.[26] The same is true of Robin Gill in his work *The Empty Church Revisited*. Gill sees decline as due to the over-supply of church buildings which could never then be filled. But he also assumes that secularity is certain to grow and religion certain to decline.[27] Woodhead and Heelas used a detailed study of the Cumbrian town of Kendal to argue that modern Britain is experiencing a 'subjective turn' away from organized Christianity towards various forms of spirituality which might be termed 'holistic'. Consequently, they argue that society may not be getting more secular, but congregational decline is seen as 'relentless'.[28] Woodhead and Catto's recent, highly nuanced, picture of British religion portrays contemporary British Christianity in terms of decline or attenuated survival.[29]

It is central to academic discourse about modern British Christianity that it is in decline – whether that decline be seen as slow or dramatic. The studies which support these conclusions beg five key questions. First, is there regional variation in the pattern of church decline or are churches across all of Britain declining? Second, is church decline happening across all churches or are some declining and others growing? Third, is church decline happening across all ethnic groups or only in some? Fourth, what is the value of different types of evidence – notably case studies compared to opinion polls and national attendance data? Fifth, how does the evidence in Britain compare with evidence elsewhere? These questions will now be examined in turn.

Regionalizing the Secularization Thesis

Discussions of modern Christian Britain have tended to emphasize regions where decline is strongest – and to neglect regions where growth has happened. Thus

---

25   C. Brown, *Death of Christian Britain*, p. 198; S. Bruce, *God is Dead*; D. Voas. and A. Crockett 'Religion in Britain: Neither believing nor belonging', *Sociology*, 39.1 (2005), pp. 11–28.
26   G. Davie, *Religion in Britain Since 1945: Believing without Belonging* (Oxford: Blackwell, 1994) and *The Sociology of Religion* (London: Sage 2007).
27   R. Gill, *The Empty Church Revisited* (Aldershot: Ashgate, 2003), p. 211.
28   P. Heelas and L. Woodhead, *The Spiritual Revolution: Why Religion is Giving Way to Spirituality* (Oxford: Blackwell, 2005), p. 41.
29   L. Woodhead and R. Catto, *Religious Change in Modern Britain* (London: Routledge, 2012), pp. 9–10.

Gill utilizes York and Wales as case studies. These are areas which have been mostly stable or declining in population, mostly lacking in economic dynamism and relatively monochrome in terms of ethnicity and culture. Yet much of the UK is experiencing population growth (often rapid growth) and economic dynamism and is increasingly diverse, both ethnically and culturally. Had Gill used London as a case study, his findings would have been markedly different – as this volume shows. Similarly Heelas and Woodhead use the Cumbrian market town of Kendal with its fairly stable, largely white, population – had they used York or Edinburgh they would not have had the same results. Brown paints a picture of a dying Christian Britain, pointing to marked decline in Scotland, but does not cite figures for Northern Ireland which offer a different ideological trajectory. Central to the findings of this volume is that church decline and growth varies markedly between different regions and towns (and, indeed, within regions and towns). Regionalizing the discussion is essential to measuring church decline or growth; where you look affects what you find.

Secularization: True for all Churches?

Studies of recent British church decline focus on what may be called 'the mainline' denominations, such as the Anglican, Methodist and Catholic churches – churches which have been in existence for centuries and whose bureaucratic structures facilitate statistical measurement. Other, newer churches (where 'new' is defined as those which came into existence during the last 100 years) are passed over. It is difficult to collect data on many such bodies, since they tend to lack overarching bureaucratic structures and they are therefore frequently absent or undercounted in statistical analyses.[30] Accurate measurement of 'non-mainline' denominations requires detailed case studies and even such research is liable to undercount. This is illustrated in the work on churches in York by Robin Gill and Rob Warner. Gill offers a highly nuanced case study of York's churches, but he focused on mainline churches and almost entirely ignored the new churches even though they have formed a large (and rapidly growing) element of the Christian community of York for several decades. Warner provides a valuable study of York's newer churches but still omits a significant number of them.[31] Detailed research shows that many new churches are growing fast nationally.[32] Consequently, a focus on 'mainline'

---

[30]   Thus, one of the key surveys of British churchgoing obtained a 30% response rate from the rapidly growing Pentecostal churches: P. Brierley, *Pulling out of the Nosedive*, p. 16.

[31]   R. Gill, *Empty Church Revisited*; R. Warner, 'York's Evangelical and Charismatics: an Emergent Free Market in Voluntarist Religious Identities', in S. Kim and P. Kollontai, *Community Identity: Dynamics of Religion in Context* (London: T. & T. Clarke, 2007) omits the following churches: York Chinese Church; York Korean Church, York Evangelical Church.

[32]   See for instance: W. Kay, *Apostolic Networks in Great Britain: New Ways of Being Church* (Milton Keynes: Paternoster, 2007).

rather than new churches means an overestimation of decline and underestimation of growth amongst British churches.

Secularization Theory and Ethnicity

Most studies of the recent history of British churches give startlingly little attention to ethnicity.[33] Whilst churches and Christians rooted in black, asian and minority ethnic communities may once have been marginal they are now a substantial section of the population as a whole and of the Christian population. It is estimated that 1,000,000 British Christians attend such churches.[34] A number of scholars seriously underestimate the significance of black, asian and minority ethnic communities in British Christianity. Bruce almost entirely ignores non-white Christians; Gill and Brown note their presence, but that is all. Heelas and Woodhead focus their research on a largely white community.[35] Such studies, which assert that the British church is declining, or even dying, are based on research which shows only that large parts of the *white* British church are declining. Black, asian and minority ethnic churchgoing is not declining; it is rapidly on the rise. Multicultural Britain has led to marked church growth in Britain. One of the unpleasant ironies of recent history has been the attempt by far-right political groups such as the British National Party to ferment hostility to black, asian and minority ethnic communities on the basis that the latter supposedly 'threaten' Britain's Christian identity. The evidence of *Church Growth in Britain* is that the exact reverse is true; Britain's churches have benefited greatly from the growth of ethnic minorities who now form a large section of church membership.

Secularization: the Conflict between National and Local Evidence

Beyond these specific questions is the larger question of the validity of national church figures and opinion poll data which form the backbone of much work on contemporary British churches.[36] Whilst such statistics have obvious value for generalization, they are highly problematic. The tendency to undercount non-mainline and new churches has already been noted.[37] More generally, just as political opinion polls are fallible indicators of voter behaviour in the polling booth,

---

[33] The following studies focus primarily on mainline denominations and/or regions with small ethnic minorities. They give little space to churches rooted in ethnic minority communities: S. Bruce, *God is Dead*; C. Brown, *Death of Christian Britain*; R. Gill, *Empty Church Revisited*; P. Heelas and L. Woodhead, *Spiritual Revolution*.

[34] See R. Warner, *Secularisation*, p. 161.

[35] S. Bruce, *God is Dead*; C. Brown, *Death of Christian Britain*, p. 2; R. Gill, *Empty Church Revisited*, p. 163; P. Heelas and L. Woodhead, *Spiritual Revolution*.

[36] S. Bruce, *God is Dead*, and C. Brown, *Death of Christian Britain*, rely heavily on such data.

[37] See p 12.

it is vital to compare the findings of large-scale surveys with what is happening in specific communities. Surveys of religious views often point to decline. Yet, as this volume shows, there is evidence of significant church growth on the ground. This is not to say that such surveys are wrong, but it is to say that British society may be growing more secular in some ways (including the ways measured by values surveys) and less secular in others (often in ways less susceptible to tabulation). One aspect of the differentiated impact of secularization is that elite culture in Britain may well be secularizing,[38] whilst other parts of British life are seeing church growth. A survey of the religious views of, for instance, BBC executives and those who clean the BBC Television Centre in London might well indicate *both* secularization *and* resacralization.

Secularization: the Global Picture

Variants of the secularization thesis have dominated debate about church growth/ decline in Britain, but debate in other countries is more diverse. In America in particular there have arisen alternative strands of opinion – most notably, what is called Rational Choice Theory (RCT), propounded most forcefully by the American academics Stark, Finke and Iannacone.[39] It is gaining traction in wider academic circles but has had little impact on British thinking. RCT argues that human beings are naturally religious, that there is an inherent demand within human beings for the 'goods' which religion offers. These 'goods' may be directly to an individual's advantage – such as communal support or a sense of inner peace – or they may be more altruistic in tone – a sense of purpose, a cause to follow. Using an economic analogy, RCT argues that humans use rational choice, balancing benefits and costs, to determine whether they make use of religion, just as individuals make choices in other aspects of life. If the 'supply' of religion is limited and/or of poor quality, (e.g., when the main provider of religion has a quasi-monopoly such as the established churches in Scandinavia and Germany), 'demand' is limited and the result is religious decline. But when there is pluralism and competing suppliers of religion, the 'supply' of religious activity is more diverse and of higher overall quality and the result is religious vitality (e.g. a pluralist society such as in the contemporary USA). This is seen as explaining the markedly more vigorous state of American Christianity compared to that of northern Europe. For RCT, faith and secularization ebb and flow, rather than one triumphing over the other. Whilst

---

[38]   One piece of evidence supporting this is a survey of the religious views of Oxford undergraduates: S. Bullivant, 'Sociology and the Study of Atheism', *Journal of Contemporary Religion,* 23.3 (2008).

[39]   An influential example of RCT is: R. Finke and R. Stark, *The Churching of America, 1776–20050: Winners and Losers in our Religious Economy* (New Brunswick, NJ: Rutgers University Press, 2005).

there have been critiques of RCT, there is a growing recognition of its explanatory value.[40]

RCT overlaps with other schools of thought. Dean Kelley led other commentators in the early 1970s with his seminal book *Why are Conservative Churches Growing?* Kelley argued that the strictness of conservative religion was facilitating growth and that excessive readiness to adapt led to decline. Others disagree with his analysis but the reality of conservative church growth amid the decline of many other churches is widely recognized.[41] A different way of picturing the same reality is to describe the religious shifts in the western world in recent decades as a shift from obligation to consumption, a shift from doing faith as a duty to doing it as an individual choice. This paradigm suggests that, in the modern west, obligation-based churches decline but consumerist-based churches grow, meaning that society can get more *and* less religious at the same time.[42] This phenomenon can even cut through denominations; thus Mitchell in this volume notes that obligation-based Catholicism in Northern Ireland appears to be struggling, whereas Harris points to Catholicism's more voluntarist vitality in London.[43] Davie in 2007 concluded that RCT had some value in Europe, but that 'far more' Europeans operated on an older model of latent belief and nominal church membership.[44] This volume suggests that religion is growing steadily more voluntarist and that RCT and these other theories have an increasing purchase on modern Britain.

In all this, it is increasingly clear that British Christianity is best understood by comparison with other societies in the context of a series of highly interconnected global religious shifts. Sociologists have for some years pondered whether it is the relative secularity of northern Europe or the relative religiosity of the USA that is exceptional. But increasingly, it can be argued that neither Europe nor the USA are dominant. Both are simply part of a wider religious mosaic, as non-western nations grow more prominent.[45] Whilst it is beyond the scope of this volume to engage

---

[40]   For a critique of RCT, see: S. Bruce, *Choice and Religion: a Critique of Rational Choice Theory* (Oxford: OUP, 1999). Evidence of the growing traction of RCT within academia can be seen in: G. Davie, *Sociology of Religion*, pp. 67ff, 76ff, 80, 82–86 and R. McClearey (ed.), *The Oxford Handbook of the Economics of Religion*, (Oxford: OUP, 2011).

[41]   D. Kelley, *Why Conservative Churches are Growing: a Study in Sociology of Religion* (Macon: Mercer University Press, 1996); the detail of Kelley's analysis is contested, but his identification of conservative church growth is widely recognised – see, for instance, H. McLeod, *Religious Crisis*, pp. 207–08; G. Davie, *Sociology of Religion*, p. 150.

[42]   G. Davie, *Sociology of Religion*, pp. 86–105.

[43]   See Chapter 15, C. Mitchell, 'Northern Irish Protestantism' and Chapter 3, A. Harris, 'Devout East Enders'.

[44]   G. Davie, *Sociology of Religion*, p. 147

[45]   P. Jenkins, *The Next Christendom: the Coming of Global Christianity* (Oxford: OUP, 2002).

with debates over globalization or 'glocalization', a key theme of contemporary British church growth is the way trends across the globe are impacting upon British church life and should inform analysis of that life. Thus Hugh McLeod, in the recent *Cambridge History of Christianity*, ponders whether the future of global Christianity will be decided not so much by developments in the west, as by developments amongst China's churches, currently seeing marked growth.[46] Immigration to Britain is much remarked upon. What remains little commented upon is the extent to which many of these immigrants are Christian – and the potential changes to church life as a result.[47] Global shifts include a shift away from the long-established denominations which dominated western Christianity in the nineteenth and much of the twentieth century towards Pentecostal and independent churches, shifts from which Europe is not immune.[48] Within Europe there is much variation; whilst countries in the north and west of Europe have seen considerable secularization (from already highly secular societies), elsewhere in Europe, especially after the fall of communism, churches have grown.[49]

Global perspectives matter both because of immigration and because neither the secularization theory nor RCT work equally well everywhere. This fits with the work of Casanova, who sees everything as exceptional – so the secularization thesis and RCT cease to be overarching theories for everywhere and become ways of explaining what is going on in specific countries. Casanova is one of a number of writers who have argued that, at least in some parts of the world, religion is being de-privatized and that society is being de-secularized and even re-sacralized.[50]

Theories tend to be narratives of great power, claiming to be meta-explications of the complexities of the universe. By their very nature they can be absorbing, reductionistic, and totalizing. Part of the trouble with secularization theories lies precisely in their universalism. Is religion on the rise? Is it declining? Answering

---

[46]   H. McLeod, 'Being a Christian at the end of the Twentieth Century', in H. McLeod, (ed.), *World Christianities, c. 1914–2000*, *Cambridge History of Christianity* (vol. IX; Cambridge: CUP, 2006), pp. 646–47.

[47]   G. Davie, *Europe: the Exceptional Case. Parameters of Faith in the Modern World* (London: DLT, 2002), pp. 104–11.

[48]   D. Martin, *Tongues of Fire: the Explosion of Pentecostalism in Latin America* (Oxford: Blackwell, 1990); D. Goodhew, 'Growth and Decline in South Africa's Churches, 1960-1991', *Journal of Religion in Africa*, XXX.3 (2000); R.S. Warner, *New Wine in Old Wineskins: Evangelicals and Liberals in a Small Town Church* (Berkeley: University of California Press, 1988).

[49]   A. Greeley, *Religion in Europe at the End of the Second Millennium: A Sociological Profile* (London: Transaction Publishers, 2003), p. xi.

[50]   J. Casanova, *Public Religions in the Modern World* (Chicago: University of Chicago Press, 1994); P. Berger, *The Desecularisation of the World: Resurgent Religion and World Politics* (Grand Rapids: Eerdemans, 1999); G. Kepel, *The Revenge of God: the Resurgence of Islam Christianity and Judaism in the Modern World* (Cambridge: Polity Press, 1994); J. Micklethwaite and A. Wooldridge, *God is Back. How the Global Rise of Faith is Changing the World* (London: Penguin, 2009).

this question at the meta- level is misleading. On one hand, religion is self-evidently in decline in some parts of Europe and the North East of America; while, on the other hand, in parts of South America, Asia and Africa it is expanding rapidly. What is needed therefore is the challenging of this hegemonic meta-narrative of 'secularization' with smaller regional accounts. For example, in Britain the narrative which dominates the popular imagery is that accounting which sees religion spiraling downward. The series of essays collected in this volume share an incredulity about this meta-narrative.

Section Three: The Chronology of British Church Growth

Insofar as there is a 'lesson of history' regarding church growth and decline, it is that Christianity has declined and grown in surprising ways across the centuries, meaning we should be wary of theories which assume faith can only shrink and not grow – or vice versa. Arguments for contemporary church decline tend to rely on the assumption that the past, especially the recent past, was very religious – a thesis which is questionable and which has the knock-on result of exaggerating the decline assumed to have happened in later decades.[51]

Whilst writers are clearly right to point to overall church decline across twentieth century Britain,[52] there was also significant church growth in some places in the first half of the century – notably in the suburbs of London, in Catholicism and in the new Pentecostal churches.[53] In addition, it is widely recognized that the period during and after World War II constituted a substantial 'blip' in the graph of decline, with a significant reinvigoration of British churches.[54] Rapid decline began in the 1960s and Brown and McLeod provide powerful depictions of the potent secularisation of that decade.[55] This said, greater attention should be given to developments in the 1960s which boosted the churches; the 1960s saw large-scale immigration, through which black majority churches were strengthened or came into being; it saw the marked growth of Orthodox churches in the UK and, via

[51]   See, for instance: P. Virgin, *The Church in the age of Negligence: Ecclesiastical Structure and the Problems of Church Reform, 1700–1840* (Cambridge: Clarke, 1989); R. Gill, *Empty Church Revisited*, pp. 19, 211 and Chapter 2 J. Wolffe and B. Jackson, 'Anglican Resurgence'.

[52]   See, for instance, S. Bruce, *God is Dead* and C. Brown, *Death of Christian Britain*.

[53]   R. Walford, *The Growth of 'New London' in Suburban Middlesex and the response of the Church of England* (Lewiston, NY; Lampeter: Edward Mellen Press, 2007); W. Kay, *Pentecostals in Britain* (Carlisle: Paternoster, 2000); Hastings, *A History of English Christianity, 1920–2000* (London: SCM Press, 2001), p. 134.

[54]   H. McLeod, *Religious Crisis*, p. 31.

[55]   H. McLeod, *Religious Crisis* and C. Brown, *Death of Christian Britain*.

the start of the charismatic movement, the 1960s saw the DNA of Pentecostalism entering the gene pool of wider British Christianity.[56]

Whilst the 1960s were, overall, the key decade of secularization in twentieth century Britain, some scholars see the 1970s as marking a shift in the other direction. Kepel pointed to the 1970s as the point when conservative religion worldwide began to fight back, when an economic slump called the idea of 'progress' into question and when a deep malaise was perceived in the world order.[57] Woodhead and Catto cogently argue that the post-war history of British faith divides into three sections: a mild religious restoration after the war; followed by substantial decline from the 1960s; followed by a marked shift at the end of the 1970s, when the dominant object of British post-war faith – the welfare state – began to appear frail and to be questioned. This was followed by further shaking of the foundations of secularity – in the form of the collapse of communism and a loss of confidence in science.[58]

The chronology outlined above provides the justification for starting this study in 1980. By this point the real shift to secular dominance in Britain had already happened. Only the delusional could ignore the marked decline in the size and power of the churches. Yet reaction to secularity was also vigorous. By exploring the 30 years since 1980 this volume explores the chronological trajectory of secularization – whether churches would continue to decline or whether they could also grow.

Section Four: Theoretical and Theological Perspectives

Theorizing about faith within the social sciences has been dominated by the figures of Marx, Durkheim and Weber. Within their thought the paradigm of secularization is a dominant motif. Marx, Weber and Durkheim model the belief that in the end religion will decline; it is an implicit (and often explicit) eschatology of church decline and secular growth. Each wrote in nineteenth century Western Europe as it modernized and secularized, and their thought should be seen as having general value but also as coming out of specific geographical and social contexts. What Marx, Weber and Durkheim might have written had they lived in China in the late twentieth century – with its mutating communism and burgeoning churches – is an interesting, but sadly impossible, question to answer.

A Brazilian friend commented to me on the resignation he witnessed among many churches in Britain, as if church decline was a given. His comment suggests that many contemporary British theologians, church leaders and churches have

---

[56]   See Chapter 7, H. Osgood, 'The Rise of Black Churches'; K. Ware, 'The Orthodox Church in the British Isles', in C. Chaillot (ed.), *A Short History of the Orthodox Church in Western Europe in the Twentieth Century* (Paris: Inter-Orthodox Dialogue, 2006); T. Saunders and H. Sansom, *David Watson: A Biography* (London: Hodder and Stoughton, 1992).

[57]   G. Kepel, *Revenge*.

[58]   L. Woodhead and R. Catto, *Religious Change*, pp. 12–15.

CHURCH GROWTH IN BRITAIN

There has been substantial church growth in Britain between 1980 and 2010. This is the controversial conclusion from the international team of scholars, who have drawn on interdisciplinary studies and the latest research from across the UK. Such church growth is seen to be on a large scale, is multi-ethnic and can be found across a wide range of social and geographical contexts. It is happening inside mainline denominations but especially in specific regions such as London, in newer churches and amongst ethnic minorities.

Church Growth in Britain provides a forceful critique of the notion of secularisation which dominates much of academia and the media – and which conditions the thinking of many churches and church leaders. This book demonstrates that, whilst decline is happening in some parts of the church, this needs to be balanced by recognition of the vitality of large swathes of the Christian church in Britain. Rebalancing the debate in this way requires wholesale change in our understanding of contemporary British Christianity.

Ashgate Contemporary Ecclesiology

The field of ecclesiology has grown remarkably in the last decade, and most especially in relation to the study of the contemporary church. Recently, theological attention has turned once more to the nature of the church, its practices and proclivities, and to interpretative readings and understandings on its role, function and ethos in contemporary society.

This new series draws from a range of disciplines and established scholars to further the study of contemporary ecclesiology and publish an important cluster of landmark titles in this field. The Series Editors represent a range of Christian traditions and disciplines, and this reflects the breadth and depth of books developing in the Series. This Ashgate series presents a clear focus on the contemporary situation of churches worldwide, offering an invaluable resource for students, researchers, ministers and other interested readers around the world working or interested in the diverse areas of contemporary ecclesiology and the important changing shape of the church worldwide.

Church Growth in Britain
1980 to the Present

Edited by

DAVID GOODHEW
Cranmer Hall, Durham, UK

ASHGATE

Published by
Ashgate Publishing Limited
Wey Court East
Union Road
Farnham
Surrey, GU9 7PT
England

Ashgate Publishing Company
Suite 420
101 Cherry Street
Burlington
VT 05401-4405
USA

www.ashgate.com

British Library Cataloguing in Publication Data
Church growth in Britain : 1980 to the present. -- (Ashgate
  contemporary ecclesiology)
  1. Church growth--Great Britain--History--20th century.
  2. Church growth--Great Britain--History--21st century.
  3. Great Britain--Church history--20th century. 4. Great
  Britain--Church history--21st century.
  I. Series II. Goodhew, David, 1965-
  274.1'082-dc23

Library of Congress Cataloging-in-Publication Data
Church growth in Britain : 1980 to the present / edited by David Goodhew.
    p. cm. -- (Ashgate contemporary ecclesiology)
  Includes bibliographical references (p.   ) and index.
  ISBN 978-1-4094-2577-9 (hardcover) -- ISBN 978-1-4094-2576-2
(pbk) -- ISBN 978-1-4094-2578-6 (ebook) 1. Church
growth--Great Britain. 2. Christianity--Great Britain--History. I.
Goodhew, David, 1965-
  BR759.C458 2012
  274.1'0828--dc23

2011050167

9781409425779 (hbk)
9781409425762 (pbk)
9781409425786 (ebk)

Printed and bound in Great Britain by the
MPG Books Group, UK.

Church decline is neither inevitable in prospect nor accurate in retrospect. This book reviews the reality of what is happening in Christian religious practice in the UK. As such it comes at a crucial time, when the Church of England appears to be gathering the will to change, and when an accurate and reasoned understanding of what is really happening, and has done so since 1980, is essential.

The Rt Revd Justin Welby, Bishop of Durham

Church Growth in Britain *is a welcome and well researched challenge to the widespread assumption that Christianity in Britain is suffering terminal decline. Without pretending that there is no significant demise in some areas or that its findings will not provoke robust debate, the "mosaic of micro-studies" in this book illustrates the vitality, depth and breath of Christianity within the United Kingdom. Its central thesis certainly reflects what I witness when visiting the parishes of the Archdiocese of Westminster. For there I see people's faith shaping their everyday lives such that Christ is truly present in the streets of our land.*

Archbishop Vincent Nichols, Archbishop of Westminster
and President of the Catholic Bishops' Conference of England and Wales

Church Growth in Britain *is a timely book with a polemic point. Contrary to received wisdom, David Goodhew and his associates argue that Christianity is thriving in Britain-but Christianity of sorts that fall under conventional radar screens. The book will draw cheers from the minority of like-minded observers, serious critical attention from a broad middle, and no doubt counterattacks from the sociological and religious establishments whose standpoints are attacked. Yet the book's most telling observations are made only partly through pointed argument and mostly through calm and informative case studies of overlooked churches.*

R. Stephen Warner, University of Illinois at Chicago, USA

What I particularly liked about this book was the way it brought out, in serious historical perspective, the very different situations in which churches find themselves according to particular environments and the kinds of strategies that revive growth. The divinity lies in the detail and there is much genuine divinity in this volume.

David Martin, Emeritus Professor, and Fellow of the British Academy

Contents

List of Figures and Tables

Figures

Tables

List of Contributors

The Revd Lynda Barley was Head of Research and Statistics for the Archbishops' Council of the Church of England, prior to her recent appointment as Truro Diocesan Secretary and Canon Pastor at Truro Cathedral.

Dr Richard Burgess is Research Fellow in the School of Philosophy, Theology and Religion, University of Birmingham.

Dr Rebecca Catto is Research Associate for the AHRC/ESRC Religion and Society Programme, based at the University of Lancaster.

Dr Paul Chambers is Senior Lecturer in Sociology and Subject Group Leader for Social Policy in the Faculty of Business and Society, University of Glamorgan.

Amy Duffuor has recently completed an M.Phil in Migration Studies at the University of Oxford.

The Revd Dr David Goodhew is Director of Ministerial Practice at Cranmer Hall, St John's College, Durham.

Dr Alana Harris is Darby Fellow in History, Lincoln College, Oxford.

The Ven Bob Jackson is lecturer at St John's College, Nottingham, a Visiting Fellow of St John's College, Durham, a church growth consultant and the former Archdeacon of Walsall.

The Revd Canon Dr. George Lings is Director of the Sheffield Centre, the Research Unit for the Church Army.

Dr Claire Mitchell is a freelance researcher, formerly a senior lecturer at the Department of Sociology, Queens University, Belfast.

The Revd Dr Colin Marsh is Ecumenical Development Officer for Birmingham Churches Together.

The Revd Dr Hugh Osgood is the Senior Minister of Cornerstone Christian Centre, Bromley, London and the founding President of Churches in Communities International.

The Revd Dr Ian Randall is Senior Research Fellow, Spurgeon's College, London and International Baptist Theological Seminary, Prague.

Professor Ken Roxburgh is St Louis and Ann W. Armstrong Professor of Religion and Chair of the Department of Religion, Samford, Alabama.

Professor John Wolffe is Professor of Religious History at the Open University.

Acknowledgements

There are a number of people who richly deserve thanks for their help in bringing the project to fruition.

First and foremost, the contributors have shown commendable patience with all that has been asked of them and considerable juggling skills in ensuring that the project was finished on time.

Michael Thate acted as my research assistant in the final stages of production. His assiduous hunting down of material, careful editing and stimulating comments have been extremely helpful in bringing the book into being.

The staff and students of Cranmer Hall and the Wesley Study Centre constitute a highly stimulating environment in which to work through the ideas propounded in this book. David Wilkinson, as Principal of St John's College, Durham provided crucial support which ensured the project could be finished. Michael Volland and Joanildo Burity provided perceptive sounding boards towards the end of the writing. David Bebbington, Grace Davie, Rodney Stark and Stephen Warner provided wise comments and encouragement at the outset of the project.

Sarah Lloyd has been the primary link with Ashgate and has been unfailingly thoughtful, encouraging and wise. Sophie Lumley, Barbara Spender and David Shervington provided crucial help in preparing the manuscript for publication.

A wide range of libraries, churches and individuals have given generously of their time in enabling the research of this volume to be drawn together. On behalf of myself and all the contributors, we wish to express our gratitude both for that help and for all that you have taught us.

My wife, Lindsey, and our children Aidan and Benjamin have shown commendable patience with a distracted husband and dad during the preparation of *Church Growth*. I am immensely grateful to them for this – and much more besides.

David Goodhew
Cranmer Hall
Durham

PART I
Introduction

Chapter 1

Church Growth in Britain, 1980 to the Present Day

David Goodhew

It is a truth almost universally acknowledged that Christianity in Britain is in decline.[1] However, not all universally acknowledged truths are actually true. *Some* churches in *some* regions are declining, but this volume shows that substantial and sustained church growth has *also* taken place across Britain over the last 30 years. This growth is large-scale; it is occurring across a wide geographical range; it is highly multi-cultural in its social reach; and it shows no sign of slowing down. The current consensus, by focusing almost exclusively on decline, is seriously mistaken. The thesis of this book is sustained by the work of an international team of scholars, working across a spectrum of disciplines, coming from a variety of theoretical and ideological perspectives.

Thus, for example, there are now 500,000 Christians in black majority churches in Britain. Sixty years ago there were hardly any. Across the 30 years since 1980 new congregations have been founded at an average of one per year in a single medium-sized northern city, the city of York. Even the contemporary Church of England is not immune from church growth. The membership of the Anglican diocese of London, the largest Anglican diocese in the country, has grown by over 70% since 1990.[2]

Such developments are no cause for ecclesiastical triumphalism, given the extent of church decline elsewhere. But this narrative of *Church Growth in Britain* subverts the dominant narrative in much of academia and the media, a narrative which heavily influences many church leaders as well as wider society. The dominant narrative assumes that there has been wholesale church decline in recent decades and that such decline is the primary reality of British Christianity. The dominant narrative, called by some the 'secularization thesis', is, in part,

---

[1] The dominant studies of contemporary British Christianity all assume decline, the only difference being whether decline is seen as gradual or cataclysmic: see works by Callum Brown, Steve Bruce, Robin Gill, Grace Davie, Linda Woodhead and Paul Heelas. These, along with the wider literature on church decline, are discussed on pp. 10–17.

[2] See Chapter 9, A. Duffuor, 'Moving Up and Moving Out'; Chapter 11, D. Goodhew, 'From the Margins to the Mainstream' and Chapter 2, J. Wolffe and B. Jackson, 'Anglican Resurgence'. See also R. Warner, *Secularisation and its Discontents* (London: Continuum, 2010), p. 161.

correct. Most 'mainline' denominations have seen large falls in support.[3] The aim of *Church Growth in Britain* is not to airbrush out such decline but to highlight the sides of the story which have been hitherto marginalized. Since church decline is widely publicized and church growth is almost totally ignored in wider debate, the focus of this volume is on church growth. Such growth is a matter of deep significance both for the churches and for wider society.

Is Christianity in Britain, overall, declining or growing? One of the key findings of this volume is that overall statistics regarding Christian churches in Britain need to be treated with considerable caution. Some attempt at an overall assessment will be offered in the conclusion, but all national figures concerning churches need to be taken with a pinch of salt. An example of the problematic nature of national statistics is provided by initial data for the 2011 British Census, which shows that, whilst only 47% of 18 to 34 year olds declared themselves to have any religious affiliation, 67% (or more) of the same age group also declared that they occasionally or regularly pray.[4] The philosopher Alasdair MacIntyre once stated that whilst the English do not believe in God, they do like to pray to Him from time to time. MacIntyre's diagnosis is well illustrated by the contradictory data of the 2011 Census.

This volume starts in a different place. *Church Growth in Britain* is contemporary church history written 'from below'. The focus is not on national statistics, nor on national leadership via bishops, synods or conferences, but on local congregations and particular neighbourhoods. This volume is a mosaic of micro-studies; from Catholics in Canning Town to Brazilian Pentecostals in York to new churches in Edinburgh. But mosaics are more than random arrangements and can portray complex realities. This mosaic of micro-studies is assembled so that it includes the global backdrop of belief. *Church Growth in Britain* offers a 'glocalized' picture, in which the local and global are interwoven. The volume focuses on congregational life and particular regions, rather than national statistics or measures of the national significance of Christianity, not because the wider picture is unimportant, but because national observations often miss local dynamics, because congregational life is at the core of Christian identity and because the argument for the secularization of Britain rests heavily on the presumption that local congregations are in deep decline.[5] The ultimate test for secularization is not what opinion polls say but what is happening out on the street.

---

[3]   See P. Brierley, *Pulling out of the Nosedive: A Contemporary Picture of Churchgoing* (London: Christian Research, 2006) pp. 21–49.

[4]   www.yougov.polis.cam.ac.uk/archive, accessed on 21 September 2011. Regarding prayer, 67% of those aged 18 to 34 said they prayed regularly or occasionally, 26% said they never prayed and 7% said they didn't know whether they prayed or not. The religious census shows that attitudes to belief are highly contradictory and that the type of question asked heavily determines the kind of result given. Any conclusions based on such data should be accompanied with an ideological health warning.

[5]   The continuing influence of a more diffuse Christian Britain has been well charted in J. Garnett (et al), *Redefining Christian Britain: Post 1945 Perspectives* (London: SCM, 2006).

This introductory chapter has four sections: first it summarizes the findings of the volume; second, it compares those findings with the secularization thesis and other theoretical perspectives; third, it offers a chronological overview, situating British church growth historically; fourth, it explores the theoretical implications of church growth for theology and for other disciplines.

Section One: Church Growth in Britain since 1980

The volume is divided into four parts: the first part (this chapter) introduces the debates about church growth and decline and summarizes this volume's contribution; the second part (Chapters 2 to 6) surveys the older, 'mainline' churches; the third part (Chapters 7 to 12) surveys new churches (where 'new' means founded within the last century); the fourth part looks at Northern Ireland, Wales and Scotland. This is followed by a brief conclusion in which the arguments are tied together and an agenda for further work is sketched.

The key findings of *Church Growth in Britain* can be summarized under the following headings.

Church Growth in London

Chapters 2 and 3 focus on London. John Wolffe and Bob Jackson explore the large-scale growth of the Anglican diocese of London during the last 20 years in which church membership has expanded by over 70%. Whilst many Anglican dioceses outside London are shrinking – some rapidly – London offers a very different trajectory. Alana Harris looks at a single Roman Catholic parish in the East End of London, showing how the latter's traditional role as a haven for immigrants is leading to dramatic (and hugely diverse) church growth in Catholic London. A number of other chapters, particularly those concerning black majority churches, point to major growth in the capital.[6] The Christian church in London is growing both in absolute terms and as a proportion of the population.[7] London, in its burgeoning Christianity, is becoming more like American cities such as New York or Chicago which are very far from being 'secular cities' (this is especially the case if we add in the growth of other faith communities).[8] Steve Bruce says of the secularization thesis, that 'what would threaten the paradigm is sustained

---

[6] See Chapter 2, J. Wolffe and B. Jackson, 'Anglican Resurgence'; Chapter 7, H. Osgood, 'Rise of Black Churches'; B. Burgess, 'African Pentecostal Growth', Chapter 9, A. Duffuor, 'Moving up and Moving Out'. and P. Brierley, *Pulling out of the Nosedive*, pp. 44–46.

[7] J. Wolffe and B. Jackson, 'Anglican Resurgence', p. 23.

[8] T. Carnes and A. Karpathakis, *New York Glory: Religions in the City* (New York: New York University Press, 2001); L. Livesey, *Public Religion and Urban Transformation: Faith in the City* (New York: New York University Press, 2000).

and widespread growth in places that were previously secular'.[9] Leaving aside the experience of nations such as Russia and China, something like this is happening in contemporary London.

Growth in Mainline Churches

Examination of London indicates that, whilst across the whole of Britain there is much evidence of decline amongst the long-established, 'mainline' denominations,[10] mainline churches have the capacity to grow in some contexts. Chapters 4 and 5 explore this phenomenon by looking at signs of life in very different sections of the mainline churches. Ian Randall explores the robust performance of the Baptist denomination across the last three decades; it is a performance which raises uncomfortable questions for the other mainline churches as to why they declined but the Baptists did not. Lynda Barley shows the continuing vitality of English cathedral congregations. Sunday worship has remained stable over recent years, but weekday worship has mushroomed. This raises the question of why traditional forms of Christian worship in cathedrals are growing when, for the most part, they are declining elsewhere.[11] More broadly, evidence of mainline growth could be extended by examination of growing networks such as New Wine, which are backed primarily by mainline congregations.[12]

In Chapter 6, Rebecca Catto explores the notion of 'reverse mission' in mainline denominations – where Christians from outside Britain are invited to boost worshipping life here. What is striking is its limited impact on mainline churches, especially compared to the huge growth of black majority churches across the same decades, as shown in later chapters of this volume. This suggests that mainline churches continue to fail to release the energies of black, asian and minority ethnic Christians within their ranks.

Church Growth and Minority Ethnic Communities

Discussion of London leads onto a recurring and central theme of the book: the very substantial growth of black and other ethnic minority churches in Britain in recent decades. This is the heart of Chapters 7, 8 and 9 but this thread runs throughout this volume. Until the 1950s, there were hardly any black majority churches in Britain. Hugh Osgood's overview in Chapter 6 shows the way this stream of Christianity began, deepened and widened as the black, asian and minority ethnic communities have grown. Richard Burgess' chapter on the Nigerian Redeemed Christian Church of God shows the same process with regard to a specific new

---

[9]   S. Bruce, *God is Dead: Secularisation in the West* (Oxford: Blackwell, 2002), p. 173.

[10] P. Brierley, *Pulling out of the Nosedive*, pp. 21–49.

[11] Ibid., pp. 52–53.

[12] B. Jackson, *The Road to Growth: Towards a Thriving Church* (London: Church House Publishing, 2005), pp. 106–10.

denomination which has shown startling energy in church planting in the last three decades. In a superb, fresh piece of research, Amy Duffuor explores a single, rapidly expanding, congregation of Ghanaian Pentecostals in Peckham as they plant a new church in the suburbs of London, facing the question of whether the social upliftment that church membership offers to members will blunt the edge of their discipleship in the long run. Black, asian and minority ethnic church growth brings challenges as well as possibilities.

Church Growth and New Churches

A further theme of *Church Growth in Britain* is the substantial growth of new churches and of new forms of church. Chapter 11 explores the city of York, showing the extraordinary shift within a single city. One congregation per year has been founded across the last three decades and the rate of foundation has accelerated since 2000. George Lings gives a history of what has been termed 'fresh expressions' of church, 'church plants' and 'emerging church' within the Church of England, showing how they have moved from being rare in the early 1980s to numbering well over a thousand and being attended by tens of thousands in the present day. He writes as a participant in this story and his chapter has something of the quality of oral history. Lings' chapter shows how Anglican churches are, in part, borrowing models conceived either outside the UK or by new, non-mainstream UK churches. He concludes that these 'fresh expressions' and church plants have great potential, but also that some are fragile. Colin Marsh closes the section on new churches by looking at the city of Birmingham, showing that those strands of Christianity which were on the margins a few decades ago – such as black majority churches and new churches – are beginning to overtake the 'mainline' churches in one major British city. This chimes with other chapters to indicate the significance of newer denominations in contemporary Britain.

The number of new churches, from all denominations, that have started up since 1980 is startling. One detailed study by Peter Brierley calculated that 2,950 new churches were started between 1989 and 2005.[13] Chapters from this book – notably those in Part 2 – reinforce Brierley's figures and suggest that this momentum was in place prior to 1989 and has been sustained after 2005.[14] Calculating the precise number of churches started in Britain between 1980 and the present is difficult; those who are the most dynamic in their ecclesiastical entrepreneurship are also the least interested in the statistical record. Based on a range of studies, it is likely that over 5,000 new churches have been started in Britain in the 30 years since 1980

---

[13] P. Brierley, *Pulling out of the Nosedive*, p. 10.

[14] See Chapter 7, H. Osgood, 'Rise of Black Churches'; Chapter 8, R. Burgess, 'African Pentecostal Growth'; Chapter 11, D. Goodhew, 'From the Margins to the Mainstream' and Chapter 10, G. Lings, 'A History of Fresh Expressions'.

– probably significantly more.[15] However, until further research is undertaken, the number of new churches in Britain cannot be estimated with precision. To put these numbers into some kind of scale, the number of new churches started since 1980 is substantially greater than the total number of Roman Catholic churches in England and equivalent to one third of all Church of England churches. It is likely that as many churches have opened as have closed in Britain during the last three decades – although within any given region the balance may tilt in the direction of decline or growth. Newspaper headlines and book covers which presuppose vast numbers of church closures are misleading in their failure to note the similarly substantial number of new churches which are opening.[16] The sheer number of churches opening and closing vividly illustrates the extent of growth *and* decline in recent British Christianity.

Church Growth, Demography and Economics

A key finding of this volume is the way that church growth in contemporary Britain is most common in areas of migration, population growth and economic dynamism. Corridors of church growth have developed alongside major economic arteries such as the A1 and the east coast mainline and the growing cities to be found on those arteries – as the chapters on London, York and Edinburgh show.[17] Paul Chambers' chapter on Wales shows how church growth can happen outside of these zones, but is significantly harder.[18] That church growth is more pronounced in areas of population growth and economic dynamism does *not* mean that growing churches are populated by the well-off. As the various chapters show, church growth connects with a wide social spectrum. Moreover, there are proven connections between societal affluence and secularity.[19] Just as the early church

---

[15]   If new churches in England had been founded at the same rate prior to 1989 and after 2005, as for the period covered by Brierley's study, then the total number founded between 1980 and 2010 would be around 5,500. This volume has shown how even detailed academic studies tend to undercount the number of new churches and that there is evidence to suggest that the rate of new church start-ups has increased during the last decade. Taken together the evidence suggests that the figure of 5,000 is probably a substantial underestimate of the number of new churches founded between 1980 and 2010. See Chapter 7, H. Osgood, 'The Rise of Black Churches'; Chapter 8, R. Burgess, 'African Pentecostal Growth' and Chapter 11, D. Goodhew, 'From the Margins to the Mainstream'.

[16]   This is the author's considered judgement, based on Brierley, *Pulling out of the Nosedive*, p. 10 and the other studies in this volume. However, much greater research is needed to achieve certainty in this area.

[17]   See Chapter 3, A. Harris, 'Devout East Enders'; Chapter 2, J. Wolffe and B. Jackson, 'Anglican Resurgence'; Chapter 11, D. Goodhew, From the Margins to the Mainstream'; and K. Roxburgh, 'Growth amidst Decline'.

[18]   See Chapter 14, P. Chambers, 'Economic Growth'.

[19]   P. Norris and R. Inglehart, *Sacred and Secular: Religion and Politics Worldwide*, (Cambridge: CUP, 2004); H. McLeod, *The Religious Crisis of the 1960s* (Oxford: OUP,

grew most strongly along trade routes, so, *mutatis mutandis*, something similar is happening in modern Britain. This is far from an automatic correlation – as the many declining churches along the 'trade routes' of Britain testify. Yet there is a connection between economic dynamism, the consequent attraction of migrants (internal and external), population growth and the growth of churches.

Church Growth as a Regional Phenomenon

Following on from the link between church growth and economic dynamism is the need to understand church growth and decline regionally. It is a crude, but correct, generalization to say that church growth diminishes the further away you get from London. Thus, the best data to support the secularization thesis is to be found in parts of the north of England, Wales and Scotland. Yet even in areas some distance from the metropolis, there are signs of growth. Chapter 11 shows the religious dynamism present in one northern city and points to similar patterns elsewhere in the north of England. Three chapters look at the special religious ecologies of Scotland, Wales and Northern Ireland. Claire Mitchell shows how Northern Irish Christianity continues to buck the secularization thesis and is showing both adaptability and vigour. Ken Roxburgh and Paul Chambers look at Scottish and Welsh churches – areas which illustrate the secularization thesis better than anywhere in Britain. Yet Wales and Scotland, by their comparative lack of population growth, limited experience of immigration and limited economic dynamism are also different from most of the UK. Even after saying all this, Chambers shows that there is significant resilience amongst Welsh churches, and Roxburgh shows significant signs of Scottish church growth in the city of Edinburgh.

Church Growth and Gender

The churches which are growing vary markedly in their attitudes towards gender, some being more conservative, some less so. But these churches also undermine preconceptions about gender roles. Harris shows in Chapter 3 how the vibrant spirituality of multicultural catholic London is, to a large degree, driven by women. Likewise, Chapter 11 shows that the new churches of York, though mainly led by men, are heavily affected by the agency of women. There is statistical evidence to suggest that churches led by women are as likely or more likely to grow than those which are not.[20] Here, as in many other parts of this volume, is an agenda for further research.

2007), p. 257; J. Hirschle, 'From Religious to Consumption-Related Routine Activities? Analysing Ireland's Economic Boom and the Decline in Church Attendance', *Journal for the Scientific Study of Religion*, 49.4 (2010).

[20]   B. Jackson, *The Road to Growth*, p. 44.

Section Two: Church Growth in Britain and the Secularization Thesis

There are a variety of academic approaches to the subject but academic agreement as to the fact of church decline is close to unanimous. Printed and electronic media and many church leaders echo these assumptions.[21] The division between contemporary academic writers on modern British religion lies in the greater or lesser degree of their pessimism, not in whether or not to be pessimistic.[22]

Secularization, as a concept, can be defined in a variety of ways. In an influential typology, Dobbelaere suggests three; the secularization of a whole society, secularization in terms of the organizational decline of churches or secularization in terms of the decline of individual subscription to Christian faith.[23] With such a division it is possible for a society to be growing more secular in terms of one measure but not in terms of another. Thus the USA is highly secular in terms of the separation of church and state yet highly religious in terms of organizational or individual activity. Conversely, many countries in northern Europe retain state-funded churches alongside profound organisational decline and widespread individual antipathy or apathy towards Christian faith. This study will focus on organizational and individual Christianity, rather than discussions of societal secularization, which has been well covered elsewhere.[24] It is perfectly possible for Britain to grow more secular by some measures and more religious by others.

Steve Bruce, Callum Brown, David Voas and other writers offer substantial arguments for why recent decades in British history represent the profound secularization of Britain, including large-scale shrinkage of the churches organizationally and in terms of individual ascription to Christian belief. Whilst Brown stresses that his *Death of Christian Britain* points not to the complete demise of Christianity but to its removal as a core narrative in British life and whilst he and Bruce disagree as to the chronology of decline, they are at one in

---

[21]   Thus, for instance, the influential Church of England report, *Mission-Shaped Church*, is predicated on C. Brown's analysis in *The Death of Christian Britain* (London: Routledge, 2001). See, The Archbishops Council, *Mission-Shaped Church* (London: Church House, 2004), p. 11.

[22]   Attempts to rebut secularization theory do exist but such rebuttals come from outside the UK: see R. Warner, *Secularisation and its Discontents*, pp. 68ff. The volume *Redefining Christian Britain* (J. Garnett et al) challenges the secularization theory by asserting that Christianity remains a key force in British life – but makes no attempt to challenge the view that churches *per se* are shrinking. The subversive writing of Bob Jackson, which has for some years pointed to areas of growth in parts of British Anglicanism, remains largely ignored by academic discourse: B. Jackson, *Hope for the Church* and *Road to Growth*.

[23]   K. Dobbelaere, *Secularisation: an Analysis at Three Levels* (Frankfurt am Main: Peter Lang, 2002). Different, but overlapping breakdowns of what secularization entails can be found in J. Casanova, *Public Religions in the Modern World* (Chicago: University of Chicago Press, 1994); and H. McLeod, *The Religious Crisis of the 1960s* (Oxford: OUP, 2007), p. 21.

[24]   J. Garnett et al, *Redefining Christian Britain*.

stressing its profundity. 'Britain is showing the world how religion as we have known it can die.'[25]

Other leading writers offer a view which is not quite as pessimistic – but hardly upbeat. Grace Davie coined the influential term 'believing without belonging' as a way of described a Britain in which the bulk of people claimed nominal Christianity but did not worship at a Christian church. In later work, Davie has preferred to speak of 'vicarious religion' as a more dilute description of the same process, whereby a majority of the British people are content that a minority practice religion for them. Davie's analysis assumes a highly secular nation. Church decline is a given.[26] The same is true of Robin Gill in his work *The Empty Church Revisited*. Gill sees decline as due to the over-supply of church buildings which could never then be filled. But he also assumes that secularity is certain to grow and religion certain to decline.[27] Woodhead and Heelas used a detailed study of the Cumbrian town of Kendal to argue that modern Britain is experiencing a 'subjective turn' away from organized Christianity towards various forms of spirituality which might be termed 'holistic'. Consequently, they argue that society may not be getting more secular, but congregational decline is seen as 'relentless'.[28] Woodhead and Catto's recent, highly nuanced, picture of British religion portrays contemporary British Christianity in terms of decline or attenuated survival.[29]

It is central to academic discourse about modern British Christianity that it is in decline – whether that decline be seen as slow or dramatic. The studies which support these conclusions beg five key questions. First, is there regional variation in the pattern of church decline or are churches across all of Britain declining? Second, is church decline happening across all churches or are some declining and others growing? Third, is church decline happening across all ethnic groups or only in some? Fourth, what is the value of different types of evidence – notably case studies compared to opinion polls and national attendance data? Fifth, how does the evidence in Britain compare with evidence elsewhere? These questions will now be examined in turn.

Regionalizing the Secularization Thesis

Discussions of modern Christian Britain have tended to emphasize regions where decline is strongest – and to neglect regions where growth has happened. Thus

---

[25]   C. Brown, *Death of Christian Britain*, p. 198; S. Bruce, *God is Dead*; D. Voas. and A. Crockett 'Religion in Britain: Neither believing nor belonging', *Sociology*, 39.1 (2005), pp. 11–28.

[26]   G. Davie, *Religion in Britain Since 1945: Believing without Belonging* (Oxford: Blackwell, 1994) and *The Sociology of Religion* (London: Sage 2007).

[27]   R. Gill, *The Empty Church Revisited* (Aldershot: Ashgate, 2003), p. 211.

[28]   P. Heelas and L. Woodhead, *The Spiritual Revolution: Why Religion is Giving Way to Spirituality* (Oxford: Blackwell, 2005), p. 41.

[29]   L. Woodhead and R. Catto, *Religious Change in Modern Britain* (London: Routledge, 2012), pp. 9–10.

Gill utilizes York and Wales as case studies. These are areas which have been mostly stable or declining in population, mostly lacking in economic dynamism and relatively monochrome in terms of ethnicity and culture. Yet much of the UK is experiencing population growth (often rapid growth) and economic dynamism and is increasingly diverse, both ethnically and culturally. Had Gill used London as a case study, his findings would have been markedly different – as this volume shows. Similarly Heelas and Woodhead use the Cumbrian market town of Kendal with its fairly stable, largely white, population – had they used York or Edinburgh they would not have had the same results. Brown paints a picture of a dying Christian Britain, pointing to marked decline in Scotland, but does not cite figures for Northern Ireland which offer a different ideological trajectory. Central to the findings of this volume is that church decline and growth varies markedly between different regions and towns (and, indeed, within regions and towns). Regionalizing the discussion is essential to measuring church decline or growth; where you look affects what you find.

Secularization: True for all Churches?

Studies of recent British church decline focus on what may be called 'the mainline' denominations, such as the Anglican, Methodist and Catholic churches – churches which have been in existence for centuries and whose bureaucratic structures facilitate statistical measurement. Other, newer churches (where 'new' is defined as those which came into existence during the last 100 years) are passed over. It is difficult to collect data on many such bodies, since they tend to lack overarching bureaucratic structures and they are therefore frequently absent or undercounted in statistical analyses.[30] Accurate measurement of 'non-mainline' denominations requires detailed case studies and even such research is liable to undercount. This is illustrated in the work on churches in York by Robin Gill and Rob Warner. Gill offers a highly nuanced case study of York's churches, but he focused on mainline churches and almost entirely ignored the new churches even though they have formed a large (and rapidly growing) element of the Christian community of York for several decades. Warner provides a valuable study of York's newer churches but still omits a significant number of them.[31] Detailed research shows that many new churches are growing fast nationally.[32] Consequently, a focus on 'mainline'

---

[30]   Thus, one of the key surveys of British churchgoing obtained a 30% response rate from the rapidly growing Pentecostal churches: P. Brierley, *Pulling out of the Nosedive,* p. 16.

[31]   R. Gill, *Empty Church Revisited*; R. Warner, 'York's Evangelical and Charismatics: an Emergent Free Market in Voluntarist Religious Identities', in S. Kim and P. Kollontai, *Community Identity: Dynamics of Religion in Context* (London: T. & T. Clarke, 2007) omits the following churches: York Chinese Church; York Korean Church, York Evangelical Church.

[32]   See for instance: W. Kay, *Apostolic Networks in Great Britain: New Ways of Being Church* (Milton Keynes: Paternoster, 2007).

rather than new churches means an overestimation of decline and underestimation of growth amongst British churches.

Secularization Theory and Ethnicity

Most studies of the recent history of British churches give startlingly little attention to ethnicity.[33] Whilst churches and Christians rooted in black, asian and minority ethnic communities may once have been marginal they are now a substantial section of the population as a whole and of the Christian population. It is estimated that 1,000,000 British Christians attend such churches.[34] A number of scholars seriously underestimate the significance of black, asian and minority ethnic communities in British Christianity. Bruce almost entirely ignores non-white Christians; Gill and Brown note their presence, but that is all. Heelas and Woodhead focus their research on a largely white community.[35] Such studies, which assert that the British church is declining, or even dying, are based on research which shows only that large parts of the *white* British church are declining. Black, asian and minority ethnic churchgoing is not declining; it is rapidly on the rise. Multicultural Britain has led to marked church growth in Britain. One of the unpleasant ironies of recent history has been the attempt by far-right political groups such as the British National Party to ferment hostility to black, asian and minority ethnic communities on the basis that the latter supposedly 'threaten' Britain's Christian identity. The evidence of *Church Growth in Britain* is that the exact reverse is true; Britain's churches have benefited greatly from the growth of ethnic minorities who now form a large section of church membership.

Secularization: the Conflict between National and Local Evidence

Beyond these specific questions is the larger question of the validity of national church figures and opinion poll data which form the backbone of much work on contemporary British churches.[36] Whilst such statistics have obvious value for generalization, they are highly problematic. The tendency to undercount non-mainline and new churches has already been noted.[37] More generally, just as political opinion polls are fallible indicators of voter behaviour in the polling booth,

---

[33]   The following studies focus primarily on mainline denominations and/or regions with small ethnic minorities. They give little space to churches rooted in ethnic minority communities: S. Bruce, *God is Dead*; C. Brown, *Death of Christian Britain*; R. Gill, *Empty Church Revisited*; P. Heelas and L. Woodhead, *Spiritual Revolution*.

[34]   See R. Warner, *Secularisation*, p. 161.

[35]   S. Bruce, *God is Dead*; C. Brown, *Death of Christian Britain*, p. 2; R. Gill, *Empty Church Revisited*, p. 163; P. Heelas and L. Woodhead, *Spiritual Revolution*.

[36]   S. Bruce, *God is Dead*, and C. Brown, *Death of Christian Britain*, rely heavily on such data.

[37]   See p 12.

it is vital to compare the findings of large-scale surveys with what is happening in specific communities. Surveys of religious views often point to decline. Yet, as this volume shows, there is evidence of significant church growth on the ground. This is not to say that such surveys are wrong, but it is to say that British society may be growing more secular in some ways (including the ways measured by values surveys) and less secular in others (often in ways less susceptible to tabulation). One aspect of the differentiated impact of secularization is that elite culture in Britain may well be secularizing,[38] whilst other parts of British life are seeing church growth. A survey of the religious views of, for instance, BBC executives and those who clean the BBC Television Centre in London might well indicate *both* secularization *and* resacralization.

Secularization: the Global Picture

Variants of the secularization thesis have dominated debate about church growth/ decline in Britain, but debate in other countries is more diverse. In America in particular there have arisen alternative strands of opinion – most notably, what is called Rational Choice Theory (RCT), propounded most forcefully by the American academics Stark, Finke and Iannacone.[39] It is gaining traction in wider academic circles but has had little impact on British thinking. RCT argues that human beings are naturally religious, that there is an inherent demand within human beings for the 'goods' which religion offers. These 'goods' may be directly to an individual's advantage – such as communal support or a sense of inner peace – or they may be more altruistic in tone – a sense of purpose, a cause to follow. Using an economic analogy, RCT argues that humans use rational choice, balancing benefits and costs, to determine whether they make use of religion, just as individuals make choices in other aspects of life. If the 'supply' of religion is limited and/or of poor quality, (e.g., when the main provider of religion has a quasi-monopoly such as the established churches in Scandinavia and Germany), 'demand' is limited and the result is religious decline. But when there is pluralism and competing suppliers of religion, the 'supply' of religious activity is more diverse and of higher overall quality and the result is religious vitality (e.g. a pluralist society such as in the contemporary USA). This is seen as explaining the markedly more vigorous state of American Christianity compared to that of northern Europe. For RCT, faith and secularization ebb and flow, rather than one triumphing over the other. Whilst

---

[38]   One piece of evidence supporting this is a survey of the religious views of Oxford undergraduates: S. Bullivant, 'Sociology and the Study of Atheism', *Journal of Contemporary Religion,* 23.3 (2008).

[39]   An influential example of RCT is: R. Finke and R. Stark, *The Churching of America, 1776–20050: Winners and Losers in our Religious Economy* (New Brunswick, NJ: Rutgers University Press, 2005).

there have been critiques of RCT, there is a growing recognition of its explanatory value.[40]

RCT overlaps with other schools of thought. Dean Kelley led other commentators in the early 1970s with his seminal book *Why are Conservative Churches Growing?* Kelley argued that the strictness of conservative religion was facilitating growth and that excessive readiness to adapt led to decline. Others disagree with his analysis but the reality of conservative church growth amid the decline of many other churches is widely recognized.[41] A different way of picturing the same reality is to describe the religious shifts in the western world in recent decades as a shift from obligation to consumption, a shift from doing faith as a duty to doing it as an individual choice. This paradigm suggests that, in the modern west, obligation-based churches decline but consumerist-based churches grow, meaning that society can get more *and* less religious at the same time.[42] This phenomenon can even cut through denominations; thus Mitchell in this volume notes that obligation-based Catholicism in Northern Ireland appears to be struggling, whereas Harris points to Catholicism's more voluntarist vitality in London.[43] Davie in 2007 concluded that RCT had some value in Europe, but that 'far more' Europeans operated on an older model of latent belief and nominal church membership.[44] This volume suggests that religion is growing steadily more voluntarist and that RCT and these other theories have an increasing purchase on modern Britain.

In all this, it is increasingly clear that British Christianity is best understood by comparison with other societies in the context of a series of highly interconnected global religious shifts. Sociologists have for some years pondered whether it is the relative secularity of northern Europe or the relative religiosity of the USA that is exceptional. But increasingly, it can be argued that neither Europe nor the USA are dominant. Both are simply part of a wider religious mosaic, as non-western nations grow more prominent.[45] Whilst it is beyond the scope of this volume to engage

---

[40]   For a critique of RCT, see: S. Bruce, *Choice and Religion: a Critique of Rational Choice Theory* (Oxford: OUP, 1999). Evidence of the growing traction of RCT within academia can be seen in: G. Davie, *Sociology of Religion*, pp. 67ff, 76ff, 80, 82–86 and R. McClearey (ed.), *The Oxford Handbook of the Economics of Religion*, (Oxford: OUP, 2011).

[41]   D. Kelley, *Why Conservative Churches are Growing: a Study in Sociology of Religion* (Macon: Mercer University Press, 1996); the detail of Kelley's analysis is contested, but his identification of conservative church growth is widely recognised – see, for instance, H. McLeod, *Religious Crisis*, pp. 207–08; G. Davie, *Sociology of Religion*, p. 150.

[42]   G. Davie, *Sociology of Religion*, pp. 86–105.

[43]   See Chapter 15, C. Mitchell, 'Northern Irish Protestantism' and Chapter 3, A. Harris, 'Devout East Enders'.

[44]   G. Davie, *Sociology of Religion*, p. 147

[45]   P. Jenkins, *The Next Christendom: the Coming of Global Christianity* (Oxford: OUP, 2002).

with debates over globalization or 'glocalization', a key theme of contemporary British church growth is the way trends across the globe are impacting upon British church life and should inform analysis of that life. Thus Hugh McLeod, in the recent *Cambridge History of Christianity*, ponders whether the future of global Christianity will be decided not so much by developments in the west, as by developments amongst China's churches, currently seeing marked growth.[46] Immigration to Britain is much remarked upon. What remains little commented upon is the extent to which many of these immigrants are Christian – and the potential changes to church life as a result.[47] Global shifts include a shift away from the long-established denominations which dominated western Christianity in the nineteenth and much of the twentieth century towards Pentecostal and independent churches, shifts from which Europe is not immune.[48] Within Europe there is much variation; whilst countries in the north and west of Europe have seen considerable secularization (from already highly secular societies), elsewhere in Europe, especially after the fall of communism, churches have grown.[49]

Global perspectives matter both because of immigration and because neither the secularization theory nor RCT work equally well everywhere. This fits with the work of Casanova, who sees everything as exceptional – so the secularization thesis and RCT cease to be overarching theories for everywhere and become ways of explaining what is going on in specific countries. Casanova is one of a number of writers who have argued that, at least in some parts of the world, religion is being de-privatized and that society is being de-secularized and even re-sacralized.[50]

Theories tend to be narratives of great power, claiming to be meta-explications of the complexities of the universe. By their very nature they can be absorbing, reductionistic, and totalizing. Part of the trouble with secularization theories lies precisely in their universalism. Is religion on the rise? Is it declining? Answering

---

[46] H. McLeod, 'Being a Christian at the end of the Twentieth Century', in H. McLeod, (ed.), *World Christianities, c. 1914–2000*, *Cambridge History of Christianity* (vol. IX; Cambridge: CUP, 2006), pp. 646–47.

[47] G. Davie, *Europe: the Exceptional Case. Parameters of Faith in the Modern World* (London: DLT, 2002), pp. 104–11.

[48] D. Martin, *Tongues of Fire: the Explosion of Pentecostalism in Latin America* (Oxford: Blackwell, 1990); D. Goodhew, 'Growth and Decline in South Africa's Churches, 1960-1991', *Journal of Religion in Africa*, XXX.3 (2000); R.S. Warner, *New Wine in Old Wineskins: Evangelicals and Liberals in a Small Town Church* (Berkeley: University of California Press, 1988).

[49] A. Greeley, *Religion in Europe at the End of the Second Millennium: A Sociological Profile* (London: Transaction Publishers, 2003), p. xi.

[50] J. Casanova, *Public Religions in the Modern World* (Chicago: University of Chicago Press, 1994); P. Berger, *The Desecularisation of the World: Resurgent Religion and World Politics* (Grand Rapids: Eerdemans, 1999); G. Kepel, *The Revenge of God: the Resurgence of Islam Christianity and Judaism in the Modern World* (Cambridge: Polity Press, 1994); J. Micklethwaite and A. Wooldridge, *God is Back. How the Global Rise of Faith is Changing the World* (London: Penguin, 2009).

this question at the meta- level is misleading. On one hand, religion is self-evidently in decline in some parts of Europe and the North East of America; while, on the other hand, in parts of South America, Asia and Africa it is expanding rapidly. What is needed therefore is the challenging of this hegemonic meta-narrative of 'secularization' with smaller regional accounts. For example, in Britain the narrative which dominates the popular imagery is that accounting which sees religion spiraling downward. The series of essays collected in this volume share an incredulity about this meta-narrative.

Section Three: The Chronology of British Church Growth

Insofar as there is a 'lesson of history' regarding church growth and decline, it is that Christianity has declined and grown in surprising ways across the centuries, meaning we should be wary of theories which assume faith can only shrink and not grow – or vice versa. Arguments for contemporary church decline tend to rely on the assumption that the past, especially the recent past, was very religious – a thesis which is questionable and which has the knock-on result of exaggerating the decline assumed to have happened in later decades.[51]

Whilst writers are clearly right to point to overall church decline across twentieth century Britain,[52] there was also significant church growth in some places in the first half of the century – notably in the suburbs of London, in Catholicism and in the new Pentecostal churches.[53] In addition, it is widely recognized that the period during and after World War II constituted a substantial 'blip' in the graph of decline, with a significant reinvigoration of British churches.[54] Rapid decline began in the 1960s and Brown and McLeod provide powerful depictions of the potent secularisation of that decade.[55] This said, greater attention should be given to developments in the 1960s which boosted the churches; the 1960s saw large-scale immigration, through which black majority churches were strengthened or came into being; it saw the marked growth of Orthodox churches in the UK and, via

---

[51]   See, for instance: P. Virgin, *The Church in the age of Negligence: Ecclesiastical Structure and the Problems of Church Reform, 1700–1840* (Cambridge: Clarke, 1989); R. Gill, *Empty Church Revisited*, pp. 19, 211 and Chapter 2 J. Wolffe and B. Jackson, 'Anglican Resurgence'.

[52]   See, for instance, S. Bruce, *God is Dead* and C. Brown, *Death of Christian Britain*.

[53]   R. Walford, *The Growth of 'New London' in Suburban Middlesex and the response of the Church of England* (Lewiston, NY; Lampeter: Edward Mellen Press, 2007); W. Kay, *Pentecostals in Britain* (Carlisle: Paternoster, 2000); Hastings, *A History of English Christianity, 1920–2000* (London: SCM Press, 2001), p. 134.

[54]   H. McLeod, *Religious Crisis*, p. 31.

[55]   H. McLeod, *Religious Crisis* and C. Brown, *Death of Christian Britain*.

the start of the charismatic movement, the 1960s saw the DNA of Pentecostalism entering the gene pool of wider British Christianity.[56]

Whilst the 1960s were, overall, the key decade of secularization in twentieth century Britain, some scholars see the 1970s as marking a shift in the other direction. Kepel pointed to the 1970s as the point when conservative religion worldwide began to fight back, when an economic slump called the idea of 'progress' into question and when a deep malaise was perceived in the world order.[57] Woodhead and Catto cogently argue that the post-war history of British faith divides into three sections: a mild religious restoration after the war; followed by substantial decline from the 1960s; followed by a marked shift at the end of the 1970s, when the dominant object of British post-war faith – the welfare state – began to appear frail and to be questioned. This was followed by further shaking of the foundations of secularity – in the form of the collapse of communism and a loss of confidence in science.[58]

The chronology outlined above provides the justification for starting this study in 1980. By this point the real shift to secular dominance in Britain had already happened. Only the delusional could ignore the marked decline in the size and power of the churches. Yet reaction to secularity was also vigorous. By exploring the 30 years since 1980 this volume explores the chronological trajectory of secularization – whether churches would continue to decline or whether they could also grow.

Section Four: Theoretical and Theological Perspectives

Theorizing about faith within the social sciences has been dominated by the figures of Marx, Durkheim and Weber. Within their thought the paradigm of secularization is a dominant motif. Marx, Weber and Durkheim model the belief that in the end religion will decline; it is an implicit (and often explicit) eschatology of church decline and secular growth. Each wrote in nineteenth century Western Europe as it modernized and secularized, and their thought should be seen as having general value but also as coming out of specific geographical and social contexts. What Marx, Weber and Durkheim might have written had they lived in China in the late twentieth century – with its mutating communism and burgeoning churches – is an interesting, but sadly impossible, question to answer.

A Brazilian friend commented to me on the resignation he witnessed among many churches in Britain, as if church decline was a given. His comment suggests that many contemporary British theologians, church leaders and churches have

---

[56]   See Chapter 7, H. Osgood, 'The Rise of Black Churches'; K. Ware, 'The Orthodox Church in the British Isles', in C. Chaillot (ed.), *A Short History of the Orthodox Church in Western Europe in the Twentieth Century* (Paris: Inter-Orthodox Dialogue, 2006); T. Saunders and H. Sansom, *David Watson: A Biography* (London: Hodder and Stoughton, 1992).

[57]   G. Kepel, *Revenge*.

[58]   L. Woodhead and R. Catto, *Religious Change*, pp. 12–15.

strategies for the Church to address the identified effects of economic rationalism, materialism and social injustice. To commemorate the twentieth anniversary of the report, the Church of England Commission on Urban Life and Faith examined the intractable resilience of economic and social inequality within inner city and outer estate communities. Its 2006 report *Faithful Cities* criticized the widening gap between rich and poor, especially along racial lines, despite multi-million pound urban regeneration projects in areas such as Docklands, Canary Wharf and the Isle of Dogs.[32] As such, it highlighted the continuing role to be played by the Christian community in addressing the effects of deindustrialization, increased migration and religious pluralism, as well as highly stratified social and economic hierarchies.

More than two decades later, one of the lasting effects of the *Faith in the City* report has been the strengthening of collaborative links in large multi-ethnic and religiously-plural cities between local activist groups, diverse church communities and agencies working to combat poverty through outreach and government-funded initiatives. Within English Catholic circles, these imperatives have received further imprimatur given the longstanding tradition of Catholic social teaching – perhaps best epitomized by the Archbishop of Westminster's successful mediation of the London Dock Strike of 1889 and Pope Leo XIII's encyclical on the dignity and rights of labour, *Rerum Novarum* in 1891.[33] These legacies of civic involvement issuing forth from religious commitment are well illustrated by the 2007 *The Ground of Justice* report by the Von Hügel Institute, Cambridge and commissioned by the Catholic Archbishops of Westminster, Southwark and Brentwood.[34] Exploring the impact of the recent influx of Eastern European Catholics on London-based parishes' services (and heightened figures for attendance at Mass), the report also emphasized the ways in which the Catholic church's parochial and social service infrastructures should be reinforced to aid these often homeless and hungry new-arrivals, providing networks for information sharing and social support, as well as a form of collectivization to protect vulnerable migrant workers from low wages and exploitative employers.

The Canning Town church studied also offers specific examples of faith-based social activism across its history, beginning in the late nineteenth century (around the time of the Dock Strikes) when the men of the parish were renowned for their staunch union support and, as Labour Party folklore has it, Keir Hardie acknowledged the role of this parish and the preaching from its pulpit as a crucial

---

[32] See: http://www.churchofengland.org/our-views/home-and-community-affairs/community-urban-affairs/urban-affairs/faithful-cities.aspx, accessed 12 July 2011. For further discussion of this report and its concept of 'faithful capital', see Chapter 8, R. Burgess, 'African Pentecostal Growth', in this volume.

[33] See M. Hornsby-Smith, *An Introduction to Catholic Social Thought* (Cambridge: CUP, 2006).

[34] See http://www.rcdow.org.uk/diocese/default.asp?library_ref=4&content_ref=1208, accessed 12 July 2011.

factor in his election as the first independent Labour MP in the 1890s.[35] A century on another parish priest – the local lad previously encountered who had imbued these histories of his former childhood parish with tales of East End activism – was one of the founding members in 1996 of *London Citizens*. Based on the Chicago model of community organising inaugurated by Saul Alinsky,[36] this organization is a diverse alliance of over 90 civil society institutions, predominantly from the faith sector, but including labour, educational and community-based organizations. Its activities have included a diverse range of campaigns spanning the London 2012 Olympics, the fight for the Living Wage and protection for migrants and asylum seekers (the 'Citizens for Sanctuary' and 'Strangers into Citizens' initiatives).[37] When asked about their involvement in parish-based activities which feed into these broader campaigns, Bianca spoke about the 'Living with other Faiths' programme and the group's visit to a local, coalition member 'Muslim church' to find out more about their prayer lives. Reflecting on the visit, she spoke of their devotion ('they closed (their) shops and so on – don't matter where they are they still – even in hospital they get a little mat and they will pray') and made comparisons between the Salat times (five daily prayers) and the Christian practice (now confined to the clergy) of the Liturgy of the Hours (Office, Lauds and Vespers). Cockney-born husband and wife team, Margaret and John take effective leadership of the The East London Communities' Organisation (TELCO) agenda, linking the activities of the parish into broader, London-wide events and campaign actions. They regale me with tales of the parish's attendance at rallies for affordable housing and recognition of the rights of migrants, as well as the success of the national living wage campaign against the big banks (in Canary Wharf and elsewhere) where the disparity between the wages of the bankers and cleaning staff supporting the operation of these buildings was publically exposed through the media. Smaller scale, profoundly local issues have also been tackled, such as the foul-smelling emissions from a nearby factory, lighting around train stations, and the worrying rise in knife-crime. For Belinda, who was a member of the group from the outset, the benefits she highlights are even more particularized – it builds community not only outside the church but also within it as 'it gets people together and gets people talking'. The former parish priest (now Vicar General) who started the initiative, Monsignor Armitage articulated a profound sense that this building of relationships of trust, understanding and mutual initiative within and across faith communities is imperative in the changed political climate of the early twentieth-first century. He attributed the co-ordinated response to the 7 July 2005 London bombings, including joint press statements and an inter-faith peace vigil on the steps of Aldgate station, to the decade-long relationships between the East London

---

[35] C. Benn, *Keir Hardie* (London: Hutchinson, 1992).

[36] S. Alinsky, *Rules for Radicals* (New York: Vintage Books, 1972).

[37] J. Wills et al, 'Religion at work: the role of faith-based organisations in living wage campaigns for immigrant workers in London', *The Cambridge Journal of Regions, Economy and Society*, 2.3 (2009), pp. 443–61.

Mosque, the Tower Hamlets Interfaith Forum and representatives of the Anglican and Catholic Hierarchy, which had been forged through *London Citizens.*

This recognition that a new century requires new initiatives has also led the Catholic Bishop of Brentwood to invite a community of young friars from New York's Bronx and Harlem districts to settle in Canning Town with the use of the parish's old hall/youth centre near to the church.[38] This small community of Franciscan Friars of the Renewal, comprised of young men all under 40 years of age and observing strict monastic rule and garb, established its mission to the East End in 2001. Here they run a soup kitchen for over 100 people four days a week and a night shelter for around 30 homeless men and a handful of women. Friar Joshua, who leads the community and is English born but has spent considerable time in the United States, contrasted this inner-city ministry to his middle-class and rural upbringing in 'middle England'. He speaks of the fundamental role of the community in Canning Town as bearing witness to God's love in an area stigmatized and stymied by poverty, family breakdown, alcohol, drug dependency and crime. These very modern ills are incorporated by him into a traditional Catholic history reaching back to the desert fathers and mothers. He speaks of Canning Town itself as 'the desert' – the area served by the community is almost isolated and cut off from the borough by the Thames and the A13 arterial – and he describes the establishment of a community here, as opposed to other 'mission territories' throughout the world, as a 'withdrawal into the wilderness'. However within this mystical tradition of seclusion, contemplation, austerity and prayer, Friar Joshua attests to the possibility of regeneration and integration within this most deprived part of London through prayer, spiritual renewal and the practice of unbounded hospitality and kindness.[39]

A very different interpretation of 'regeneration', predicated on the express intertwining of religion and politics and the church's intrinsic responsibility to shape the social order, is shared by an increasing number of ethno-religious groups who have sought representation in local politics. The Labour Party has dominated this area of London since its inception at the turn of the twentieth century and, on the amalgamation of East and West Ham to form the Borough of Newham in 1965, the party of Keir Hardie continued to enjoy a largely uninterrupted 60-nil majority in Council Chambers.[40] While the tradition of Christian Socialism re-emerged as a force through an independent charismatic fellowship of Labour

---

[38]   For discussion of the work of similar religious orders in New York, see R. Orsi (ed.), *Gods of the City: Religion and American Urban Landscape* (Indiana: Indiana University Press, 1999).

[39]   For similar theological musings, see, for example: E. Graham and S. Lowe, *What Makes a Good City? Public Theology and the Urban Church* (London: Darton, Longman and Todd, 2009).

[40]   G. Smith, 'Faith in Local Government: The Emergence of Religion in the Politics of an Inner London Borough, 1975–2006', *Politics and Religion Journal*, 4.2 (2010), pp. 157–82.

Party activists in the early 1980s,[41] the movement from class-based to religiously-informed identity politics can be more precisely dated from the late 1990s with the formation of the Christian People's Alliance (CPA). Drawing upon the European tradition of Christian Democracy, and constituting one of the most effective challenges to the Labour Party, this collection of Evangelical Christians fielded over 20 candidates in the 2006 local council elections. One of the most successful CPA candidates, Alan Craig, worked for a number of years as the youth work manager of the Mayflower Family Centre – an Anglican-based settlement founded by *Faith in the City* powerhouse Bishop David Sheppard and located merely two streets away from the Franciscan Friars initiative in Canning Town. On a platform centred on fair and affordable housing and 'family' values (chiefly contra homosexuality and abortion), Craig won his seat in 2002 and was re-elected to the Council in 2006 (with two other CPA candidates), polling over 6,500 votes in the mayoral election.[42] In 2008 he stood as a candidate against Ken Livingstone and Boris Johnson in the London mayoral elections, coming sixth with 1.68% of first preference votes. CPA draws much of its support from the burgeoning African population in the south and west of the borough, many of whom are members of Black Majority evangelical and Pentecostal churches. Similar constituencies have also been mobilized with a recent charitable foundation in July 2007 – the 'More than Gold' broad-based Christian initiative crossing church denominations and Christian agencies. Comprising the Church of England's Archbishops' Council; the Roman Catholic Bishops' Conference of England and Wales, the Free Churches Federal Council, Churches Together in England, the Evangelical Alliance, Afro-Caribbean Evangelical Alliance and Transform Newham (and cross-denominational evangelical Protestant organizations), this Christian charity is co-ordinating programmes of outreach, hospitality and service surrounding the Olympic games so that the churches can play their part in supporting the national effort and give witness to their Christian apostleship.[43] This initiative or the *London Citizens* alliance in which many Catholic parishes throughout the capital participate, given its congruence with 'social teaching' traditions and conceptions of the 'common good', contrasts with the CPA. Its self-consciously sectarian mobilization of religion as a salient marker for expressions of communal identity and ethnic differentiation has made the express articulation of religion within the political sphere intensely controversial for a nation that 'doesn't do God'.

---

[41]   G. Dale, *God's Politicians: the Christian Contribution to 100 years of Labour* (London: HarperCollins, 2001).

[42]   It is significant that in this 2006 election, Labour Councillors fell to 54 with three Respect Party (all Muslims, one of whom was a former Labour councillor and mayor) and the three CPA councillors. However, in the 2010 elections, when the UK Labour government was defeated, the Labour vote in Newham saw a resurgence and it 'regained its 60-nil in the Council Chamber', Smith, '*Faith in Local Government*', p. 159.

[43]   http://www.morethangold.org.uk/, accessed 12 July 2011.

Conclusions

There are a number of suggestive conclusions that can be drawn from this study of the transformation of Catholicism in London since the 1980s. Firstly, Britain's ethnic composition has dramatically shifted over these decades as a consequence of the unprecedented scale and pace of global migration,[44] with often little-appreciated consequences for religious communities as some of the world's 'oldest transnationals'.[45] Not only does this require greater attention to the dynamics of religious affiliation throughout the migratory process which scholars, particularly in the United States, are starting to address,[46] but it also requires more sensitive methodologies to examine the impact of interactions between settled and newly-arrived Catholics, and between Christians and other people of faith, on religious lives and social identities within (and beyond) the institutional, congregational realm.[47] This examination of the reanimation and renewal of forms of Catholic extra-liturgical religious life provides an example of the importance of moving beyond merely statistical, quantifiable and measurable factors such as church attendance when considering the growth and transformation of contemporary religiosity. In seeking to engage with the subjectivities and lived religious lives of contemporary Catholics in the East End of London, this case study asks different questions to those posed by traditional sociologists of religion who are committed to the secularization thesis[48] by paying attention to the ways in which Catholicism is intertwined into 'the everyday lives and identities of a large proportion of the world's population, affecting not just those who migrate or belong to a religious community'.[49] This methodological approach to the study of 'lived religion'[50] not only reveals fascinating continuities but also areas of devotional experimentation

---

[44]   S. Spencer, *The Migration Debate* (Bristol: The Polity Press, 2011).

[45]   S.H. Rudolph and J. Piscatori, *Transnational Religion and Fading States* (Oxford: Westview Press, 1997), p. 1.

[46]   See, for example: M. Vasquez and M.F. Marquardt, *Globalising the Sacred: Religion Across the Americas* (New Jersey: Rutgers University Press, 2003).

[47]   S. Warner and J. Wittner (eds), *Gathering in Diaspora: Religious Communities and the New Immigration* (Philadelphia: Temple University Press, 1998).

[48]   S. Bruce, *Secularization: In Defence of an Unfashionable Theory* (Oxford: OUP, 2011). For a sustained critique of the secularization thesis, see J. Garnett, M. Grimely, A. Harris, W. Whyte and S. Williams (eds), *Redefining Christian Britain: Post 1945 Perspectives* (London: SCM Press, 2007), Chapter 1.

[49]   O. Sheringham, 'Everyday Transnationalism: Religion in the Lives of Brazilian Migrations in London and Brazil', *University of Newcastle, Geographies of Religion Working Paper* #2 (2010), p. 22.

[50]   D. Hall (ed.), *Lived Religion in America: Towards a History of Practice* (Princeton: Princeton University Press, 1997), pp. 3–21.

and transformation,[51] drawing attention to the ways in which newly-arrived migrants can find within Catholic institutional structures and congregational networks avenues for 'refuge, responsibility and resources'.[52] As Hagan and Ebaugh conclude, this attention to the '"agency" component of the migration process stress(es) the creative ways in which migrants use the institution of religion and its beliefs and practices to organize the entire migration process, from decision-making to the development of transnational activities.'[53] From the spiritual resources of the Divine Mercy novena, to the Nigerian burial contributions of the Union of Catholic Mothers through to the activism of *London Citizens* to create a pathway into citizenship (through 'regularization' or a 'conditional amnesty') for long-term undocumented migrants, Catholic parishes in London are adapting to serve and support the spiritual and material needs of their diverse congregations.

This case study also speaks to emerging theoretical approaches which acknowledge the return of religion, faith communities and spiritual values to the centre of public life and the role of urban locations as places/spaces for negotiation across religious and secular boundaries.[54] Through an interdisciplinary examination of these 'postsecular cities', as Beaumont and Baker call them,[55] particularly one that is sensitive to the ways in which believers speak about their motivations for community involvement or political action[56] and subjectively spatialize their homes and neighbourhoods,[57] new perspectives emerge on the role of 'faith in politics'.[58] This recalibrated analytical lens is even more important given the ways in which British Governments since the 1990s have explicitly encouraged religious

---

[51]　M. McGuire, 'Embodied Practices: Negotiation and Resistance' in Nancy Ammerman (ed.), *Everyday Religion. Observing Modern Religious Lives* (Oxford: OUP, 2007), pp. 169–86.

[52]　C. Hirschman, 'The Role of Religion in the Origins and Adaptation of Immigrant Groups in the United States', in A. Portes and J. DeWind (eds), *Rethinking Migration: New Theoretical and Empirical Perspectives* (New York/Oxford: Berghahn, 2007), pp. 391–418.

[53]　J. Hagan and H. Ebaugh, 'Calling Upon the Sacred: Migrants' Use of Religion in the Migration Process; *International Migration Review*, 37.4 (2003), p. 1147.

[54]　A. Dinham, R. Furbey and V. Lowndes (eds), *Faith in the Public Realm. Controversies, Policies and Practices* (Bristol: The Polity Press, 2009).

[55]　J. Beaumont and C. Baker (eds), *Postsecular Cities: Space, Theory and Practice* (London: Continuum, 2011).

[56]　G. Smith, 'Faith in Community and Communities of Faith? Government Rhetoric and Religious Identity in Urban Britain', *Journal of Contemporary Religion*, 19.2 (May 2004), pp. 185–204; F. Tubergen, 'Religious Affiliation and Participation among Immigrants in a Secular society: a Study of Immigrants in the Netherlands', *Journal of Ethnic and Migration Studies*, 33.5 (2007), pp. 747–65.

[57]　D. Garbin, 'Embodied spirit(s) and charismatic power among Congolese migrants in London', in A. Dawson (ed.), *Summoning the Spirits: Possession and Invocation in Contemporary Religion* (New York: IB Tauris, 2010), pp. 40–57.

[58]　L. Jamoul and J. Wills, 'Faith in Politics', *Urban Studies*, 45.10 (2008), pp. 2035–56.

groups to engage in government-third sector 'partnerships',[59] to seek funding for community projects and, in a context of economic privation, to deliver essential social services on a voluntary or reduced-funding basis. In the wake of 9/11 and 7/7, political and academic attention shifted to the problematic role of religion within 'prevent' and 'community cohesion' agendas,[60] but more recent scholarship is now exploring the ways in which religious affiliation may allow for the formation of relationships which 'do not negate cultural, religious, ethnic or gendered differences but see people as capable of relationships of experiential commonalities despite differences'.[61] This has been termed a 'cosmopolitan sociability', defined as 'forms of competence and communication skills that are based on the human capacity to create social relations of inclusiveness and openness to the world'.[62] As Glick Schiller, Caglar and Guildbrandsen have recognized within a North American and European context, religious communities may allow for affiliation, identification and incorporation 'beyond the ethnic lens' and a 'shared humanity across lines of ethnic, national and political differences'.[63] Nevertheless, as the emergence of the CPA illustrates, with its implicitly exclusivist emphasis on a globalized Evangelical Protestant theology, 'some forms of openness, such as those constituted by religious discourses, may ultimately depend on developing rhetorics and practices of difference that create new forms of closure'.[64] In its various forms, religion has been recognized by New Labour and Coalition governments alike as a source of 'social capital' useful for the regeneration of London and the renewal of communitarian, 'big society' politics.[65] As this chapter illuminates, it is imperative for scholars to move beyond the analytical 'restrictions of a liberal consensus of separate public-political and private-religious spheres' and to recognize the dynamics of a 'political pluralism that, by necessity, includes constituencies of

---

[59]   R. Furbey (et al), *Faith as Social Capital: Connecting or Dividing?* (Bristol: Rowntree Foundation, 2006).

[60]   See A. Davey and E. Graham, 'Inhabiting the Good City: The Politics of Hate and the Urbanism of Hope' in Beaumont and Baker (eds), *The Postsecular City*, pp. 120–36 and 154–67.

[61]   N. Glick Schiller, T. Darieva and S. Gruner-Domic, 'Defining Cosmopolitan Sociality in a Transnational Age. An Introduction', *Ethnic and Racial* Studies, 34.3 (2011), p. 403.

[62]   N. Glick Schiller et al, 'Defining Cosmopolitan Sociability', p. 402.

[63]   N. Glick Schiller, A. Caglar and T. Guildbrandsen, 'Beyond the Ethnic Lens: Locality, Globality and Born-Again Incorporation', *American Ethnologist*, 33.4 (2006), pp. 612–33.

[64]   N. Glick Schiller et al, 'Defining Cosmopolitan Sociability', p. 412.

[65]   Most recently see C. Baker and G. Smith, '*Spiritual, religious and social capital – exploring their dimensions and their relationship with faith-based motivation and participation in UK civil society*', Summary working paper, Manchester: William Temple Foundation, 2011 http://www.wtf.org.uk/activities/documents/-BAKERANDSMITH270810.pdf, accessed 12 July 2011.

the religious and faithful'.[66] Within such an analysis, it will be necessary to try to incorporate the 'everyday' cosmopolitan sociability of Bianca (with her door-knocking and cups of tea) and Martha (with comfort and silent prayers at hospital bedsides) alongside the pragmatic, programmatic and public activities of *London Citizens* to ensure a 50% affordable housing legacy in the 2012 Olympic Park. This approach will also ensure that when analyzing 'church growth' in Britain in the last 40 years, attention will be paid not only to the diversification and (in some areas) the growth of Catholic congregations but also to the ways in which Catholicism may be inflected into the everyday lives, identities and collective activities of many more within the British population, beyond those who have migrated here recently or regularly sit in a pew on a Sunday.

---

[66] J. Holloway, 'The Space that Faith Makes: Towards a (hopeful) Ethos of Engagement' in P. Hopkins, L. Kong and E. Olson (eds), *Religion and Place: Identity, Community and Territory* (New York: Springer, forthcoming). For the beginning of this engagement, and diverse lines of interpretation, see, for example: J. Habermas, 'Notes on post-secular society', *New Perspectives Quarterly*, 25.4 (1998), pp. 17–29.

Chapter 4
Baptist Growth in England

Ian M. Randall

In England and Wales, according to the Census of 1851, Baptist churches attracted well over half a million worshippers.[1] By comparison with earlier growth, the twentieth century Baptist experience in England was marked on the whole by decline. Whilst there are a range of churches and groups of churches which regard themselves as 'Baptist', in this study I will restrict myself to churches in membership of the Baptist Union of Great Britain (BUGB), which amounts to over 2,000 churches, the overwhelming majority of which are in England. For churches in England affiliated to BUGB (I will use the terms 'English Baptists' and 'Baptist Union' as shorthand), the period from 1980 to 2010 was one in which a number of new missional trends became significant and in which growth can be observed.[2] This growth has been in numbers attending services. Formal membership has declined but attendances have been greater than the membership. According to Callum Brown in *The Death of Christian Britain*, from the 1960s Christianity in Britain went on a downward spiral and the Christian-centred culture that had conferred identity on Britain was rejected.[3] But groups of 'Dissenters' such as Baptists have seen themselves as counter-cultural and the 'downward spiral' theory does not fit Baptist experience in the period being studied here.

Local Churches and Growth

In the 1980s, a significant number of English Baptist churches witnessed a measure of numerical progress – after years of decline. As early as 1979, Lewis Misselbrook, then beginning work in the Baptist Union's Mission Department, said that in the mid-1970s it would have been difficult to find a dozen English Baptist churches that were growing steadily, whereas now there were about 200.[4] Growth in membership of the churches in the Baptist Union in 1984 was the largest for

---

[1] J. Briggs, *The English Baptists of the Nineteenth Century* (Didcot: Baptist Historical Society, 1994), p. 264.

[2] For the whole of the twentieth century, see I. Randall, *The English Baptists of the Twentieth Century* (Didcot: Baptist Historical Society, 2005).

[3] C. Brown, *The Death of Christian Britain* (London: Routledge, 2001), pp. 1, 193.

[4] L. Misselbrook, 'Perspective on Growth', *Mainstream Newsletter*, No. 1 (March 1979), p. 2.

60 years. Baptisms in that year were 1,900 more than the 1983 figure, with 8,159 people being baptized. A further increase in Baptist membership was reported in 1987 against a background of general decline in historic mainline denominations.[5] Wider influences were at work. Mission England, which took place nationally in 1984 with the American evangelist Billy Graham as its leading figure, played an important part in the growth that took place.[6] Baptists were heavily involved in 1984, and again in Billy Graham's meetings in Sheffield in 1989. The total attendance at the 1984 stadium meetings across the country was over 1,000,000 people and approaching 100,000 responded to Graham's appeal.[7]

In part, such growth was the product of deliberate effort. Paul Beasley-Murray, who was minister of Altrincham Baptist Church and then Principal of Spurgeon's College in London (the largest English Baptist training college for ministers and lay people), noted that 'in the 1980s a new spirit of optimism and commitment to church growth and church planting emerged'. One reason for this, according to Beasley-Murray, was Baptist involvement in the church growth movement.[8] There was also considerable interest among English Baptists in the 1980s in 'church growth' theories.[9] At Altrincham, membership grew from 93 in 1971 to over 200 by 1980. Membership doubled again in the subsequent years. Based on experiences at Altrincham and on a survey of 330 Baptist churches, Beasley-Murray and Alan Wilkinson produced *Turning the Tide*, offering a model for growth.[10] In the same period, Baptists such as Derek Tidball helped start the British Church Growth Association, whose inaugural meeting was held at Baptist Church House, London, whilst Roy Pointer worked through the Bible Society to create church growth materials which were influential in many Baptist churches, urging churches to deploy leadership, utilize small groups, define evangelistic tasks, and identify members' ministries in an effort to seek growth.[11]

There were examples of both small and large Baptist churches that were growing in the 1980s. Some were newly planted, such as a church in mid-Sussex which started meeting in the home of two medical doctors, David and Helen Skipp, in 1977 and which, by 1980, had outgrown a youth centre in Haywards

---

[5]   *Baptist Times* [hereafter *BT*] (31 December 1987), p. 7.

[6]   *BT* (6 February 1986), p. 1.

[7]   G. Reid, *To Reach a Nation* (London: Hodder & Stoughton, 1987), pp. 56, 61.

[8]   P. Beasley-Murray, *Radical Believers: The Baptist Way of Being the Church* (Didcot: Baptist Union, 1992), p. 118.

[9]   Church growth thinking from a Baptist perspective was dealt with in *Signs of Hope: Report of the Denominational Enquiry Group* (London: Baptist Union, 1979).

[10]   P. Beasley-Murray and A. Wilkinson, *Turning the Tide* (London: The Bible Society, 1981).

[11]   I. Randall, *Educating Evangelicalism: The Origins, Development and Impact of London Bible College* (Carlisle: Paternoster, 2000), p. 177; *Renewal* No. 95 (October/November 1981), p. 4; R. Pointer, *How Do Churches Grow?* (Basingstoke: Marshall, Morgan & Scott, 1984), pp. 7, 115–41.

Heath with seating for 150 people. Other examples of similar significant rates of growth in the South included Locks Heath, Hampshire. In the centre of Cambridge, under the preaching and the pastoral leadership from 1980 of Michael Quicke, the congregation at St Andrew's Street Baptist Church more than quadrupled, with congregations exceeding 500.[12] Often individual churches across the country began extension work. In the Midlands, West Bridgford Baptist Church, Nottingham, under the leadership of Peter Nodding, engaged in starting new congregations.[13] A similar approach to Baptist church planting was developed in Peterborough under the leadership of Stephen Ibbotson.[14] Initiatives were reported in the weekly *Baptist Times*.[15] An example of growth in the West Country was Zion, Creech St Michael, which grew from 35 members in the early 1980s to 175 by 1986.[16] In the Northern Baptist Association, where there were 224 baptisms in 1985 (more than in any year since 1923), the Association Secretary, David Neil, considered that the Association's churches generally accepted principles of church growth and renewal.[17] A number of new Baptist causes across the country received financial support from Baptist Home Mission funds to enable them to call a minister.[18]

As early as 1982, before church planting became a widespread topic for denominations in the UK, the Baptist Union had launched a church planting initiative.[19] At a later Baptist Union conference (1990) on church planting, which attracted 40 specialists, Geoffrey Reynolds, the Southern Area Baptist Superintendent (BUGB at that time had geographical 'Areas' and regional Associations within those), stressed the importance of regional Baptist Associations having their own church planting strategies.[20] This was based on his own experience. Industrial and office development had resulted in very substantial residential growth in the Thames Valley and around Swindon and Baptist churches established new congregations in these areas. Not all the Area's church planting ventures had succeeded but Reynolds could report on significant numbers of new

---

[12] M. Quicke, *360-Degree Preaching* (Carlisle: Paternoster Press, 2003), p. 13.

[13] Peter Nodding later wrote *Local Church Planting* (London: Marshall Pickering, 1994).

[14] Graham Doel has analysed Baptist church planting: G. Doel, *Church Planting in the Baptist Union of Great Britain, 1980–2010: A Critical Study*, University of Manchester MPhil thesis (2010).

[15] *BT* (19 July 1990), p. 5. I am grateful to Geoffrey Reynolds for his comments.

[16] *BT* (11 April 1985), p. 7; (6 March 1986), p. 7.

[17] *BT* (1 May 1986), p. 21.

[18] *BT* (28 January 1980), pp. 8–9.

[19] *BT* (17 November 1982), pp. 1, 7.

[20] See G. Reynolds, *First Among Equals: A Study of the Basis of Association and Oversight Among Baptist Churches* (Bath: Berkshire, Southern and Oxfordshire and East Glos. Associations, 1993); cf. I. Randall, '"Counsel and Help": European Baptists and Wider Baptist Fellowship', *Journal of European Baptist Studies*, 11.1 (2010), pp. 25–35.

churches. Considerable sums of money were raised through the Associations for new church premises and – as elsewhere – Home Mission 'initial pastorate' grants made a major contribution towards the support of ministry. Different models of church planting were offered at this conference.[21] Following the conference a Baptist Church Planters Group was set up and 'Planting Papers' produced.[22]

In 1992 it was calculated that, in the period since 1980, Baptists across the various Areas of the Baptist Union had been involved in the planting of 183 new churches, with the Southern Area leading the field (37 new churches), followed by the North West (22), then the North East and London (19 each), the South East (17) and the Eastern Area (16). The other Areas averaged a dozen newly planted churches each.[23] In the mid-1990s, however, there were doubts about whether this demanding rate of church planting could be significantly increased and the doubts proved to be justified. There were also tensions over denomination-specific church planting. Baptists like Hugh Cross, Ecumenical Moderator for Milton Keynes, argued that all new churches should be ecumenical, which had tended to be the pattern in Milton Keynes and other new towns. But others in the denomination, such as David Spriggs, then Evangelism Secretary at the Evangelical Alliance, and Stuart Murray, who taught Evangelism and Church Planting at Spurgeon's College, did not share this view.[24] Despite some uncertainties, nearly 200 Baptist churches were planted during the 1990s.[25]

In the years from the later 1990s, it was evident that Alpha courses, which provided a setting within which people were introduced to the Christian faith over a period of weeks, had helped to create a new approach to evangelism in many Baptist churches. Alpha was a product of Holy Trinity Church, Brompton, London, and spread initially through the charismatic evangelical constituency. In 1997 almost 5,000 Alpha courses were being run across the world, including 350 in Baptist churches in Britain. A year later this figure had risen to 500.[26] Many of these churches were sympathetic to the charismatic spirituality of Holy Trinity Brompton. In an article in 2002 on the impact of Alpha on Baptist churches, Darrell Jackson, Mission Adviser at the Baptist Union, estimated (from surveys undertaken) that over 1,000 Baptist Union churches were using Alpha. His research indicated that churches using Alpha were 'significantly more likely to be seeing increases in membership and attendance at worship than those that were

---

[21]   *BT* (19 July 1990), p. 5.

[22]   G. Doel, 'Church Planting', pp. 71–4.

[23]   *BT* (2 April 1992), pp. 8–9.

[24]   *BT* (22 July 1993), p. 9; For Stuart Murray's thinking, see *Church Planting: Laying Foundations* (Carlisle: Paternoster, 1998).

[25]   *BT* (2 December 1999), p. 1

[26]   D. Hilborn, *Picking up the Pieces* (London: Hodder & Stoughton, 1997), pp. 210–14; S.J. Heard, *Inside Alpha* (Eugene, OR.: Wipf and Stock, 2010).

not running Alpha'.[27] Over a period of 30 years, Baptists moved from the large-scale Mission concept to the idea of small groups that enabled people to explore Christianity and undertake a spiritual journey at a pace appropriate for them.

Leadership and Growth

The expectation of those examining the Baptist Union in the 1980s was that inspirational leadership would help churches to move forward.[28] In the early 1980s new energy came into the Union through the launch of a group called Mainstream. The first Mainstream newsletter affirmed wholehearted commitment to the Gospel 'as expressed in the [Baptist] Union's Declaration of Principle' – 'That it is the duty of every disciple to bear personal witness to the Gospel of Jesus Christ, and to take part in the evangelisation of the world'.[29] Mainstream was publicly launched at a late night extra at the 1979 annual Baptist Assembly and attracted 700 people, many of them ministers or lay leaders. David Coffey, the Mainstream secretary, who became the Baptist Union's Secretary for Evangelism in 1988 and later the General Secretary of the Union, interviewed several Baptist ministers about their experiences of church growth and Paul Beasley-Murray spoke on this topic.[30] Mainstream contributed to a vision for renewal and advance that was being fostered among many Baptist ministers, especially younger ministers. At one stage in the early 1980s all the members of the Mainstream executive were also members of the Baptist Union Council, the Union's central forum.[31]

Many within Mainstream were finding themselves in tune with developments in wider British evangelicalism and, unsurprisingly, many Baptists were deeply involved in pan-evangelical enterprises such as the Evangelical Alliance, which was growing swiftly in this period,[32] or the Christian convention, Spring Harvest, which began in 1979 and was attended by around 50,000 people by 1988. [33] In 1991 it was noted that a recent census had shown that 84% of Baptists identified

---

[27] D. Jackson, *The Impact of Alpha on Baptist Churches* (Didcot: Baptist Union, 2002), p. 6.

[28] Report in November 1980 from the committee on the General Secretaryship, held with the *Minutes of the Baptist Union Council*, Angus Library, Regent's Park College, Oxford.

[29] *Mainstream Newsletter*, No. 1 (March 1979), p. 1.

[30] *BT* (5 May 1979), p. 4.

[31] D. Coffey, 'Mainstream', *Mainstream*, No. 63 (September 1998), p. 5.

[32] J. Edwards, 'The Evangelical Alliance: A National Phenomenon', in S. Brady and H. Rowdon, eds, *For Such a Time as This* (London: Scripture Union, 1996), p. 53.

[33] *BT* (22 April 1982), p. 1; (10 May 1984), p. 15; (27 March 1986), pp. 1–2; P. Beasley-Murray, 'Renewal in Baptist churches', *Renewal*, No. 130 (March 1987), pp. 27–8; D. McBain, *Fire over the Waters: Renewal among Baptists and others from the 1960s to the 1990s* (London: DLT, 1997), p. 135.

themselves as evangelical. The census also showed growth of 2% from 1985 to 1989 in Baptist attendance.[34] The fact that many Baptist leaders were identifying with pan-evangelicalism helped to attract into Baptist churches people looking for an evangelical community. Baptist church growth both contributed to and gained from the dynamism of wider evangelicalism in Britain in the 1980s.

The numbers of people coming out of theological training and entering Baptist ministry were increasing in the early 1980s and this was another factor stimulating growth. The number of churches seeking ministers was also increasing. About 40 Baptist churches now had an assistant minister or were looking for one, which represented a considerable increase in the number of team ministries.[35] This was a trend that would continue. Often these team ministries led to growth. The ability of churches to support more ministers was partly due to an underlying increase in prosperity in Britain.[36] Baptist colleges continued in the 1990s and up to 2010 to have high levels of men and women training as Baptist ministers. Thinking about training changed, especially as more mature students entered colleges. In 1989 the average age of students entering Spurgeon's College was 32.4 and three-quarters had already served as assistant ministers, elders or deacons. Only about a quarter were from Baptist backgrounds, indicating how Baptist churches were attracting people – among them future leaders – from outside their own ranks.[37] Paul Beasley-Murray developed Spurgeon's Adaptable Leadership Training Programme (SALT). Later Spurgeon's began Church Planting and Evangelism training. At Northern Baptist College in Manchester, Ernest Whalley further developed congregational-based training. Similar moves took place at the Baptist colleges in Oxford and Bristol. At Regent's Park College in Oxford, Malcolm Goodspeed, Baptist minister in Woolwich, became tutor in mission and lay training, partly in response to a report – *Half the Denomination* – about the many small Baptist churches.[38]

The question of how to lead ecumenical congregations in which Baptists were partners became the subject of increasing discussion.[39] An example in Yorkshire of a Local Ecumenical Project (LEP) which grew rapidly was in Sheffield: St Thomas's Anglican Church and Mulehouse Road Baptist Church in Crookes began joint worship in 1977 when the Anglican building was undergoing extensive

---

[34]   *BT* (26 April 1991), p. 6.

[35]   Paper by Donald Black, *Ministerial Supply and Demand*, for Baptist Union Council, 26 September 1980; *BT* (4 June 1981), p. 2.

[36]   For figures see A. Halsey and J. Webb, eds, *Twentieth-Century British Social Trends* (Basingstoke: Macmillan, 2000), p. 328.

[37]   *BT* (21 December 1989), p. 10.

[38]   *BT* (3 July 1980), p. 7; (21 Feb 1985), p. 1.

[39]   K. Jones, *Baptismal Policy in LEPs: A Discussion Document* (Leeds: YBA, 1983, revised 1989).

refurbishment. An LEP was inaugurated in 1982.[40] St Thomas Crookes, as it was called, later achieved fame and then notoriety for its Nine O' Clock Service which boomed and then bust.[41] The church recovered and experienced further significant growth, planting another Anglican-Baptist congregation, St Thomas Philadelphia, led from 2004 by a Baptist minister, Paul Maconochie. This has multiple missional communities across the city.[42] Jonathan Edwards, who had earlier been minister of an Anglican-Baptist-URC ecumenical partnership (Southgate Church, Bury St Edmunds),[43] followed David Coffey as the Baptist Union General Secretary. The Baptist Union produced *With Charity and with Conviction*, encouraging Baptist participation in LEPs – provided Baptists could teach and practise believer's baptism.[44] The Union was identifying itself with an evangelical and ecumenical vision but considered that a clear vision for ecumenism in the next century was lacking.[45]

Baptist leadership in the twenty-first century has – as Peck foresaw – not had ecumenism as a major denominational concern. This is not because of a significant anti-ecumenical spirit in Baptist Union life; generally, Baptist ministers and churches strongly opposed to ecumenism have left the Union. Towards the end of the first decade of the twenty-first century, the Baptist Union published a document, *2020 Vision*, which looked forward to the year 2020. This publication suggested that other issues, such as spiritual growth and mission, are seen by most Baptists to be of greater importance than ecumenism.[46]

Movements of Church Renewal

The stress by Edwards on the 'infilling' of the Spirit is indicative of the way spiritual renewal, and in many cases specifically charismatic renewal, was an ingredient contributing to Baptist growth, just as it has become a powerful force in British Christianity.[47] Douglas McBain, later the Baptist Area Superintendent for London,

---

[40] R. Warren, *In the Crucible: The Testing and Growth of a Local Church* (Crowborough: Highland Books, 1989), Chapters 8 and 9).

[41] R. Howard, *The Rise and Fall of the Nine O' Clock Service* (London: Mowbray, 1996).

[42] http://www.stthomaschurch.org.uk/our_story, accessed 24 June 2011.

[43] A. Cross, *Baptism and the Baptists: Theology and Practice in Twentieth-Century Britain* (Carlisle: Paternoster Press, 2000), p. 303.

[44] D. Sparkes (ed.), *With Charity and With Conviction* (Didcot: Baptist Union, 1984), pp. 12, 14.

[45] *SecCheck*, 14 (Summer 1996), p. 2.

[46] *The Baptist Union of Great Britain: 2020 Vision* (Didcot: Baptist Union, 2007), pp. 2, 14, 15.

[47] D. Bebbington, *Evangelicalism in Modern Britain: A History from the 1730s to the 1980s* (London: Routledge, 1995), p. 229.

suggested in 1981 that it was largely from churches affected by charismatic spirituality that new candidates for ordained ministry in many denominations, including the Baptist Union, were coming and he saw the charismatic movement as having potential to renew Baptist life.[48]

By the early 1980s several Baptist congregations, for example Gold Hill, Chalfont St Peter and Commercial Road, Guildford (later the Millmead Centre), were emerging as models of Baptist renewal. Developments at Gold Hill had been featured in the *Baptist Times* in 1974. Jim Graham, the minister, reported congregations of 500 people in the morning and 300–400 in the evening. Church membership was just over 300 at that time. He described the evening services: 'We have a lot more spontaneity in praise and freedom in worship ... There would be an opportunity for the Gifts of the Spirit to be used. The main Gift used in the evening services so far has been prophecy ... Perhaps the most significant evening service is our evening communion service which would now probably run for two hours with much freedom.'[49] Features within the charismatic movement, identified by a 1978 Baptist Union report on charismatic renewal report – for example, committed fellowship, use of spiritual gifts, participatory worship and financial giving – all had commonalities with features of Baptist life. The charismatic movement also offered informal expressions of spirituality that mirrored cultural changes. Contemporary worship music, for example, became the norm. For Baptists as well as others 'renewal created a Christian version of the counter-culture.'[50] The most prominent Baptist exponents of charismatic renewal all offered a vision of church growth. In 1989 80% of the students at Spurgeon's College saw themselves as charismatic in their spirituality.[51]

For many Baptists in the 1980s John Wimber, leader of the Vineyard Christian Fellowship in Los Angeles, brought an intensified form of charismatic renewal coupled with a stress on mission which was appealing. Wimber had been influenced by Church Growth but came to believe that an essential element in evangelism was 'signs and wonders', as in the ministry of Jesus and in the Acts of the Apostles. He advocated 'power evangelism' and 'power healing'. The best-known leader within the Anglican charismatic movement, David Watson of St Michael-le-Belfry in York, gave his backing to Wimber in 1981.[52] A series of 'Wimber meetings' in Britain took place, with an international conference in 1984 in London.[53] In Lytham St Anne's, Ansdell Baptist Church hosted Wimber and his team for a

---

[48]   D. McBain, 'No Gentle Breeze: Baptist churchmanship and the winds of change' (*Mainstream*, 1981), pp. 6, 14, 17, 32; D. McBain, *Fire over the Waters: Renewal among Baptists and others from the 1960s to the 1990s* (London: DLT, 1997), p. 122.

[49]   *BT* (5 September 1974), p. 7.

[50]   D. Bebbington, *Evangelicalism in Modern Britain*, p. 233.

[51]   *BT* (21 December 1989), p. 10.

[52]   For David Watson see T. Saunders and H. Sansom, *David Watson* (London: Hodder & Stoughton, 1992).

[53]   McBain, *Fire over the Waters*, pp. 89–96.

weekend. When an associate of Wimber's climbed into the pulpit and said 'Come, Holy Spirit', the results were remarkable. Nigel Wright, then the Ansdell minister, later recalled: 'Within seconds the Spirit of God had fallen upon a large proportion of the congregation'.[54] Ansdell went from 62 to 198 members under the leadership of Nigel Wright.[55] Brian Butcher, pastor at Banbury Baptist Church, reported that after a Wimber Conference he and his wife had shared their experiences with their church and had seen 'God move across the congregation'.[56] Inevitably Wimber's approach produced widely differing reactions. But when he returned to Britain in 1985, he attracted 7,500 people to seminars in Brighton, London and Sheffield. Many were Baptists. [57]

Some Baptist churches in this period linked themselves with new groups such as that led by Terry Virgo (New Frontiers), prominent examples being Bracknell Baptist Church, Berkshire and Queen's Road, Wimbledon. When Ben Davies went to Bracknell as minister in 1964 the church was a small village congregation. Sustained growth led to the building of a 1,000-seater building.[58] Some Baptist churches left the Baptist Union to join these new groups. If they had stayed in the Union, Baptist growth would have been greater. Nigel Wright, in a key book, *The Radical Kingdom*, was critical of 'Restorationism' (a term Terry Virgo and others used) for its rigid views of ecclesiology and he argued for a view of renewal that embraced the whole church.[59] Among Restorationist churches and some Baptist churches the most dramatic event of the 1990s in the area of spiritual experience was 'the Toronto Blessing', which originated at a Vineyard Christian Fellowship in Toronto and arrived in Britain, at Holy Trinity, Brompton, in May 1994. People began to 'laugh in the Spirit' and exhibit physical contortions. *The Times* journalist, Ruth Gledhill, reported on the 'Toronto Blessing' as a nickname for 'mass fainting'.[60] A number of Baptist churches were soon affected, notably Queen's Road, Wimbledon, Lewin Road in Streatham, Herne Hill and Bookham, Surrey.[61]

The Toronto Blessing did not appear to result in significant church growth and over subsequent years the emphasis in many Baptist churches changed from

---

[54] N. Wright, 'A Pilgrimage in Renewal', in T. Smail, A. Walker and N. Wright, *Charismatic Renewal: The Search for a Theology* (London: SPCK, 1993), p. 27. See also, N. Wright, 'A Baptist Evaluation', in D. Pytches, ed., *John Wimber: His Influence and Legacy* (Guildford: Eagle, 1998), pp. 244–56.

[55] I. Sellers, ed., *Our Heritage: The Baptists of Yorkshire, Lancashire and Cheshire, 1647–1987* (Leeds: Yorkshire Baptist Association and Lancashire & Cheshire Baptist Association, 1987), p. 152.

[56] B. Butcher, 'Wimber at Westminster', *Mainstream Newsletter*, No. 19 (April 1985).

[57] *BT* (14 November 1985), p. 6.

[58] *BT* (2 February 1989), p. 7.

[59] N. Wright, *The Radical Kingdom* (Eastbourne: Kingsway, 1986), pp. 19, 140.

[60] R. Gledhill, 'Spread of Hysteria Fad Worries Church', *The Times* (18 June 1994), p. 12.

[61] *BT* (30 June 1994), p. 2.

dramatic events in worship to relationship and fostering community. For some, an influence was the discovery of the powerful community life of the sixteenth-century Anabaptists.[62] Nigel Wright advocated the values of these 'Baptist' believers as potentially helpful in finding a more radical contemporary Baptist identity. He spoke warmly in 1992 about the formation of an Anabaptist Network.[63] The combination of believer's baptism and the church as a community of believers was seen as highly relevant in a post-Christian society. This, however, was not an exercise simply in looking to the past. Baptists increasingly saw their churches as places to which contemporary people could belong, before they necessarily believed in the Christian faith or considered Baptist principles as important. There was a distinct preference in Baptist churches, as Darrel Jackson found in his research, for 'relational discourse' over 'denominational discourse'.[64] To the extent that Baptist congregations have been able to renew a sense of relationship they have been able to connect with a significant need that people have been feeling. In recent years 'belonging' has been central to many people's experience of affiliating with a Baptist congregation.[65]

At the same time, there was a renewed interest in the role of larger churches. Baptist churches with large congregations at the turn of the century included Gold Hill, Trinity Hill, Sutton Coldfield and Tonbridge, Kent. Each of these churches regularly attracted over 700 people to Sunday worship.[66] In the Baptist study *2020 Vision*, Roger Martin, who had seen church growth in each of his pastorates and was at that time the minister of Stockton Baptist Church, argued for the benefits of large churches. About 14% of Baptist churches had an attendance in excess of 350. Martin suggested that, in such churches, hurting people found anonymity whilst exploring a journey of healing; that there were resources of trained lay personnel; that teaching could take place in a more formal setting; that there were more young people who could form peer groups; and that a larger multi-functional team could undertake specialist ministries.[67] Research by Darrell Jackson on 'Finding Faith Today' showed that Baptist churches with a membership of over 300 were twice as likely to be growing as any other size of church, but he also suggested there was a significant element of 'transfer' growth.[68] In overall terms, however, the majority

---

[62]   I. Randall, 'Baptist-Anabaptist identity among European Baptists since the 1950s', in J. Briggs and A. Cross, eds, *Baptists and the World: Renewing the Vision* (Oxford: CBHH and BHS), pp. 133–51.

[63]   *BT* (24 Sept 1992), p. 10.

[64]   D. Jackson, 'The Discourse of "Belonging" and Baptist Church Membership in Contemporary Britain' (University of Birmingham ThD thesis, 2009), p. 125.

[65]   There has been much said about belonging before believing, as well as believing without belonging. cf. G. Davie, *Religion in Britain since 1945: Believing without Belonging* (Oxford: Blackwell, 1994).

[66]   *BT* (18/25 December 2003), p. 1. The attendance at Gold Hill was 1,200.

[67]   *2020 Vision*, p. 10.

[68]   D. Jackson, 'Finding Faith Today' (25 May 2002), p. 4.

of those joining Baptist churches did so following profession of faith, often linked with baptism as a believer.[69]

Mission in a Changing Society

Baptists were very aware in the period examined here of the rapidly changing face of British society. Some societal problems in the 1980s were seen as linked with high levels of unemployment and several Baptist churches assisted in the organization of work experience for young people. Concern about deprivation led the Yorkshire Baptist Association, through its Secretary Keith Jones, to arrange consultations on poverty. A Baptist mill-owner from Huddersfield proposed a scheme in 1986 to train unemployed young people as dry stone wallers.[70] A number of churches and groups were inspired by the ground-breaking example of community action at Bunyan Baptist Church, Kingston-upon-Thames, where the church launched the Kaleidoscope Youth and Community Project under the leadership of Eric Blakebrough. The Kaleidoscope youth club, advice centre, hostel and other ministries were featured in two television documentaries and Blakebrough wrote about his experiences of mission to those in the drug scene in London.[71] In central Cambridge, at St Andrew's Street Baptist Church, a centre was opened which served 4,000 people each week, including those who were homeless and jobless, and the full-time church staff team grew to 14.[72] Those Baptists who were socially involved were often those most acutely aware of the degree of social fracture in Britain. Riots in the 1980s showed the tension existing in parts of inner-city Britain. Stuart Cook at Solon Road, Brixton, and Stanley Woods JP in Handsworth, Birmingham were among Baptist ministers reaching out to ravaged communities. In Rochdale a Baptist couple, Graham and Kate Routley, developed community work among the large Asian population.[73]

Baptist mission in the 1990s, therefore, was marked by social action as well as evangelism and this trend was set to continue. David Coffey, as he became General Secretary of the Union in 1991, stated: 'I understand Mission to mean church planting and evangelism, social action and prophetic protest, a world mission commitment and a Kingdom of God awareness of international affairs and environmental concerns.'[74] Oasis Trust, directed by Steve Chalke, took several initiatives. The Trust became responsible for Haddon Hall, a Baptist church near

---

[69]   Ibid., p. 9.

[70]   *BT* (6 March 1986), p. 9.

[71]   E. Blakebrough, *No Quick Fix* (Basingstoke: Marshall Pickering, 1986).

[72]   M. Quicke, *360-Degree Preaching* (Carlisle: Paternoster Press, 2003), p. 13.

[73]   A Report by Graham and Kate Routley, 1 January 1980, Baptist Union Council papers; Sellers, ed., *Our Heritage*, p. 149.

[74]   *BT* (25 March 1991), p. 8; conversation with David Coffey, 17 July 2002.

London Bridge facing closure. In 1990 it opened a new hostel for the homeless.[75] Another initiative by Chalke, Christmas Cracker restaurants, raised about £1,000,000 in 1990 for social projects in Africa and India. Christmas Cracker had 420 outlets over the Christmas period, with thousands of young people involved. The seed-bed of the idea was a restaurant that Chalke set up during his ministry on the team of Tonbridge Baptist Church. The BBC produced a documentary about what was done.[76] Later Oasis Trust began training youth specialists for work in church and community settings. Help for holistic mission initiatives was available through Baptist Union Home Mission 'Green Shoots' grants and through funds available under what was called 'Against the Stream', a scheme to help fund projects in needy areas. The first 'Against the Stream' grants were made to Baptist churches in Toxteth and in Dagenham, East London.[77]

There were also issues connected with the younger generation and their view of the church. In his study on 'Finding Faith Today', Jackson noted that the percentage of those under the age of 19 in Baptist churches was not very different from the percentage in the English population as a whole and that those in this age group represented about one-third of all baptisms conducted in Baptist churches.[78] However Kathryn Morgan, a regional minister with the Southern Counties Baptist Association, drew attention in *2020 Vision* to the decrease in numbers of children in Baptist churches. She also noted that although Baptist churches had more people in the 20–44 age group (pro-rata) than some other denominations, nonetheless many local Baptist churches reported a lack of single people in their 20s. Some Baptist churches were seeking to address this through 'Fresh Expressions' of church or 'Emerging churches'.[79] Many churches premises were renovated and made more 'user-friendly' and also multi-purpose. An unexpected result from research undertaken in this period into those newly baptized in Baptist churches was that 25% of them were over 50 years of age.[80] This was in line with the theme of a book by Roger Standing, Tutor for Mission, Church Planting and Evangelism at Spurgeon's College. In *Re-Emerging Church*, published in 2008, Standing spoke about the way in which a generation that had an early awareness of Christianity but had not been involved in the life of the church community was approaching retirement and, in some cases, re-engagement with Christianity was evident.[81]

---

[75]   *BT* (8 March 1990), p. 3.

[76]   *BT* (21 March 1991), pp. 1, 9; (19 Dec 1991), pp. 11–12.

[77]   *BT* (5 May 1994), p. 3; (28 July 1994), p. 3.

[78]   D. Jackson, 'Finding Faith Today', pp. 6–7.

[79]   *2020 Vision*, p. 6.

[80]   D. Jackson, 'Finding Faith Today', p. 7. The way the Baptist community has been at work with older people is covered in Ian Knox, *Older People and the Church* (Edinburgh: Continuum, 2002).

[81]   R. Standing, *Re-Emerging Church: Strategies for Reaching a Returning Generation* (Abingdon: BRF, 2008).

The increasing diversity of British society in the 1980s presented its own set of challenges. In 1988, as President of the Baptist Union, Colin Marchant spoke of the great changes in West Ham during the four decades he had been working there. There were now more Muslims than Methodists and Baptists were outnumbered by Hindus and Sikhs. Mission had to recognize this new situation.[82] The multi-faith, multi-ethnic background was illustrated when Jay Chauhan was appointed by the West Midland Association to work in mission in the region. He was born in Kenya and was a Hindu by family background. Some Baptist churches were now multi-ethnic churches, for example Small Heath, Birmingham. It opened an Advice Centre for Asians. The Small Heath minister, Bill Dixon, was white, but the number of black Baptist ministers gradually increased. Desmond Gordon, for example, served with the Baptist Missionary Society in Trinidad from 1974-9 and then became minister at Church End, Finchley, London. Another black minister, Glenford Gordon from Birmingham, became pastor at Acock's Green, Birmingham in 1988. Although much inner-city Baptist church growth was among those whose roots were in the Caribbean or Africa, significant ministry was also taking place through and among people whose background was elsewhere. Fred George from Sri Lanka settled as minister at East Barnet in 1969. In 1996 Fred George – soon to be Baptist Union President – proposed a motion at the Baptist Council affirming the contribution of different races and cultures and acknowledging racism as sinful.[83]

One response in the 1990s to the challenge of under-churched, culturally diverse and economically deprived areas of the inner city was Urban Expression (UE). Although not an explicitly Baptist initiative, a number of its formative leaders, such as Juliet Kilpin, Urban Expression Coordinator, have been Baptist ministers. UE is widely recognised as Anabaptist in ethos and approach. Its most formative thinker has been Stuart Murray, whose work on mission in a 'post-Christendom' context has been influential, perhaps especially resonating with Baptists who have historically opposed the Christendom model of the church.[84] From 1997, UE deployed small church planting teams in London, expanding from there to Manchester, Glasgow, Birmingham, Stoke and Bristol and from this a number of new churches gradually developed from scratch. Urban Expression is one of the sponsors of the Crucible training course which is seeking to 'equip Christians to follow Jesus on the margins'.[85] Although not part of UE, 'Church from Scratch' in Southend has similarly been seeking to reach out in an under-churched area.

---

[82] *BT* (28 April 1988), pp. 1, 2, 3; cf. C. Marchant, *Signs in the City* (London: Hodder & Stoughton, 1986), pp. 88–9.

[83] *BT* (28 March 1996), p. 3.

[84] See S. Murray, *Post-Christendom* (Carlisle: Paternoster Press, 2004); *Church After Christendom* (Carlisle: Paternoster Press, 2004).

[85] http://www.anabaptistnetwork.com, accessed 25 May 2011. See J. Kilpin and S. Murray, *Church Planting in the Inner City: The Urban Expressio Story* (Cambridge: Grove Books, 2007).

It was established by Peter Dominey, a Baptist Union accredited evangelist, and Dominey described in 2007 how it had grown from three adults to 60 adults in its first four years. The process of evangelism is described by Dominey as the 'long, long journey walking alongside people who know nothing about Jesus'.[86]

The most spectacular examples of church planting and of rapid growth in this period have been among black-majority Baptist congregations. Kingsley Appiagyei in West Norwood reported that, when he came from Ghana to study at Spurgeon's in the late 1980s, a group of eight people began to meet in his flat. By 1991 the group had become a Ghanaian Baptist Fellowship of 180 in West Norwood, London. A year later, when this congregation was applying to join the Union, there were 350 worshippers, 95% of them Ghanaian.[87] Another predominantly Ghanaian congregation, Calvary Charismatic Baptist Church, which began in 1994 with Francis Sarpong as minister, had almost 400 members two years later. Loans from the London Baptist Property Board and the Union Corporation helped this church to acquire a former car showroom for worship.[88] These two churches became the largest in the Baptist Union, each with over 2,000 members. Kingsley Appiagyei became President of the Baptist Union in 2009.

A large number of ethnically diverse Baptist congregations began to emerge and many of these were growing in the 1990s. Willesden Green, London, with Philip Robinson as minister, more than doubled in size during the 1990s, to over 600 members. Growth was also seen in Birmingham. Clifford Fryer reported in 1992 on Cannon Street Memorial, Handsworth, a 280-member church that was 80% black and was part of the Birmingham Baptist Inner City Project. The Project missioner, Christine Parkinson, ran 'create and celebrate' days for black and Asian leaders, mostly aged under 35. Another Birmingham church, Small Heath, was converting a derelict property into shops and accommodation for single women and their children.[89] In 1994, a group of African Caribbean churches in London and the Midlands, the Progressive Baptist Convention of Europe, joined the Union.[90] A black minister who was to become the first black woman President of the Baptist Union, Kate Coleman, became a minister in Camden in 1996, later moving to Birmingham.

A Missional Denomination?

The major focus of this examination of Baptist growth from the 1980s has been local church and regional life. However, the churches belong to a national

---

[86]   G. Doel, *'Church Planting'*, p. 91.

[87]   *BT* (11 March 1991), p. 11. K. Appiagyei, 'Reaching Africans in London: An Ethnic Ministry', *The Baptist Ministers' Journal*, 238 (April 1992), pp. 6–10.

[88]   *BT* (20 June 1996), p. 1.

[89]   *BT* (16 July 1992), p. 6.

[90]   *BT* (17 November 1994), p. 3.

Union, and this last part of the study will look at the role of the Baptist Union as a factor in church growth. At the Baptist Union Assembly in 1977, after the annual report on 'the state of the Union', Douglas McBain asked from the floor that the Union examine 'the reasons for our numerical and spiritual decline'. McBain's intervention took the platform by surprise. Although Ernest Payne, Union President that year, was resistant to the motion, after Paul Beasley-Murray raised questions there were hurried consultations and a resolution was passed that an enquiry group should look at issues of Baptist decline.[91] Professor John H.Y. Briggs of the History Department at Keele University (later Pro Vice Chancellor of Birmingham University) chaired the group and the report, *Signs of Hope*, produced in 1979, represented an important analysis of Baptist life. Decline from 1952 to 1977 was delineated. The report expressed concern about churches that were 'closed in outlook', but concluded that 'there does seem to be ... an unwillingness to be bound by precedent, a new concern to proclaim the eternal gospel in terms relevant to the contemporary scene, and a greater willingness to serve the needs of the community in the name of Christ'.[92]

Although it was not entirely evident at the time, this period represented a turning point. In 1982 Bernard Green came from local church pastoral ministry to be General Secretary of the Union. Two years before that he wrote an article on 'What Baptists Ought to be Thinking about in the Next Ten Years'. Green urged, among other things, exploration of the purpose and place of Baptist Associations in education and training, inspiration, fellowship, evangelism, social responsibility and prayer; a critical examination of the life of local churches; and creative involvement in 'the struggles of humanity'.[93] His outline of hopes and aims was well received and set an agenda. Green was followed by 48 year old David Coffey as Secretary, with 39 year old Keith Jones as Deputy Secretary.[94] After their appointment they engaged in a 'Listening' process across the Union. Coffey and Jones later spoke of the vibrant Listening Day meetings as 'an adventure in spirituality'.[95] Out of these came 'Towards 2000', a 10-year plan designed to take Baptists forward with a common mission strategy in which evangelism was central.[96]

Missional issues – such as how well equipped Baptist churches were to undertake contemporary mission in a postmodern context in Britain – were then

---

[91]   *BT* (28 April 1977), p. 3; (12 May 1977), p. 5; P. Beasley-Murray, 'The Assembly: A Deliberative Body?', *The Fraternal*, 180 (July 1977), p. 19.

[92]   *Signs of Hope: Report of the Denominational Enquiry Group* (London: Baptist Union, 1979), pp. 8, 9, 25, 44.

[93]   B. Green, 'What Baptists Ought to be Thinking about in the Next Ten Years', *The Fraternal*, 191 (April 1980), pp. 3–6.

[94]   *BT* (15 March 1990), p. 1.

[95]   *SecCheck*, Issue No. 9 (Summer 1994).

[96]   *Baptist Leader*, Issue No. 3 (Summer 1992); *A Ten Year Plan Towards 2000: Incorporating the National Mission Strategy* (Didcot: Baptist Union, 1993).

addressed at a Denominational Consultation held at Swanwick in 1996, only the third such Baptist consultation held since World War II. It was David Coffey's hope that mission would be the focus of discussions but he was also well aware of the fact that there was frustration with the internal functioning of the Union.[97] By now there was a widespread concern about how to be relevant to a new cultural climate. At the 1996 Consultation the importance of re-imagining the Union was emphasized, as was the need to create a new structural framework for associating within the Union. To what extent, then, did changes within the Union in the 1990s produce, as David Coffey and Keith Jones hoped, a new thrust in mission? Over the period 1989 to 1998 the churches in the Baptist Union had an increased Sunday attendance of 2%. Grace Baptists and Gospel Standard Strict Baptists declined in this period. Independent Baptist attendance (many independent Baptist churches had formerly been in the Union) however, increased by 27% to 24,400.[98]

Further detailed work was commissioned by the Union on baptisms and attendance figures by region. In Yorkshire, for example, it was noted that Baptist congregations had grown by 19% during the 1990s after a fall of 6% in the 1980s.[99] Nationally, baptisms were up by 15% in 1997 compared to the year before.[100] Writing in 1998, Darrell Jackson noted that in the previous two years, although baptisms had increased, Baptist membership had continued to decline. There were indications of more people attending Baptist churches, but many were not becoming members.[101] A year later, Jackson's analysis of the changing relationship between attendance and membership was confirmed. Research showed that, against a background of a 14% decline in churchgoing in the 1990s, attendance at Baptist churches had grown by 13%.[102] Between 1989 and 1998 regular attendance at Baptist churches had increased from an estimated 162,000 to 167,500 and a report spoke of 'Bucking the Trend'. Over the same period, however, church membership had decreased from 161,400 to 144,900.[103]

Looking at the period 1998 to 2003, David Coffey pointed to the increases in regular attendance at worship and in the numbers of baptisms performed. These had increased by 20% and 26% respectively in those five years but, given the continued decline in membership, he commented: 'It would seem it is our inability to attract a committed membership to the local church that is the most challenging

[97] D Coffey 'The Denominational Consultation', *Baptist Leader*, Issue No 13 (Winter 1995), pp. 1-2.

[98] P. Brierley, *The Tide is Running Out* (London: Christian Research Association, 2000), p. 39.

[99] *BT* (16/23 December 1999), p. 5.

[100] *BT* (1 January 1998), p. 1

[101] *BT* (19 November 1998), p. 5.

[102] *BT* (2 December 1999), p. 1.

[103] 'Bucking the Trend', in M. Blyth (ed.), *Joined Up Thinking: Membership* (Didcot: Baptist Union, 2004).

statistic.'[104] A Baptist Union research report was commissioned in 2003 and this looked at issues of numbers and also what it meant to people to belong to a Baptist church. Results showed that members and attendees of Baptist churches valued the relationships they found or hoped to find in the congregation more than they appreciated denominational identity. This was particularly true for the rising number of individuals opting for regular attendance without formal membership. Not surprisingly, a sense of belonging was frequently nourished by involvement in small groups, which were to be found in almost all Baptist churches.[105] In the same period the Union called a Consultation on Church Planting and out of this the Incarnate Network was formed to communicate stories about church planting practice, to foster networking, to promote church planning strategies and to help practitioners to learn from and develop their practice.[106]

Many churches in the Baptist Union, as they came to the end of the first decade of the twenty-first century, had been planted or had experienced some significant advance over the previous 30 years, but the results for 2002–2008, as presented in the *Baptist Times* for 19 February 2010, were decidedly mixed. Church attendance on the first Sunday in December had risen by 3% during these years, roughly in line with growth in population. The number of regular Baptist churchgoers was probably higher than this figure as many were worshipping less than weekly or attending church on a day other than Sunday. There was an increase in teenagers attending Baptist churches (up by 9%) or otherwise in contact with congregations (up by 21%), but church membership fell by 7%, baptisms by 23% and children under 14 in contact with Baptist churches by 8%. The number of members in 2008 was 139,000, considerably less than the total of those attending services.[107] This indicates, perhaps, different ways of 'belonging' to Baptist churches and potential for growth.

Conclusion

Within Baptist life the period examined here has been one in which there have been many examples of local church growth. Wider influences have been at work, such as the Billy Graham campaigns of the 1980s. But in many cases the initiatives have been local. Movements of renewal have been significant for Baptists, especially charismatic renewal. David Bebbington argues that, up to the 1960s, many chapels – Baptist and others – were retreating before secularizing forces and that the charismatic movement brought 'rejuvenating change' and new

---

[104] D. Coffey, *A Missionary Union: Past, Present and Future Perspectives: The Dr G R Beasley-Murray Memorial Lecture 2006* (London: Spurgeon's College, 2006), p. 6.

[105] Analysed in Jackson,'The Discourse of "Belonging" and Baptist Church Membership', Chapters 5 and 6.

[106] G. Doel, 'Church Planting', pp. 102–04.

[107] *BT* (19 February 2010), p. 1.

confidence.[108] This was true for a generation of Baptist ministers and lay leaders. There was also a consistent desire to engage in relevant mission, not simply to be concerned with inner renewal. Baptist growth has been connected with a blending of Baptist identity into a broader charismatic-evangelicalism, with Alpha courses as an important ingredient in that process. Baptist identity has not been seen as linked to a 'Christendom' model of church, but rather to a missional one.[109] In a context in which church decline was given great publicity in society at large, the challenge of shaping communities that were effective in mission was seen by Baptists in England as of paramount importance. The vision was worked out in holistic mission, church planting and increasingly through multi-ethnic congregations. Baptists have seen more people attending their churches but have also faced the issue of declining membership.[110]

---

[108]   D. Bebbington, 'Evangelism and Spirituality in Twentieth-Century Protestant Nonconformity', in A.P.F. Sell and A.R. Cross (eds), *Protestant Nonconformity in the Twentieth Century*, p. 215.

[109]   *BT* (23 Sept 1999), p. 11.

[110]   *BT* (19 February 2010), p. 1.

Chapter 5

Stirrings in Barchester: Cathedrals and Church Growth

Lynda Barley

Cathedrals have a particular place in the history of Britain and in contemporary British society. This chapter will focus on the 42 English cathedrals of the Church of England but even here the contribution of each cathedral to Church and society is unique. The Queen has jurisdiction over the Royal Peculiar churches which include Westminster Abbey. Roman Catholic and Orthodox Churches have their own cathedrals but, in the lives of the majority of English residents, it is the image of their Church of England diocesan cathedral that comes to mind with the headline 'Cathedrals and Church Growth'. In the minds of the public cathedrals are associated with bishops and consequently with the bishop's throne in the diocesan cathedral. In many respects English diocesan cathedrals bear the hallmarks of being places of Christian tradition and are representative of institutional religion, although some cathedrals might challenge such generalizations.

Since the 1980s the Research and Statistics department of the Archbishops' Council (formerly the Statistics Unit of the Church of England Central Board of Finance) has gathered and monitored congregational statistics from the English cathedrals. Over time the statistics have been actively developed to reflect more accurately the daily ministry and mission of cathedrals in their local neighbourhoods. With the permission of the Association of English Cathedrals (AEC) we shall bring together the emerging story from these statistics and from the trends within them, reflecting too on the wider social and religious context in which these cathedrals operate in contemporary society. The statistics collected across recent years suggest a dramatic rise in attendance at worship across the last decade and reveal a changing role for cathedrals which is of increasing interest to researchers. This chapter will argue that English cathedrals at the beginning of the twenty-first century are in good health and of ongoing significance to wider society, with a view to stimulating further religious sociological and theological reflection.[1]

---

[1] This chapter complements the work of S. Platten and C. Lewis, (eds), *Dreaming Spires: Cathedrals in a New Age* (London: SPCK, 2006).

Christian Heritage Attractions

Cathedrals have historically been key features in defining the status of a city and, as population mobility has altered and neighbourhoods have grown, some cathedrals, like Bradford, have consequently emerged from their roots as parish churches. Others, for example York Minster, have monastic roots and a number, like Salisbury cathedral, attract pilgrims travelling together to explore journeys of faith. More modern cathedrals, for example at Guildford, were designed as mother churches to accommodate large gatherings for worship and celebration. Cathedrals are frequently the largest public building in their city and will be sought as a venue for university graduation ceremonies or local festivals, concerts and exhibitions. All the English cathedrals have experienced an increase in such bookings and in the last 15 years or so have particularly embraced the need for professional business arms to their operations. Since the turn of the millennium annual returns to the AEC have shown that 1,600,000 people every year have enjoyed the setting of their local cathedral for over 5,000 public events. Our cities have come to benefit from each cathedral hosting, on average, between three and five public events every week throughout the year.

In recent years it has become a controversial subject of debate that a number of cathedrals feel the need to charge visitor fees or request voluntary donations towards the upkeep of the building. Despite this development visitor numbers remain high and cathedrals estimate that around 12,000,000 people visit English cathedrals each year, necessitating the assistance of 15,000 volunteers (on average 350 per cathedral). Canterbury Cathedral, York Minister and St Paul's, London (alongside Westminster Abbey) are consistently among the top 20 or so visitor attractions in Britain reported by the Association of Leading Visitor Attractions.[2] Three of the English cathedrals (Durham, Westminster Abbey and Canterbury) are World Heritage sites and a number of other cathedrals across the country are also major national tourist attractions. Winchester cathedral, for example, is a frequent inclusion on day tourism trips from London to this city. Such popularity as sources of heritage tourism has prompted cathedrals to consider how to marry a careful business model in this area with their desire to offer Christian hospitality. The growth of public interest in spirituality since the turn of the millennium is well documented[3] and has prompted cathedrals to develop spiritual tours and programmes with the aspiration of turning tourists into pilgrims. Southwark cathedral, for example, has taken a simple step in recent years by offering a brief leaflet explaining the spiritual significance of the Christian symbols in the cathedral.

Since the 1990s cathedrals have discovered particular opportunities to develop as attractions for younger visitors. In British schools the curriculum focus on

---

[2]   www.alva.org.uk/vistor_statistics, accessed 10 September 2011.

[3]   See L. Barley, *Time to Listen: Christian Roots, Contemporary Spirituality* (London: Church House Publishing, 2006), pp. 3–9.

spiritual, moral and cultural education has provided opportunities for cathedrals to offer their historic perspective on Christian spirituality and religiosity. Promoting educational programmes through the development of education centres has become more popular across many cathedrals, including those located in less than obvious tourist locations. Every year English cathedrals now host 300,000 children and young people visiting through organized educational events. A number of cathedrals employ education officers to develop this work and to broaden their provision for visitors to connect with the cathedral's spiritual heritage. They are, in turn, discovering that a child's enthusiasm can be a worthwhile draw, encouraging the wider family circle to make subsequent visits.

In 2009 the AEC co-sponsored a national cathedral visitor survey with English Heritage, Ecclesiastical Insurance Group, Garfield Weston and a number of smaller charitable funders.[4] In this study it was not altogether surprising to discover that the cathedral building itself was the most significant attraction for four in ten (41%) of visitors but of greater significance for our discussion here is that one in ten (10%) were primarily attracted by the opportunity to reflect and be thoughtful (often about a loved one). Overall, visitors to cathedrals report high satisfaction levels. Six in ten (58%) rate their visit very good, a proportion which increased by over 10% as they participated in what the cathedral had to offer.

Spiritual Ministry

The highest levels of satisfaction among cathedral visitors were reported by those in the 2009 survey who had actively engaged in the cathedral's spiritual ministry. Seven in ten visitors (68%) who had time to light a candle and pray rated their visit as very good while the highest satisfaction rating was offered by those who attended a cathedral service. Three in four (74%) of visitors who attended a service of worship rated the visit overall as very good. We shall reflect further on cathedral worship but at this point it is worth noting the attraction that cathedral worship is to those beyond the regular congregation, to those who come to the cathedral as visitors and who take the opportunity to engage with its spiritual ministry. Where visitors had the opportunity to attend a service the music, the choir and the time to pray were most frequently highlighted.

Alongside heritage tours the ministry of prayer candles, prayer boards and spiritual tours is growing at a fast rate. Six in ten (59%) found time during their visit to light a candle or say a prayer and even among those who 'just looked around' the cathedral, four in ten (45%) also prayed or lit a candle. One cathedral verger has commented that he could not accommodate any more candle stations which was a regret, not least because the associated donations generated more

---

[4]   Opinion Research Business (ORB) *English Cathedral National Visitor Survey* for the Association of English Cathedrals (March 2010).

income than anything else in the cathedral. Wakefield cathedral, for example,[5] has taken the challenge of spiritual connectivity further by offering a popular audio spiritual tour which incorporates an opportunity to reflect at a prayer station.

Cathedrals are responding positively to what appears to be a growing spiritual appetite among their visitors. It has to be acknowledged that a cathedral visit is particularly appreciated by older people and those who regard themselves as Christians but it is certainly not restricted to regular churchgoers. The 2009 cathedral visitor survey revealed that two in three described themselves as a spiritual or religious person, that eight in ten consider themselves Christian while four in ten attend church ònce a month or more often. Although these statistics are higher than their counterparts across the general public,[6] it is clear there are still significant numbers of people who are more attracted to cathedrals by aspects of their Christian heritage than by dimensions of Christian spirituality. The ambience of the cathedral, its atmosphere, peacefulness and calm was cited as the most appreciated aspect of their visit by one in four (27%) of visitors while over half cited various aspects of the building. In an age of supposed growing secularization English cathedrals attract visitors primarily as places of Christian heritage tourism but within this framework they are gaining confidence to make connections with contemporary spirituality.

Social Capital

English cathedrals are seen by many as icons of the traditions of Christendom across England. Over the last 30 years, in common with much of urban England, the cities in which they have been planted have generally grown in population, commerce and business. Their status has meant that universities and business have often sought to attract attention by promoting the status of their location as that of a 'cathedral city'. Cathedrals are only too aware that their presence attracts people to their city. Surveys in the early years of the twenty-first century at Wells and at Truro included a question that asked tourist visitors to name the most important factor that had persuaded them to come to the city. It was estimated that three in four (78%) of people who visited Wells primarily did so to visit the cathedral and approaching one in four (23%) at Truro noted that the main reason was specifically to visit the cathedral.[7] Links between cathedrals and their cities seem strong. Cathedrals and other city churches bring social capital to their host

---

[5]   See L. Barley, *Time to Listen: Community Value* (London: Church House Publishing, 2007), pp. 47–9.

[6]   See L. Barley, *Time to Listen: Christian Roots*, pp. 3–9.

[7]   Quoted in ECOTEC Research & Consulting Ltd, *The Economic and Social Impact of Cathedrals in England* (June 2004), p. 36.

city and take their civic links seriously.[8] Their role hosting civic functions has grown in significance in recent years and they actively build links with the city mayor and local council.

In 2004 English Heritage joined with the AEC to commission a study to assess the economic and social impact of Anglican cathedrals in England.[9] The study used an analytical framework focussing on flows of expenditure to assess the economic impact associated with cathedrals. They examined the financial expenditure of the visitors they attracted and the way these flows worked through the local economies, generating incomes and employment in the process. The study also endeavoured to estimate the extent to which the presence of the cathedral influenced individuals to visit the local area and to capture the social impact of cathedrals through education, volunteering, social and community activity.

Thirty-nine English cathedrals provided information and a number of case studies were conducted to formulate a typology of the various roles and impact of different types of cathedral:

- Large, international importance
- Medium-sized historic
- Medium-sized modern
- Urban
- Parish church

The calculations suggested that cathedrals accounted for a total visitor spend in their areas of £91,000,000 per year with a total impact on local spending of £150,000,000 per year. They directly employed 2,000 people and their impact on local employment in visitor and related activities was around 5,500 people full-time equivalent (FTE). Even the 'Parish church' category resulted in, on average, 25 FTE in employment while the 'Large, international' category generated, on average, 460 FTE.

Cathedrals bring the vitality of employment and economic health to their cities and, like churches, are key parts of their local neighbourhoods. National surveys over the last decade reveal that a consistently high proportion (85%) of adults in Britain have visited a local church or chapel for some reason over the previous year[10] compared to 46% who have visited an historic house/garden, and 51% who have visited a cinema.[11] Across the turn of the third millennium local churches

---

[8] See *Commission on Urban Life and Faith, Faithful Cities: A Call for Celebration, Vision and Justice* (London: Methodist Publishing House and Church House Publishing, 2006), pp. 76–88.

[9] ECOTEC Research & Consulting Ltd, *The Economic and Social Impact of Cathedrals in England* (June 2004).

[10] Opinion Research Business (ORB) *Surveys for the Archbishops' Council* (October 2001–2009).

[11] Quoted in, *Faithful Cities*, p. 97.

and other places of worship have continued to feature strongly in community life. They have adapted to their changing social context and their presence remains an integral part of local community living that quietly persists in English daily life.[12]

Government funders too have taken a close interest in historic places of worship and sought to map the most vulnerable and target their resources. They have been interested to explore the appetite of the public for the community role of places of worship. In a national survey sponsored by English Heritage and the Church of England in 2003, seven in ten (72%) adults in Britain considered a place of worship to be an important part of the local community; six in ten (63%) agreed that places of worship should be more actively involved in the local community, while seven in ten (69%) felt that places of worship should be more accessible to the local community and a similar proportion (72%) agreed that places of worship provide valuable social and community facilities.[13] This positive picture has particularly encouraged cathedrals and churches to keep their doors open for community use and spiritual reflection. Malcolm McLaren, a punk rock manager, observed in an interview: 'Church is the most fantastic place. It's sanctuary. They should be open 24 hours a day. They're the only place left in London where you don't have to buy anything.'[14]

Cathedrals, in particular, are open to all every day of the year. They host exhibitions, concerts, civic and public events, conferences and meetings, university graduation ceremonies and school functions. They offer a unique community resource which is distinctive and also growing in popularity. In 2000, at the turn of the millennium, when footfall figures were first collected, English cathedrals attracted over 907,000 people to public or civic events and by 2010 this number had grown significantly to 1,600,000. The public role of cathedrals and churches in creating social capital and contributing to community cohesion remains strong and cathedrals have found their growing connections with their localities to be mutually beneficial.

Open Worship

Although cathedrals and churches are valued as places of historic interest and community resource, their role as centres of worship and prayer in local communities is even more strongly marked out. Back in the 1980s the impact of cathedrals on this area of national life was waning. Sunday worship attendance levels were steadily declining alongside those of local parish churches. Between 1986 and 1987, for example, adult attendance at cathedral worship on a typical Sunday

---

[12]   One particularly interesting example is documented by T. Jenkins, *Religion in Everyday Life: An Ethnographic Approach* (New York/ Oxford: Berghahn Books, 1999).

[13]   Opinion Research Business (ORB) *Surveys for the Archbishops' Council* (October 2005).

[14]   Quoted in, *Faithful Cities*, p. 78.

dropped by nearly 5% to 13,700 and the numbers of children and young people attending decreased by almost 14% to just 2,300. This pattern continued alongside declines in the traditional counts of cathedral communicant numbers, baptism and electoral roll figures. Although there were some successes in individual cathedrals for individual years the general picture of decreasing cathedral congregations mirrored that in local parishes across England in the 1980s and into the 1990s.

Professor Grace Davie,[15] in commenting on contemporary religious practice in western countries, has observed differing sociological factors developing together. Tensions between cultural heritage and the growing number of secular alternatives impact significantly on cathedral ministry. Davie also suggests a growing vicarious religion and the replacing of individual obligation to attend worship with a shift towards a confessional consumerist attitude towards churchgoing. For Davie the decline in religiosity must be interpreted against this changing sociological context. Church attendance counts in the 1980s and earlier do not represent the same phenomena as they do at the beginning of the twenty-first century. The apparent decline in churchgoing does not directly point to a wholesale rejection of the Christian faith in favour of secularism.

Whilst public religion seems to have become increasingly secularized there are those who maintained their faith in the role of cathedrals in religious life. The Very Revd Oliver Twisleton-Wykeham-Fiennes, on his retirement as dean of Lincoln cathedral in 1989, is recorded as saying 'It is because of the enormous opportunities for the proclamation of the gospel which cathedrals provide … it is an exciting time for cathedrals.'[16] It was in 1996 that the first statistical signs of a reversal in fortunes appeared as adult attendance at cathedral Sunday services of worship grew by 1%. The equivalent measure for children and young people continued to decrease annually by 2.6% until 1999 when there was a sudden increase back to former levels of around 2,400. By this time adult attendance had climbed further to 15,400 but no one foresaw the subsequent and most significant statistics that would emerge with the introduction of counting across the week, from Monday to Saturday.

At the turn of the millennium, Sunday congregation sizes in cathedrals were recorded at a high of 16,200. Many people were attracted to church services over the course of this special, for some more 'spiritual', year but the figures dropped to a recorded level of 15,500 in 2001 and are now registered a little higher in 2010 at 15,800. There appears to be little relationship between these trends and those that have emerged from monitoring attendance at services over the remainder of the week. This has increased at such a surprising rate that in the 10 years over which they have been monitored congregational attendance is recorded as more than doubling, from 4,900 in 2000 to 11,600 in 2010. For adults, children and young people, attendance at services held between Mondays and Saturdays now adds 85% to Sunday attendance levels (nearly a doubling of attendance levels)

---

[15] G. Davie, *The Sociology of Religion* (London: Sage, 2007).

[16] *Daily Telegraph* newspaper obituary (30 June 2011).

and forms an increasingly significant aspect of cathedral ministry among the working population and visitors. This growth is apparent in all types and locations of cathedral from north to south, inner city to medium sized tourist attraction. The availability of accessible worship in open cathedrals throughout the week is attracting spiritual pilgrims at times that are more convenient to contemporary lifestyles.

Traditionally cathedrals have not sought to cater to any great extent for young people and children in their regular congregations but, alongside the positive focus on educational events, a number of cathedrals have associated schools and choirs which offer increasing opportunities for ministry among young people. The numbers attending worship are not large and add just over a quarter (27%) to attendance levels, but here again there has been a significant increase primarily in midweek attendance. Whilst Sunday attendance figures for children and young people under 16 years of age have remained static since counting was initiated in 2000, the number of youngsters attending during the week has more than doubled to 4,500.

Cathedrals are places where large congregations are not unusual and a national survey in 2004 revealed that congregation sizes at the main Sunday service were four to five times the numbers at the next best attended regular service (that is, excluding specially arranged services). Not surprisingly, larger cathedrals attracted the largest congregations but all cathedrals regularly experience congregational sizes measured in the hundreds:[17]

- Large, international   380
- Medium   228
- Urban   207
- Parish church   170

In 2003, when asked what they thought of their local church or chapel, eight in ten (84%) of adults in Britain considered it to be a place of worship and seven in ten (73%) a quiet place or sanctuary. This compared to lower proportions, around one in two who considered it to be a social and community venue (56%) or a historic place (53%). Worship is also primarily at the heart of cathedral life and further statistics confirm that despite the increased secularization of public life in England participation levels in all regular services of worship are surprisingly healthy. On average, over 20 services take place each week in each cathedral with Sunday services attracting the highest numbers.[18] Attendance levels at regular services have doubled over the last decade from 1,000,000 recorded in 2000 to approaching 2,000,000 people in 2010. In addition to these regular services there are also numerous specially arranged services that in the same period have

---

[17]   ECOTEC Research & Consulting Ltd, *The Economic and Social Impact of Cathedrals in England* (June 2004), p. 46.

[18]   Ibid., p. 43.

consistently added around 1,000,000 attendees each year. Civic services, funerals and memorial services, weddings and baptisms dominate these specially arranged services which range from around 80 each year in 'Parish church' cathedrals to 140 in 'Medium-sized' cathedrals.[19]

Whatever their historic foundation the heart of cathedral life centres on daily worship and in this respect the statistics show that cathedrals are experiencing significant growth. Cathedrals traditionally offer professionally led worship which is more formal in its style. In addition to the continued success of its English choral tradition cathedrals are able to offer other worship experiences of a high standard. They draw many churchgoers who want to connect with Christian spirituality at a time convenient to them. Exeter cathedral hosts an authorized fresh expression of church[20] on Saturday evenings that successfully attracts younger people by incorporating imaginative styles of contemporary worship under the title 'Night Church'. Southwark cathedral provides different worship experiences that attract students and young people from the vicinity of South London, some of which are traditional and while others are more contemporary, for example a Service of Light that attracts students and young people. Other cathedrals are developing more quiet and contemplative services of various Christian spiritual traditions while others are broadening the appeal of their regular worship by, for example, introducing children's groups and crèches. St Paul's London led the way for a number of cathedrals in 2000 by hosting a prayer labyrinth which has also become popular across Christian conference venues and churches.

An example of church growth in a single cathedral can be found in Bradford Cathedral. This cathedral had some difficult years at the beginning of the millennium. The figures for the number of adults attending each week (including attendance at all services, Sunday and weekday and including one-off services) reflect this – but they also reflect substantial growth in recent years.

2000	314
2001	320
2002	311
2003	308
2004	232
2005	214
2006	224
2007	484
2008	457
2009	494
2010	610

---

[19]   Ibid., p. 44.

[20]   Mission and Public Affairs, Archbishops' Council, *Mission-Shaped Church: Church Planting and Fresh Expressions of Church in a Changing Context* (London: Church House Publishing, 2004), pp. 43–83.

The main cause of the growth is the increase in attendance at one-off acts of worship. Sustained work in the city and diocese began to bring organizations into the cathedral for special services, such as 600 Scouts on St George's Day, the creation of new carol services and so forth. There was a further jump in 2010 in the number of such one-off events, up to 51 services from 28 in 2009. The number of individual worshippers has not risen so strongly: a steady stream of newcomers has been balanced by older members who have died, moved away or become too frail to attend. Nonetheless the electoral roll has increased in the last five years from about 150 to 200. David Ison, the dean of Bradford, explained it in this way:

> I think that this represents two things: one is the greater openness of organizations to having a spiritual dimension to, and affirmation of, their life together. The other is that more individuals are willing to come with a familiar group and to come to a cathedral where they have some relationship ... [21]

Faithful Capital

Cathedrals have a wide ministry among those who are not regular churchgoers, those who might consider themselves to be outside their walls. We have seen that attendances at regular services of worship and specially arranged services have increased significantly over the last decade but it would be hasty to overstate the impact of this on the number of regular attenders. Surveys among cathedral congregations reveal that they attract many from other churches, as well as people who have over time drifted away from churchgoing. The attraction of cathedral worship to these people is attributed to a variety of factors, including accessible, professionally led services and a greater acceptance of more passive participation. Cathedral services can often be a more comfortable places for hesitant newcomers than many local parish congregations where their presence may be more noticeable and generate a stronger interest from other congregation members.

The significance of cathedral buildings as powerful symbolic cultural presences and icons of Christian spirituality in their locality is not to be underestimated. We see this most clearly when a national tragedy occurs and candles are lit outside the cathedral. The reaction to events such as the wedding of Prince William and Catherine Middleton and the death of Princess Diana most obviously identify Britain as a nation that values its corporate Christian memory. There has been a growth, for example, in the contemporary phenomena of candles and roadside shrines. Local tragedies and disasters further afield (e.g. tragic accidents, terrorist attacks, overseas tsunamis and earthquakes) are frequently marked with the informal public placing of flowers or a public religious memorialization. In 2010 Exeter cathedral overflowed into the precinct when thousands attended the funeral of a local sporting hero.

---

[21]   Information from David Ison, 8 November 2011.

The term 'faithful capital' was first used in 2006 by the Commission on Urban Life and Faith in a document produced by the Anglican and Methodist churches and intended as a call for Christians to engage more effectively with Britain's urban centres. The authors use the term 'faithful capital' to describe the distinctive contributions the church and individual Christians in local communities can make to wider social capital through corporate worship, caring for others and commitment to human dignity and social justice. The authors argue that 'faithful capital,' found in abundance in communities of faith, is crucial for the survival and sustenance of urban life.[22] Cathedrals bring faithful capital in their spiritual presence, in their religious practice and in their wider witness to the local community through social and community involvement. Bradford cathedral has a particular ministry in promoting inter faith dialogue and cooperation while Southwark cathedral, among others, actively supports the work of a homeless charity. In this respect they could be said to be no different to other faith communities who are active in their neighbourhood but at the same time such work reveals a more holistic ministry for cathedrals which may be surprising to some.

To reflect the outward face and faithful capital that cathedrals bring to their neighbourhoods, the AEC requested particular information from its members in 2010. Numbers were sought to quantify the involvement of cathedrals over the year in events and forums that promote community faith cohesion. The enquiry discovered that cathedral clergy supported over 3,500 events in the community and across the diocese while their choirs supported 320. They were involved in 420 inter-faith forums and events alongside 990 ecumenical events. Consequently, on average, English cathedrals bring faithful capital to their communities through their individual involvement each year in around 80 events, 10 inter-faith forums and over 20 ecumenical events. As a consequence of the increasingly pluralistic nature of English society, the majority of cathedral deans can evidence a considerable and recent growth in this role alongside their already significant role in hospitality for public and civic events and the like.

The mission and ministry of cathedrals at the beginning of the twenty-first century is complex, unique and evolving in response to the needs of English society. They remain at the centre of city and diocesan life but their influence in the wider community is growing. They attract a wider range of people than most local churches and offer a greater breadth of hospitality and experience incorporating Christian heritage, religion and spirituality. At no time is this better seen than at Christmas when Christian religious observance and inherited traditional spirituality come together. Over the Christmas Day in 2008, 24 hour

---

[22] Commission on Urban Life and Faith, *Faithful Cities: A Call for Celebration, Vision and Justice* (London: Methodist Publishing House/Church House Publishing, 2006), pp. 3, 1. For a discussion of the concept of 'faithful capital', see C. Baker, 'Blurred encounters? Religious literacy, spiritual capital and language,' in A. Dinham, R. Furbey and V. Lowndes (eds), *Faith in the Public Realm: Controversies, Policies and Practices* (Bristol: The Policy Press, 2009), p. 112.

attendance at cathedral worship reached a high of over 121,600 following a rise of approaching a third (29%) since 2000. On average each English cathedral attracts congregations of approaching 3,000 on Christmas Eve/Day. Of still further note is that Westminster Abbey added a further 5,000 to these figures.

Winter weather and the close proximity of Christmas Day to the holiday weekend has reduced attendance levels in recent years but attendance over the Advent season prior to Christmas has grown just as significantly. In 2000, when attendance levels were first monitored over Christmas Eve/Day, 94,300 adults, children and young people attended Christmas services in cathedrals and 630,500 attended Advent carol services and related events. Steady growth saw Advent attendances recording a rise of nearly a quarter (24%) over the first seven years of the new millennium to reach 778,800 in 2008, on average 18,500 for each cathedral. In recent years cathedrals have exercised a considerable and growing public ministry at Christmas which has been fully embraced by cathedral staff whose approach has been restricted primarily by the capacity of the buildings.

Congregations are not only consistently larger at Christmas than at any other time of the year but they are more diverse in their make-up. A small scale exploratory survey undertaken by the author in partnership with six cathedrals in 2006–08 revealed that there was a more even balance of men and women than in other services and that most people lived within half an hour's travel time of the cathedral. Only 10% of people attended these services alone and they generally attracted people of middle years, aged 35 or over. Around half had previously attended a service at the cathedral but were not regular churchgoers while others were frequently people who had visited the cathedral during the year to see the building, listen to the music or for quiet reflection. Christmas worship appeals to many who have attended church as children and regard themselves as Christians and as spiritual or religious people.

Cathedrals are responding positively to the demand for Christmas worship by integrating traditional religion with contemporary spirituality. Christmas crib services are attracting younger families and cathedrals appear to be enjoying the challenges that all this brings. Rochester cathedral has for some years broadcast its carol services into the shopping precincts because it cannot accommodate more people inside the building. Some cathedrals have introduced ticket restrictions and offer multiple services to manage the popularity of their Christmas worship but demand increases each year. Cathedrals are often at capacity for Christmas midnight services or special carol services and such is the popularity of these that even a large cathedral like St Paul's, London now relays carol services into the cathedral precincts.

Embracing Pluralism

Despite apparent external appearances English cathedrals are in many respects in tune with our changing English society. Their attitude towards their public has altered in recent years towards a willingness to respond meaningfully to the religious needs of contemporary individualized spirituality. The commitment of cathedrals to bringing the treasures of inherited religion to the best of emerging expressions of Christianity offers a high quality shop window to the Church of England. They appeal to many churchgoers as well as to the considerable proportion of people who consider themselves to have drifted away from church (and Sunday School), 'the dechurched'.[23] At least one in two adults in Britain would place themselves in this category while a growing proportion of around three in ten, generally younger people ('the unchurched'), have no experience of church or Sunday School.[24] The success of cathedrals in social connectivity and in fresh expressions of church reveals a further surprising confidence to embrace the challenges here too.

Alongside English society the established Church is experiencing significant change and the constancy of its cathedrals is a welcome reassurance that the Church should not lose its nerve. The Church of England's public face meets an increasingly pluralistic nation which values the presence of churches and cathedrals. Across the British population six in ten (63%) would be concerned if their local church did not exist and whilst this rises to 74% among those of Christian allegiance it remains a substantial proportion (38%) among both those aligned to other faiths and those of no faith.[25] English cathedrals are places where local and national religious life meets, where the sacred meets the secular and this provides them with a unique perspective into the future. They offer examples of future church life to enrich the Church and a confidence to respond positively to contemporary society. Church growth has surprised cathedral clergy and staff who frequently express the view that whilst they seek to be professional in their ministry they are doing nothing special.[26] Perhaps that perspective is the key to their growth. Cathedrals take the religious needs of all their congregations seriously and seek as directly as possible to marry these with the needs of the outsider. They welcome all comers and point the way for churches to embrace with confidence an increasingly pluralistic future.

---

[23]   Mission and Public Affairs, Archbishops' Council *Mission-Shaped Church: Church Planting and Fresh Expressions of Church in a Changing Context* (London: Church House Publishing, 2004), pp. 38–9.

[24]   Composite result by the author from British Social Attitudes, ORB and other national surveys 2002–5.

[25]   Opinion Research Business (ORB) *Surveys for the Archbishops' Council* (October 2003).

[26]   S. Platten and C. Lewis, (eds) *Dreaming Spires.*

Chapter 6

Reverse Mission: From the Global South to Mainline Churches

Rebecca Catto

This chapter draws upon my PhD research, completed in 2008, a sociological investigation of 'reverse mission' in Britain.[1] As the first piece of in-depth qualitative research undertaken with missionaries associated with this phenomenon in the UK, my doctorate was necessarily exploratory, comprised of interviews and participant observations with engaged individuals, complemented by discourse analysis. Here I present a selection from it, illustrating the variety of interactions with mainline churches in reverse mission. Hence I would like, at the outset, to thank participants for their contributions (names and details have been changed to protect identities as far as is possible). The fieldwork was conducted mainly in England, between 2005 and 2007.

Reverse mission is generally regarded as having 'taken off' around the early 1980s and is an aspect of British church life which may be seen to be growing. Matthews Ojo defines it as:

> [t]he sending of missionaries to Europe and North America by churches and Christians from the non-Western world, particularly Africa, Asia and Latin America, which were at the receiving end of Catholic and Protestant missions as mission fields from the sixteenth century to the late twentieth century.[2]

Hence, reverse mission denotes a change in the direction of mission between 'the global North' and 'the global South'.

These are, of course, sweeping geographical generalizations which do not map precisely onto reality. Nevertheless they endure as useful, albeit problematic, shorthand for communicating continuing inequalities and asymmetric power relations between two parts of the globe connected to colonialism. It has become something of a truism that Christianity is growing in the global South whilst it

---

[1] R. Catto, *From the Rest to the West: Exploring Reversal in Christian Mission in Twenty-first Century Britain* (unpublished PhD thesis: University of Exeter, 2008).

[2] M. Ojo, 'Reverse Mission', in Jonathan J. Bonk (ed.), *Encyclopedia of Mission and Missionaries* (New York: Routledge, 2007), pp. 380–82, p. 380.

is declining in the global North.[3] From the work of Barrett *et al*,[4] it does appear that though it may continue to be Europe (including Russia) which has the largest number of Christians globally, the next three largest continents in terms of numbers of Christians are Latin America, Africa and Asia, with Christian membership growing at a faster rate in these regions. So drawing a North/South divide in terms of Christian demographics seems plausible and this is part of the story as to why, since the late twentieth century, there has been a movement of Christian personnel from the Global South to Britain specifically. There is an increase in numbers of committed, often young, people willing and able to travel, wishing to evangelize the 'dark continent of Europe' and give 'back', combined with an increased desire among British churches and organizations to learn from examples of growth and success.

A lot of the work so far related to the phenomenon of 'reverse mission' has focused upon African Initiated and Pentecostal-Charismatic Churches[5] (not necessarily discrete categories) in the West.[6] Hence the research presented here differs somewhat with its focus on mainline churches. The term 'mainline church' comes from the US and denotes historic Protestant churches which are generally theologically and politically liberal and associated with the (white) middle class. I conducted fieldwork within the Church of England, Methodist and Baptist Churches (alongside some comparative work with independent congregations). It is useful to focus upon mainline churches because of their distinct colonial heritage and enduring place – physical, cultural and institutional – in British society, despite drops in attendance. They provide contrasts with and similarities to independent immigrant congregations.

Are mainline churches welcoming Christian personnel from the global South in order to try to help them pull 'out of the nose dive'?[7] I now present research

---

[3] L. Sanneh and J. Carpenter (eds), *The Changing Face of Christianity: Africa, the West and the World* (New York: Oxford University Press, 2005); P. Jenkins, *The New Faces of Christianity: Believing in the Bible in the Global South* (New York: Oxford University Press, 2006).

[4] D. Barrett, G. Kurian and T. Johnson, *World Christian Encyclopedia*: Vol 1. The world by countries: religionists, churches, ministries (Oxford: Oxford University Press, 2001); D. Barrett, T. Johnson and P. Crossing, 'Missiometrics 2007; Creating Your Own Analysis of Global Data', *International Bulletin of Missionary Research*, 31.1 (2007), pp. 25–32.

[5] For a discussion of these terms, see B. Meyer, 'Christianity in Africa: From African Independent to Pentecostal-Charismatic Churches', *Annual Review of Anthropology*, 33 (2004), pp. 447–74.

[6] For example, A. Adogame, 'A Home Away from Home: The Proliferation of Celestial Church of Christ in Diaspora – Europe', *Exchange*, 27.2 (1998), pp. 141–60; G. ter Haar, *Halfway to Paradise: African Christians in Europe* (Cardiff: Cardiff Academic Press, 1998) and R. Burgess, A. Duffuor and H. Osgood in this volume.

[7] P. Brierley, *Pulling out of the Nose Dive. A Contemporary Picture of Churchgoing: What the 2005 English Church Census Reveals* (London: Christian Research, 2006).

conducted with Christians from a range of countries which may be classified as part of the global South who are fulfilling a variety of roles across England. This research helps address this question and communicate the multifaceted nature of reverse mission within the UK.

Case Studies

The Melanesian Brothers and Sisters

The Melanesian Brothers and Sisters' 2005 'Mission to the UK' consisted of 24 people: 20 men and four women travelling around Britain between May and August 2005. There were two Sisters of the Church, two Melanesian Sisters, two Franciscan Brothers, and the rest were from the Melanesian Brotherhood. The group stayed in Chester, Exeter and finally London performing at Anglican services, outdoor events, in schools, care homes and prisons. The former Bishop of Chester had met the Archbishop of the Anglican Church in Melanesia at the 1988 Lambeth Conference and thus established a link. The then suffragan Bishop of Birkenhead moved to become Bishop of Exeter and so an historic link was re-established. John Coleridge Patteson – who is widely credited with having consolidated Anglicanism in Melanesia before being murdered on one its islands in 1871 – had come from the parish of Ottery St Mary within the Exeter Diocese.

When they came out on stage for their first public appearance in Exeter as part of its annual festival, one of the brothers announced 'We are here on a mission.' before the group proceeded to perform melodic and uplifting Melanesian songs about Jesus, God, love and peace, as well as the region. They were well received by the crowd. Another performance, in a field just outside a Devonshire village, had quite a different tone. The group performed a Passion Play, which is a significant part of Melanesian Christianity, dramatically recreating Jesus' crucifixion. One brother repeatedly exhorted the crowd: 'let God change you from his enemies into his friends', communicating a stronger message. They performed it throughout the mission, including in St Martin in the Fields in London, as well as a play about the prodigal son, which was often performed in schools.

One of the British organizers of the Exeter leg of the mission informed me that reaching out to young people was an express intention of the mission. She thought it would be good for British young people to meet young people who come from a much more socially deprived country and are happy in their commitment to celibacy, poverty and obedience.[8] The organizers also arranged a series of 'Modern Martyr' lunches where people involved in the Church could meet and talk to the Brothers who had been involved in peace negotiations between government forces

---

[8]   These are the vows men take when they become members of the Melanesian Brotherhood (for a fixed term), B. Macdonald-Milne, *The True Way of Service: The Pacific Story of the Melanesian Brotherhood 1925-2000* (Christians Aware: Leicester, 2003).

and rebels in the Solomon Islands during its recent civil war. Seven brothers had been murdered in April 2004 whilst on a peace mission to the rebels and this experience had deeply affected the Brotherhood.

So we see that the mission was designed to reach out to those within the Church of England, as well as the wider community. In my initial conversation with one Brother, he mentioned Bishop Patteson twice, and told me that they were here to show the fruit of his mission through coming back to England, to Christians. Another spoke of Bishop Patteson's sacrifice and their now being on a mission here to help, to strengthen the faith in Britain. Indeed, 'personal and corporate renewal'[9] in the Church in England was a major motivation for the mission. This implies something lacking in the Church of England. A female British volunteer with the mission from Chester told me:

> the work of the Church of England has become poor. There are Ministers and Bishops who have given up hope of a fruitful church and are happy to believe it is in decline. There are 100s of congregations who go to church because of routine, not because of God ... and the congregations are old.

Frequently the Brothers made reference to the absence of young people in British churches contrasted with the vivacity of Sunday services in Melanesia. The popular divide drawn between declining Christianity in the North and thriving Christianity in the South was thus played out. Part of the motivation for inviting the Brothers and Sisters was the relative success of their church.

It was difficult to gauge whether the mission itself was a success or not (a recurrent theme in the research). Certainly public events appeared well attended and the Brothers and Sisters warmly received. The volunteer from Chester quoted above also told me that she had taken one elderly man's testimony after the St Martin in the Fields performance and she herself had been moved to train for ministry. Following on from the mission five people in the Exeter Diocese and 21 in the Chester Diocese were moved to become Companions to the Melanesian Brotherhood which involves committing oneself to support the Brotherhood through prayer, as well as materially. Thus, perhaps the mission helped the Church to grow spiritually rather than in numbers.

The Brothers and Sisters were invited to Lambeth Palace at the end of the mission and the Archbishop of Canterbury had already become a Companion having visited Melanesia in 2004. So a reversal, or at least great shift from previous relations, may be seen to have taken place in the mission, with Anglicans from what was once a peripheral mission territory being welcomed to the core and reaching out to the struggling 'mother church'. However, a Melanesian bishop now leading a parish in Devon sounded a warning note in our interview. He critiqued the concept of 'reverse mission' for implying a proud mentality – pride

---

[9]   M. Langrish, 'Drama at the Palace', *Melanesia News*, 57, Winter 05/06 (2005), pp. 1–2.

on the part of the West in the former dominance of colonial missions and pride on the part of non-Westerners believing that they have the better situation and solution. He preferred the term 'partnership' and pointed out that, though they live very busy, modern lives, his British parishioners are deeply committed to his church. There are still more members of the Church of England than people in the entire Solomon Islands and church statistics in the Solomon Islands (the part of Melanesia where he was based) are very unreliable. The bishop also highlighted the persistent social problems in Melanesia: high unemployment, low education and deprivation: it is not some exotic paradise for Christians.

In sum, we must be wary of easy distinctions between religiosity in a Northern country and religiosity in a Southern country. Nonetheless, the Brothers and Sisters' identity as coming from a much poorer region with strong historical and colonial connections to Britain and vibrant Anglicanism does seem to have been a significant factor in their mission. Whereas they came temporarily for a couple of months trying to reach out to as many people as possible, the bishop is settled living and ministering in Devon. This raises the question of the line between ministry and mission and I move on now to present what is quite a different form of mission.

Maria and Mateo

Mateo and Maria are a couple from an independent Evangelical church in Peru who arranged through Latin Partners to migrate to work as mission partners in a major city in North West England. Latin Partners is a branch of the British Evangelical missionary organization Latin Link which generally engages in arranging missions to Latin America. However, Latin Partners works to place Latin Americans in receiving churches in the UK. On their website they state:

> In this country we increasingly need to communicate our faith effectively within the context of our relationships. Latin Americans find cross-cultural personal evangelism much more natural than many do in churches in Britain and Ireland. Our experience has confirmed that Latin Americans find considerable rapport with ethnic minorities. This is partly due to sharing a common experience of marginalisation and political instability, but also from some common ground in their respective cultures, such as the value given to hospitality and the extended family.[10]

Mateo and Maria separately felt called to evangelize Muslims and so, after they married, wished to undertake this mission together. They see Britain as neutral territory in which to experience working with Muslims. Unsurprisingly, this is challenging work which they are not always publicly open about locally. Mateo

---

[10]   http://www.latinlink.org.uk/National-Sites/UK/Who-we-are/Our-Members/Latin-Partners accessed 31 March 2011.

has been studying Islam and Arabic at a local university and they have formed various friendships with Muslims. Maria runs an English class for Muslim women at the recently established, local Anglican church in a deprived urban setting to which they are attached, and this has become well attended. Once again, impact in terms of numbers converting to Christianity is negligible but relationships are being developed. Mateo queries the need to invite missionaries from Latin America to conduct their type of mission in the UK, but then, as Latin Partners does, he sees benefits:

> the church here says "we need you here, you are part of the solution of this country", because, our pastor say, that this country needs, that more people come from South America here to preach. Why from South America? It's because here since 11-9, since 11 September ... there [is] a war between Americans or British with Muslims so that Muslims doesn't want to remain too much friendly with the British people or American people, but if they see us, we have similar colour in the skin, we, like them, we come from poverty countries and like them we are not, we are not from here. Our background is from another place, so they are more open to us ...

Here we see then that their identity as from a country in the global South is also significant. In our interview Maria and Mateo continued to discuss how some people are interested in talking to them simply because they speak Spanish. The mission might not be considered such an example of reversal as that of the Melanesian Brothers and Sisters, because they are reaching out to Muslims rather than the 'indigenous' population. However, in contrast to the Melanesian Mission, theirs is funded by their Peruvian sending church and they are nonetheless having an impact upon their host Anglican church. I observed their welcome and how much they were appreciated at Sunday services I attended with them.

Mateo and Maria discussed Peru's inheritance from British and American Christianity, albeit negatively. They think that Evangelical Christians in Peru have learned incorrectly about mission from British and American missionaries. They say that there is overemphasis on preaching and church-planting in Peru rather than cross-cultural mission (Mateo's words are in italics):

> They have the wrong concept about mission, for example, what they have learned? They have learned that mission is going to the station to preach. This is not mission, this is evangelism, but they think that this is missions. *For [them] mission is give some papers for some activity in the church*, and go to the park and give to the people. 'I made mission. I went to the park, and I give some papers to people about Jesus', but this is not mission, this is evangelism, but they learn wrong, so their concept is wrong.

Such attitudes mean that missions to other countries like theirs are not popular. Their home church community struggles to understand their lack of success in terms of conversion in Britain.

Apparently, Peruvian churches are not generally interested in funding missions to Britain as they see it as a Christian country. However, since being in Britain, Mateo and Maria report having experienced a massive culture shock and have observed in particular the decline of Christianity. Consequently they now see Britain as in need of mission with Anglican churches closing down, becoming mosques, shops etc: 'England is very, very difficult for missionaries from other countries, especially for South Americans ... for people thinking England is Christian ... and the British, some say "we are grandfather of mission, so we don't need you."' They have settled as part of a deprived neighbourhood, raising a young family. Though they are working in a more socio-economically developed nation-state, they encounter challenges and struggles, both religious and material.

Mateo complained about the administrative and managerial work he is obliged to do in the church for his minister of religion visa as he finds it a frustrating distraction from the missionary task in hand. He sees there being a change in the meaning of mission now that poor people are working in developed countries. It is contradictory. Peru has historically received missionaries, and now that they, Mateo and Maria, have undertaken this new missionary task they have to renew their identity and concept of mission (Mateo sees it as partnership) and battle for their mission to be accepted by their home church.

According to Mateo, there is a danger that Latin Americans who have migrated to conduct mission in Britain become nothing more than economic migrants. As they are obliged to work very hard to support themselves in such an expensive country, they become despondent with their lack of success. He contrasted a Brazilian friend who has managed to found a church in London in his spare time with an Argentinian one who appears to have lost impetus entirely.

It seems that Maria and Mateo have observed more decline than growth in a mainline church in Britain since moving to the UK. It would also appear that migrating from the global South to try and conduct mission in Britain on a longer-term basis is decidedly challenging, because of economic, social and cultural barriers and perceptions in one's home and host communities. Yet, through their sheer presence Maria and Mateo are invigorating their local, mainline church and they are part of a local Christian scene engaging in small-scale creative projects such as 'Messy Church' and a touring bus providing activities for teenagers aimed at making Christianity more accessible.

Now we move from the experiences of a younger Latin American couple to those of a senior Indian man.

Jerome

Jerome is from the ecumenical Church of South India. He was originally invited by a group of churches in the Midlands in order to conduct mission, helping cross ethnic divides, and has since lived in Britain for over a decade. He is now principal of an Anglican theological college in the South West and has founded his own ecumenical mission agency staffed by Christians from the global South, supporting such Christians to work in the global North. Jerome employs the terms 'the global North' and 'the global South' explicitly in his discourse, but rejects the word mission for having too much colonial baggage and so being 'positively unhelpful'. Nonetheless, the aim of his agency is to try to reach out to the 'Caucasian indigenous people of this land [Britain].'

As Mateo and Maria did, Jerome draws attention to the difficulties and challenges of missionary work in the North:

> Well, to work in the West you need to have a very strong faith first of all to sustain you. Secondly, a clear reason for what you believe, to be able to give clear, simple, spontaneous reasons as to why I believe what I believe. Thirdly, a preparedness to suffer physically. It's cold out here. It's gloomy out here. Socially I won't have a supporting community. I will be picked on, because I am a minority. I'll have to learn a new language. I will be misunderstood, so I have to be prepared to endure hardships and suffer. I'll have to invest a huge amount in imagination, and develop skills, build on my social skills in developing friendships with people who don't want to be my friends. I'll have to be prepared to eat this wretchedly bland food, and look like I'm enjoying it. I'll have to learn to value and appreciate what people in this part of the world value and appreciate, and resist the temptation to say "we do things much better at home", to be less judgmental and much more open to people. These are just some things.

When he and another man from India were both made principals of British theological training colleges, there was talk of an 'Indian takeover'. He said:

> Sure, you experience racism, you experience being patronised by people. I still do. I'm the principal of this college. When people first see me they think I must be a student here, or I might be the cook here or whatever. It's so funny when people first meet me, the way they treat me, and when they realise I'm the principal, the way their jaw drops and the way they treat me then.

Jerome makes explicit in these quotes the issue of racial difference and inequality which pertains in missions from South to North. They show that migrating to work in a more developed country does not necessarily mean one is going to have an easier time. Jerome bemoaned British priests being more caretakers of monuments than ministers.

He said he tries to model the joy and happiness that living a Christian life can bring. He certainly has become part of the mainline British Christian establishment and his work bringing missionaries from the global South to work in Britain would seem to indicate something of a reverse mission. The agency is, after all, aiming to reach out to non-Christian, 'indigenous' Britons.

Another form of Christian activity within a mainline British denomination, which may not be so straightforwardly considered mission from the global South is now considered.

Korean Methodists

Ministering to a congregation is not necessarily a missionary activity. Hence when designing a project to investigate reverse mission, it was not my original intention to study diaspora congregations. Yet as the research progressed I found that talk about mission from the global South often implies diaspora congregations, especially Pentecostal-Charismatic ones, and so this dimension was added to the study. I did also conduct fieldwork with a diaspora congregation which is part of a mainline church: a group of Korean Methodists in a South Western city. It has been well documented that South Korea is one of the fastest growing Christian missionary sending nations in the world since the end of the Korean War in 1953 and subsequent increased ease of travel to and from the country.[11] Seoul's Yoido Full Gospel Church is alleged to have the largest congregation in the world.[12] The Korean Methodist Church may be smaller than this, but it nonetheless has many more members than the British Methodist Church.

The British Methodist church I attended had decided to employ a Korean pastor after a couple of Korean families began to attend. The two resident Korean pastors employed during my period of fieldwork at the church each received funding from their home church in Korea, as well as from the British church. The Korean congregation has its own Korean-language service fortnightly with around 35–40 people attending. The Koreans who come commonly do not know very much English at all, at least at the outset, and so are separated from the British congregation by language. The church makes a concerted effort to bridge this gap. For example, the full text of the sermon is supplied in Korean at the services where Koreans and English-speakers worship together.

The church has grown into something of a Korean cultural centre for the South West and the British pastor said that he is happy with this. I was given three examples of Koreans who had converted to Christianity whilst living in Britain and attending the church. Here we see non-Western Christians being converted in Britain rather than in their home countries.

The term 'non-Western' is used here because it is questionable whether South Korea can be counted as part of the global South. Asia is usually associated as part of the global South in the discourse, but geographically South Korea is in

---

[11]   G. Davie, *Europe: the Exceptional Case: Parameters of Faith in the Modern World* (London: Darton, Longman & Todd, 2002); P. Jenkins, *The Next Christendom: the Coming of Global Christianity* (Oxford: Oxford University Press, 2002).

[12]   K. Kim and S. Kim, *Christianity as a World Religion* (London: Continuum, 2008).

the Northern rather than the Southern hemisphere. It follows the Southern pattern of comparatively rapid Christian growth since the twentieth century, but it is a nation-state with a relatively high UN Human Development Index score. Also, the Methodist Church was brought to South Korea by American, not British, missionaries from the Northern and Southern Methodist Churches from 1884 onwards and South Korea has undergone a different experience of colonization with Japan, rather than the Western powers. Hence this case does not present a classic example of reverse mission from the global South.

This Methodist church is itself unusual in bucking the trend by being a mainline church which is growing. In our interview, the British pastor made reference to Grace Davie's model of growing churches in Europe:[13]

> the two kinds of churches that ought to be growing are either authoritarian evangelical fundamentalist churches which we certainly are not as ... I would describe the Methodist Church as liberal evangelical ... so we don't fit Grace's model there. Her other model is that of cathedrals and places where you can come and go as an individual in absolute anonymity ... and we manifestly don't fit that ...

He did cite the fact that they happen to have stumbled on a niche in the local church market with the Koreans as one of the reasons the church is growing. He thinks it makes the church a more welcoming place for other nationalities as well. The British pastor also told me that other churches invite the Korean pastor and members of the Korean congregation to come and talk and perhaps sing. People are interested in the Koreans because 'they bring a different perspective and a different culture, and a different approach ...'

So the Koreans do have something of an impact beyond their own diaspora congregation. They have increased the church's congregation, given the church an appealing international character and reach out to other churches. They have built relationships across the congregation, facilitated by the church's approach. A Korean congregation member commented to me that usually they would just rent a church hall in the afternoon and thus have little interaction with the local congregation. I heard from British congregation members about the friendships they still maintain with former members who have moved back to Korea. Yet, in the shared services I attended, I did not observe much mixing and there were some indications of resentment from members of the British congregation, of Koreans treating the church as a social rather than religious place. These observations echo Wilkinson's finding that there are ongoing divisions between Canadian and Korean congregations within the Pentecostal Assemblies of Canada.[14]

---

[13] G. Davie, *Religion in Europe: A Memory Mutates* (Oxford: Oxford University Press, 2000).

[14] M. Wilkinson, *The Spirit Said Go: Pentecostal Immigrants in Canada* (New York: Peter Lang, 2006).

This somewhat contrasting example shows how international, if not necessarily Southern, Christians can contribute towards church growth in a mainline British church via a congregation rather than through explicit mission, but diaspora congregations have their difficulties. This was brought home to me by fieldwork at a particular church in a North Western city. Pastor Peter is a Nigerian Christian who has seen his African congregation grow exponentially since arriving in Britain. Their independent Pentecostal-Charismatic church outgrew various temporary locations and was looking for a permanent home (as Burgess, Osgood and Duffuor's chapters in this volume indicate, finding appropriate premises is a perennial issue for black majority churches in Britain). This is when Peter met the pastor of an ailing local British Baptist church which was facing closure because of its dwindling congregation. The team joined forces, giving Pastor Peter's congregation a home and saving the church building. However, now only the Baptist minister herself attends, along with a few members from the former congregation. Peter told me that one elderly female Baptist had stopped coming because she was too scared of black people.

This vignette is an example of Christians from the global South helping a mainline church to survive, but not really to grow as such. Peter and his congregation live with serious economic pressures, immigration worries and racism in Britain, reminding us once again how hard mission to Britain can be. Pastor Peter told me that he does regard himself as a missionary reaching out to Britons as well, but that this is an incredibly slow, hard process. He recounted being shocked to meet a British man who had never been to church, but said:

> God has sent us to revive his church. We are not just preaching the Gospel to them ... the Gospel is in the land ... already, but what we are doing is reviving them, and the seed has been sown years back. The seed is slowly dying, and it needs watering ...

Interestingly, in this volume, Randall shows that there has been growth driven by other factors within the Baptist Union of Great Britain, as well as acknowledging the contribution of African and Caribbean leaders and congregations.

Evangelizing the Heathen North

Non-Western Christians arriving in Britain encounter a surprising lack of Christian knowledge, practice and architecture, but enduring structures and potential. They may also encounter thriving pockets, as the South Koreans I have described.[15] The examples presented here indicate how highly varied and difficult to typify

---

[15]   This picture of overall decline punctured by pockets of growth in mainline churches is reflected in Kenneth Roxburgh's observations from Edinburgh in this volume (see Chapter 13).

contemporary missions to Britain are. Their presence and activities challenge a stereotypical definition of mission as charity and conversion, yet success can be difficult to gauge, not least in terms of numbers. In this book, Burgess, Chambers, Duffuor, Osgood, Lings and Roxburgh document a whole range of churches encountering difficulties in reaching out to 'unchurched' populations.

If they are not necessarily winning converts, then what does the work of 'reverse missionaries' from the global South with mainline churches in Britain comprise? We have seen the Melanesian Brothers and Sisters engaging with the Anglican Church locally and with the wider British public through a series of meetings and events and a Melanesian bishop working as a parish priest in the Church of England. Mateo and Maria are aiming to convert Muslims but also supporting their local Anglican church and forming friendships. Jerome is principal of a theological college. The Korean pastor in the British Methodist church is ministering to a diaspora congregation and they are interacting with the local congregation and other British churches. Pastor Peter has helped save a shrinking Baptist church whilst growing his own congregation: the work is incredibly varied within as well as between denominations.

In this chapter I have oscillated between the terms 'North' and 'South' and 'West' and 'non-West' and also employed the heavily loaded term 'indigenous'. These labels can perpetuate as well as communicate inequalities. The notion of 'reverse mission' can imply a 'pride mentality' as critiqued by the Melanesian bishop.

Ogbu Kalu, writing in the1975 issue of the *International Review of Mission* dedicated to the moratorium debate started by the Reverend John Gatu, General Secretary of the Presbyterian Church of East Africa in 1971, suggested that reverse mission perpetuates previously unequal relations: 'The palliative is that some of the converted from among the "billions" should move in "reverse flow" to achieve mutuality and preserve the historical pattern. This is a rather clever survival tactic.'[16]

Mateo and Maria's Peruvian church is funding their mission and the Korean pastors' home churches have paid for half of their posts. Yet, the impetus came from Britain, as it did in Jerome's case, with British churches also funding his initial mission. The Melanesian mission was organized and funded by the host dioceses in Britain. As Kalu had already pointed out in 1975, the power and control remain with the Western centres.

British mainline congregations may be wealthier but they are also, generally, older and smaller and looking for help from the global South. Missions from the 'South' to British mainline churches are distinctive (compared to the activities of independent immigrant congregations) because questions of race and class immediately confront the incoming Christian personnel within their host church, as do historic institutional structures, a colonial inheritance and visible decline competing with memories of previous power and growth.

---

[16]   O. Kalu, 'Not Just New Relationships but a Renewed Body', *International Review of Mission*, 66.254 (1975), pp. 143–7.

Conclusion

Reverse mission, despite persisting structural and socio-economic inequalities, does represent a divergence from the previously dominant understanding of Christian mission as flowing from the civilized West to the 'heathen rest'. The data presented here and throughout the volume indicate that mainline churches in Britain are certainly responding to changes in relation not only to domestic social developments but also to processes of globalization and shifting Christian demographics. Christians migrating to the UK, to study, work or explicitly undertake a mission, are not replacing, or recruiting sufficient numbers to replace, those leaving mainline churches. Nonetheless, they are challenging and changing preconceptions, as Gatu did in 1971 and John Sentamu may be seen as doing today. It seems that the growth of Christianity in the 'global South' and of immigrant congregations has made mainline churches in Britain take notice and realize that they also have something to learn in what is a period of transition for them and for wider society.[17]

---

[17] L. Woodhead and R. Catto (eds), *Religion and Change in Modern Britain* (Routledge: London/New York, 2012).

PART III
New Churches

Chapter 7
The Rise of Black Churches

Hugh Osgood

This chapter gives an overview of the growth of Black Majority Churches in Britain since 1980.[1] The scope of the topic is confirmed by the fact that the next chapter examines the British development of just one African Church grouping (The Redeemed Christian Church of God). That a single grouping can grow rapidly within a strand of British church life without in any way dominating that strand is noteworthy.

Setting the Scene

By 1980 British Black Majority Church life had already passed through a number of phases.[2] The labels used by Joel Edwards in his contribution to the 1993 book *Britain on the Brink* were: the inception of Afro-Caribbean church growth (1950–65), the period of consolidation (1960–75) and the period of initiation (1975–1985/8). The picture Edwards paints is of a diversity of church life burgeoning out from common experiences. He wrote with conviction of a Caribbean diaspora (at the time Black Majority Churches were predominantly Caribbean) triumphing over challenges that ranged from a sense of transience (experienced by senior diaspora members on their arrival in the 1950s) to questions of identity (affecting their teenage British-born children in the 1970s). He recorded that between 1960 and 1975 '[g]rowing congregations bought derelict church properties, upgraded their ministerial status and established national Headquarters and autonomy'.[3] He

---

[1]   'Black Majority Churches' was adopted in the 1990s as the preferred term for churches serving the Caribbean (i.e. Afro-Caribbean) diaspora and/or the African diaspora. For consistency it is used throughout this chapter.

[2]   R. Gerloff, *A Plea for British Black Theologies: The Black Church Movement in Britain and its transatlantic cultural and theological interactions*, Part 1 (Frankfurt: Peter Lang, 1992), pp. 55–6; J. Edwards, 'The British Afro-Caribbean Community' in M. Eden (ed.), *Britain on the Brink: Major Trends in Society Today* (Nottingham: Crossway Books, 1993), pp. 107–11; M. Sturge, *Look What the Lord has Done! An Exploration of Black Christian Faith in Britain* (Bletchley: Scripture Union, 2005), pp. 84-96; J. Aldred, '*The Development of BMCs*', presentation given as part of the CTBI consultation with BMCs, 23 November 2002.

[3]   J. Edwards, Afro-Caribbean, p. 109.

also indicated that in the same period 'a keen interest in social and political issues began to develop.'[4]

The Caribbean churches in Britain in 1980 were not, in his view, churches birthed by default in response to racist attitudes but churches that 'came into being to fulfil spiritual, social and cultural needs which otherwise would have gone unmet'.[5] These were churches with a missionary awareness and an inner-city consciousness, prepared to be salt and light in urban Britain.[6] Their diversity came from different levels of success in attaining personal goals against a backdrop of stereotyping within a society that could produce what Edwards described as 'lethal doses of economic deprivation, marginalisation, institutional and personal racism'.[7] These were brave churches, serving where they were set, providing support for their members and expanding in the process. A MARC Europe survey identified a 20% growth in Caribbean churches from 1975 to 1979, a growth which could not be explained by immigration, as that had reduced markedly following the immigration acts of 1962, 1965, 1968 and 1971.[8] The signs were that, despite all the difficulties, Black Majority Churches were finding a renewed relevance within the Caribbean diaspora community.

Two further insights about the pre-1980s Black Majority Churches come from Mark Sturge. Writing in 2005, he sub-divides Edwards' categories and sees Black Majority Churches as having passed from an initial 'scattered' phase into 'community' and 'denominational' phases before reaching Edwards' 'consolidating' phase. He then adds a 'restless' phase as a sub-phase of Edwards' 'initiation' phase, pointing out that one aspect of this restlessness was that, by 1980, Black Majority Churches were beginning to look for ways of working together.[9] His identification of denominationalism and the desire for collaboration are helpful. Most Caribbean church-planting prior to 1980 was either carried out in conjunction with Caribbean-based denominations (often with American headquarters) or undertaken by leaders within the British Caribbean community who had new denominations in mind as they planted fresh clusters of diaspora churches.[10] The large, single, independent Black Majority Church, drawing people from a wide geographical area, was not the dominant feature prior to 1980. Local congregations serving specific geographical diaspora communities under different denominational umbrellas were much more the pattern.[11] Nonetheless,

---

[4]   Ibid., p. 109.

[5]   Ibid., p. 104.

[6]   Ibid., p. 107.

[7]   Ibid., p. 107.

[8]   Ibid., p. 110.

[9]   M. Sturge, *Look*, pp. 84–96.

[10]   New Testament Church of God, Church of God of Prophecy and Church of God in Christ all have USA headquarters.

[11]   Sturge lists 22 Black Majority Church denominations in Britain by 1980, M. Sturge, *Look,* pp. 91–93.

collaboration has consistently proved to be the key to greater civic recognition and socio-political engagement.

The Second Wave

Although it is difficult to ascribe an exact date to the start of a second wave of Black Majority Church growth in Britain in which African-led church-planting came to the fore, 1980 serves well. There was evidence of this new phase emerging in the mid-1970s and there were much stronger indications of it developing by 1985. Clearly with such a rapid increase in African diaspora churches throughout the 1980s and on into the first decade of the new millennium, the integration of the resultant new churches, both into the existing Black Majority Church scene and into the wider expressions of British church life, has to be considered.

It is perhaps not surprising that the first churches to be planted as this new phase was heralded were those that would cater for a more African-traditional experience of church life not mirrored here in Britain. Whilst Africans who had attended Catholic, Anglican, Methodist and Baptist churches in their home nations could readily be assimilated within Britain's historic denominations – albeit frequently with support from the Ghanaian Christian Fellowship or the Overseas Fellowship of Nigerian Christians – those from the Aladura churches were not so easily accommodated.[12] Some of the first African denominations to plant in Britain, therefore, were the Cherubim and Seraphim Church (1965), the Aladura International Church (1970) and the Celestial Church of Christ (1974).[13] Before the end of the decade other West African denominations had followed: Christ Apostolic Church Mount Bethel (1974), Church of Jesus Christ Apostolic (1975) and Christ Apostolic Church of Great Britain (1976).[14] Perhaps more significant for future growth patterns however was that the 1970s and early 1980s saw the establishing of some individual African churches that were intentionally non-denominational. These churches grew from prayer groups established by professional African residents who, as leaders within their diaspora communities, felt constrained to provide culturally-familiar fellowship for those looking for support from their fellow nationals.[15]

Black Majority Church growth from 1980–2010 continued to involve a mixture of church-planting approaches but was increasingly affected by West Africa's

---

[12]   Aladura churches tend towards formulaic prayers and distinctive ceremonies, some wearing white *soutanes* for worship.

[13]   *BMCs Directory 2003/4*, pp. 139–41.

[14]   Ibid., pp. 141–2.

[15]   H. Osgood, '*African neo-Pentecostal Churches and British Evangelicalism 1985–2005: Balancing Principles and Practicalities*' (PhD, School of Oriental and African Studies, University of London, 2006), pp. 88–94.

1970s evangelical campus revival.[16] More African church leaders were sent to establish branches of existing African-based ministries; a respected professional gathered more fellow nationals; some who were sent to plant transferred themselves out of their original church grouping in order to church-plant independently and others who came to train in British Bible Schools planted churches on graduation. Throughout the period, a whole tranche of churches was planted by people who, having arrived in Britain to work professionally, used their initiative to start completely new, independent congregations. Each of these patterns needs to be illustrated and the labels 'constrained to plant', 'sent to plant', 'transferred to plant', 'trained to plant' and 'called to plant' will serve to distinguish the categories.[17] In the midst of the illustrations, space has to be given to reflect on how British Black Majority Churches as a whole handled the transition from being mainly denominational and locally-based to, at least in most of Britain's major cities, a broader mix. The change led to the denominational churches existing alongside a multiplicity of independent churches and non-locally-minded mega-churches functioning alongside community-conscious congregations. In conclusion, some paragraphs will need to be devoted to the wider aspects of Black Majority Church integration, particularly how white majority churches have handled aspects of the Black Majority Churches' rise.

Constrained to Plant

Although not the major contributor to African-initiated church growth, the pattern wherein a professional African resident would, as a respected community leader, feel obliged to respond to requests to draw together fellow nationals, had some early significance. One example from the 1980s which has continued to have impact is that of the Ghanaian lawyer (and subsequently politician) Samson Kwaku Boafo.

Boafo had gained a London law degree and was practising as a solicitor in Hackney before beginning to draw together his fellow nationals. In 1984 nine people met with him for prayer at 72 St Paul's Road, Tottenham, near the Tottenham Hotspur football ground.[18] By 1985 the gathering, which had come to include Nigerians as well as Ghanaians, was sufficiently large to warrant a move to St Saviour's Church, Chalk Farm, and the organization took the name Universal Prayer Group (UPG). Three years later, in 1988, Boafo acquired a church building in Grove Street, Edmonton and ran this in conjunction with offices and a bookshop at 328 High Road, Tottenham. He held three Sunday services in the new church

---

[16]   M. Ojo, '*Campus Christianity in West Africa*', (PhD, London University, 1987).
[17]   H. Osgood, '*African*', p. 88.
[18]   Ibid., p. 91.

building, which became known as Edmonton Temple, the congregation numbering around 1,200.[19]

In 1994 Boafo, who had increasingly travelled to and from Ghana, moved back permanently to pursue a career in politics and to oversee the churches he was establishing in Kumasi and Accra.[20] The work in Britain stayed under his control with two elders, who had been with him from the early days in St Paul's Road, serving alongside him and the day-to-day oversight being handed over to a Ghanaian UK Bible college graduate, Sam Ohene-Apraku. In 1998, Shadrach Ofosuware, son-in-law to Boafo, set up a South London branch, South London Temple. Significantly, both the UK churches birthed from this early initiative are now furthering the mega-church trend which has brought a new dimension to Black Majority Churches from the early 1990s and on into the 21st century. Since 2000 Edmonton Temple has refurbished a large cinema complex in Wood Green, North London and become the Dominion Centre.[21] In 2010 South London Temple, having been renamed the Freedom Centre International, purchased and refurbished a former cinema in Welling, South East London.[22]

The resident professionals who responded to the requests from their fellow Africans in the early 1980s were seeking 'to fulfil spiritual, social and cultural needs which otherwise would have gone unmet', in much the same way as Edwards observed was the case with Caribbean church-planters 30 years earlier.[23]

Sent to Plant

The 1970s saw some remarkable church growth in Nigeria following the Biafran War. Existing churches, such as the Redeemed Christian Church of God, grew rapidly and many other new churches came into being. Deeper Christian Life Ministry began in 1973 as a Bible study fellowship in the University of Lagos and then spread through Nigeria as a whole.[24] The impact of Deeper Life, as it became known, was all the greater for having started as a para-church movement that attracted many from denominational churches who stayed committed when Deeper Life Bible Church was birthed. It is not surprising, given the relative ease of immigration from West Africa prior to 1988, that with such a large membership in Nigeria, a significant number of Deeper Life members relocated to Britain. On arrival some sought to link with fellow Deeper Life members and others worshipped with white majority or Black Majority Churches near their new homes. The Deeper Life leadership in Nigeria soon saw the need to send a senior leader

---

19   Ibid., p. 91.

20   Ibid., p. 92.

21   http://www.dominioncentre.org, accessed 20 March 2011.

22   http://www.freedomcentreinternational.org, accessed 20 March 2011.

23   J. Edwards, Afro-Caribbean, p. 104.

24   M. Ojo, '*Campus*'.

to Britain to gather its scattered membership and chose Pre Ovia who arrived in London in 1985, having previously served Deeper Life in Kano, northern Nigeria, where he had worked as an engineer before becoming a zonal leader.[25]

The first meeting place Ovia secured for Deeper Life in London was the Rockingham Estate Community Hall at Elephant and Castle. Growth was assured when the founder of Deeper Life, Dr William Kumuyi, visited in August 1986 and held a 'crusade' at Westminster Chapel, unintentionally filling the building with Nigerians.[26] Despite its evangelistic intent it was seen by some as an African diaspora event designed to guard against spiritual lapse, a particular Deeper Life concern given the church's commitment to conservative dress, teetotalism, frugal home furnishings and avoidance of worldly entertainment, none of which were as high on the agenda of most other churches in Britain.

From the Rockingham Estate Community Hall the Deeper Life London branch moved to St Botolph's Church in Lombard Street in the City and then in 1988 relocated to Borough Road, London SE1. A decentralization programme, implemented in 1991, saw the merging of house fellowships on a locality basis to form eight satellite churches. The timing proved appropriate as many who had arrived from Nigeria as singles were now married with children and were beginning to put down roots in local communities. In South East London the Deeper Life house fellowships in Ladywell, New Cross, Deptford and Brockley joined together and bought a large Anglican church on the South Circular Road in Dulwich.[27]

By the turn of the millennium some London boroughs had several Deeper Life congregations and churches had also been established in Gravesend, Watford, Leeds, Newcastle, Liverpool, Huddersfield, Nottingham, Birmingham, Manchester and Dublin, though many still used public halls or other churches' buildings.

Deeper Life was not the only Nigerian church to send its existing church leaders to Britain to gather or plant in the 1980s. New Covenant sent Titus David in 1986, whilst Foursquare, a Pentecostal denomination with American missionary links, had sent Matthew Ashimolowo in 1985. David saw his task as one of planting rather than gathering and the London branch of New Covenant Church started in September 1986 with just four people, meeting in the Rockingham Estate Community Centre as Deeper Life moved out.[28] Far from being a negative reflection on New Covenant, which has since grown significantly in Britain with new adherents joining and existing members immigrating, the initial low numbers demonstrate the other side of the 'sent to plant' pattern. A few other African churches have been so keen to claim a British branch that they have sent church-planters as missionaries and announced the existence of 'our British congregation', even before the church-planter has been able to make any headway.

---

[25]   H. Osgood, '*African*', p. 95.

[26]   M. Ojo, '*Campus*', pp. 305–6.

[27]   H. Osgood, '*African*', p. 95.

[28]   Ibid., p. 98.

Generally there is a balance in the 'sent to plant' model between a desire to 'break new ground' and a desire to provide 'a home away from home'. When the Church of Pentecost, which has a history in Ghana stretching back to British Apostolic Pentecostal missionaries in the 1930s, planted its London branch in 1988 under the local leadership of Kwame Blackson, it followed the usual model of seeking to be relevant whilst maintaining its existing identity. However, in 1994 it affiliated with Britain's Elim Foursquare Gospel Alliance to become the Elim Church of Pentecost, unusually prioritizing its new context at the expense of its original identity.[29]

As new churches have continued to come into being in Africa, so the 'sent to plant' pattern has continued in Britain, either with a view to gathering emigrated members or to extending influence through establishing a new work. Many of the large West African churches, even those started since the late 1980s, now have at least one branch in Britain. Those that do not still establish British links as their senior pastors in Africa accept invitations to speak at conferences organized by their friends now resident in Britain.

Transferred to Plant

Whereas many Nigerian university students in the 1970s embraced Deeper Life's modest lifestyle as a radical alternative, the students of the 1980s were looking for something equally radical that was more in tune with their hopes for self-improvement.[30] They found in the Word of Faith emphasis, gaining popularity amongst America's television evangelists, an understanding of prosperity that fitted well with their 'upwardly-mobile' aspirations and as a result the face of West African Christianity changed: many independent churches were established and links between Africa and America became more common. The 1990s saw the change repeated through much of the continent. Britain was affected too with many more people planting independent African diaspora churches and even some who had previously been sent to plant transferring away from their original allegiances to plant afresh. This was true for both David and Ashimolowo.

---

[29]   E. Anim, '*A Paradigm Shift in the Theology of Salvation: an Examination of Cultural and Socio-Economic Effects on the Soteriology of the Church Of Pentecost with Special Reference to the Elim Church of Pentecost in Britain*' (MA, All Nations Christian College, Hertfordshire, 1999).

[30]   R. Marshall-Fratani, 'Mediating the Global and Local in Nigerian Pentecostalism', in A. Corten and R. Marshall-Fratani (eds), *Between Babel and Pentecost: Transnational Pentecostalism in Africa and Latin America* (Bloomington: Indiana University Press, 2001), pp. 84–5.

Ashimolowo left Foursquare to start Kingsway International Christian Centre (KICC) in September 1992.[31] The church began with 300, using rented accommodation in Holloway. They subsequently purchased a building in Darnley Road, Hackney where they eventually accommodated 1,000 people, maximizing their capacity by holding four services on Sundays.[32] Within a few years the pressure of increasing numbers and challenges with parking prompted the purchase of a former warehouse property in Waterden Road, Hackney where the new main auditorium could seat 4,000.[33]

Ashimolowo is able to attribute much of KICC's growth to its independence from denominational ties. As a leader he has been able to exercise greater freedom in decision-making, to use a more personalized presentational style to motivate his members and to harness conferences, public relations and broadcasting to give KICC a strong and distinctive identity.[34]

As KICC has grown its annual conference, the International Gathering of Champions, has become one of London's largest church events, with motivational guest speakers and soloists coming from both Africa and America. The marketing for this, as for all aspects of KICC's ministry, has been extremely professional. In broadcasting, KICC followed Cornerstone Christian Centre onto the Identity Channel in 1994 and then onto Christian Channel Europe. Later, in 1997, when Premier Christian Radio was re-formed out of London Christian Radio, a former Capital FM 'DJ' in the KICC congregation opened the way for Ashimolowo's broadcasts. Now KICC has its own television station and has planted multiple churches with large congregations in both Ghana and Nigeria making KICC something of an international brand.[35]

Internal Relations

Although the considerable contribution to this second wave made by those who were trained to plant and 'called' to plant has yet to be highlighted, sufficient commentary has been made in assessing the effect of this second wave of Black Majority Church growth on internal Black Majority Church relations. It is particularly important to make the assessment at this stage lest the impression be given that the rise in Black Majority Churches from 1980 onwards was entirely an African phenomenon. As already intimated, the scene was set for a significant

---

[31] Unattributed, 'Birth of KICC', *Winning Ways* (special edition for Matthew Ashimolowo's 50th birthday, March 2002), p. 5.

[32] Ibid., p. 5.

[33] Rosman records 'some six thousand worshippers attended a three-hour service' to open the Waterden Road premises on 23 August 1998. D. Rosman, *The Evolution of the English Churches 1500-2000* (Cambridge: CUP, 2003), p. 316.

[34] H. Osgood, '*African*', pp. 115-7.

[35] http://www.kicc.org.uk, accessed 20 March 2011.

rise in Black Majority Church influence even ahead of the 1980s/90s' numerical increase in Britain's African diaspora. Both Edwards and Sturge indicate that by 1980 the Black Majority Churches were beginning to look for ways of working together to increase their civic and inter-church involvement.[36] The internal unity emerging within the Black Majority Churches by the mid-1990s contributed significantly to a rise in their public profile.

By 1980 the emergence of the Afro West Indian United Council of Churches (established 1977) and the Council of African and Afro-Caribbean Churches (established 1979) confirmed a desire for a representative Black Majority Church voice.[37] In 1984 a distinctly evangelical voice was added when the West Indian Evangelical Alliance came into being. Although its name change in 1989 to the Afro-Caribbean Evangelical Alliance still indicated a mainly Caribbean diaspora membership, it was increasingly aware of African voices, not least because David of New Covenant, in seeking to maintain links with the likes of Ashimolowo and Ovia, had set up a small Nigerian Ministers' Fellowship. When, in 1991, the Afro-Caribbean Evangelical Alliance changed its name for a second time to become the African and Caribbean Evangelical Alliance (ACEA), the Nigerian Ministers' Fellowship ceased to function in order to co-operate. The significance of this final name change was underscored by Edwards when he stated that '[b]efore Black consciousness of the 1960s and the growing Afro-centric movements of the late 1970s, most Caribbean Christians were unwilling to be linked to an African identity'.[38]

Such was the progress with the integration process that, in 1994, ACEA's three-year-old annual 'Accord' conference was replaced by 'Highway', a conference focussing on black identity issues.[39] Highway's organizer, Les Isaac, appointed a young Nigerian pastor, Paul Ogedengbe, as his vice-chairman for the event. Four years on, in the lead up to the 1998 celebrations for the 50th anniversary of the arrival of MV Windrush, the ship that brought the first wave of post-war workers from the West Indies, an ACEA conference was confident to address possible tensions between the African and Caribbean communities head-on. ACEA's magazine highlighted the conference as follows:

> In the run up to the Windrush Celebrations ACEA took the bold step of calling on the Black Majority Churches to unite. Billed as *a plea for unity, understanding and reconciliation among African, Caribbean and the wider Black Majority Churches in the UK,* Rosemarie Davidson-Gotabed, Racial Justice Co-ordinator for the London Baptist Association, says: "sociologically we are divided as

---

[36] M. Sturge, *Look*, pp. 84–96.

[37] J. Edwards, Afro-Caribbean, pp. 109, 111; M. Sturge, *Look,* pp. 95–6.

[38] J. Edwards, *Lord, Make Us One – But Not All the Same: Seeking Unity in Diversity* (London: Hodder and Stoughton, 1999), p. 51.

[39] Unattributed, 'Black Church Builds For Future', *Idea* (January–March 1996), p. 14.

Africans, African-Caribbeans and 'Black other'. We must leave these boxes that have kept us apart and present new models for church and the wider society as we search for a multicultural Britain at ease with itself."[40]

As African and Caribbean contributors spoke, the 'boxes' became harder to define. Whilst one speaker said, 'the Caribbean Churches were large and credible organisations and the way they exercise[d] their social responsibility made them the stabilising force within the community', another emphasized the strengths of the African churches, citing their youth and dynamism, the high proportion of educated professionals in their memberships and the determination of their leaders.[41] The African speaker then went on to stress the advantage of being 'free from legalistic and historical baggage', with 'less controlling boards that allow for greater freedom and for the decision-making process to be more decisive and prompt' and it increasingly felt as if the comparison was being made between denominationalism and independence, with the ethnic nature of the argument breaking down.[42] By 1998 it was not only clear that large African churches, such as Deeper Life and the Redeemed Christian Church of God, had a measure of corporate functionality, but also that a significant number of Caribbean diaspora leaders, such as Mark Goodridge and John Francis, had moved away from Caribbean denominationalism to set up large independent churches that were indistinguishable, at least in style, from their African counterparts.

Perhaps the one event that did more than any other to bring down barriers between the denominationally-minded and the independently-minded, as well as between Africans and Caribbeans, was the annual Mission to London. This started at Earls Court Two in the summer of 1992 with American evangelist Morris Cerullo assembling a large cast of international speakers who won the support of most of London's African churches, as well as that of members of the Caribbean denominations, and attracted delegates from throughout Britain and Europe. One researcher, Nancy Schaefer, described it as embodying 'the competing tensions between commonality and diversity, the global and the local at one and the same time … tailored to a specific 'niche' in the UK religious market place; that is urban African Caribbean and African migrant churches.'[43]

Ashimolowo's presence on the platform from 1993 onwards helped to bring local African leadership to the event and, when the chairmanship of Mission to London passed from Cerullo to Colin Dye of Kensington Temple in 1996, Ashimolowo continued to attend as a guest speaker, as did Cerullo. In 1998, however, Cerullo

---

[40]   Unattributed, 'Africans and Caribbeans do Belong Together – Conference Told', *Focus* (September-November 1998), p. 5.

[41]   Ibid.

[42]   Ibid.

[43]   N. Schaefer, 'Morris Cerullo's London Revivals as "Glocal" (neo-) Pentecostal Movement Events', *Culture and Religion: An Interdisciplinary Journal*, 3.1 (May 2002), pp. 103–23.

preached at Ashimolowo's Gathering of Champions, an indication that Gathering of Champions (also a summer conference) was growing at Mission to London's expense. For the August 1999 event, Ashimolowo's vacant place on the original three person steering team was taken at Dye's request by three other London church leaders: John Francis of Ruach, Agu Irukwu of Redeemed Christian Church of God and Sam Larbie of Camberwell Elim Church.[44] Dye mandated this new team to organize three 'regional meetings' around the capital during the 'MTL week' as a lead-up to what was to be the largest ever Mission to London, planned for August 2000. However, the August 2000 event never happened. Many church leaders who engaged with Mission to London miss the unity in evangelism that it created amongst African and Caribbean churches.

Although Mission to London drew some of its support from outside the capital, expressions of African and Caribbean unity have often been regional rather than national. In response to the 1980s' Birmingham riots, a group of key leaders in the city formed the Black-led Churches Liaison Committee. In 1998 it was formalized as the Council of Black-led Churches and served as a 'unifying agency at the heart of Black Christian faith in the Midlands' with over 200 churches engaged and representing more than 30,000 Christians.[45] The West Yorkshire African Caribbean Council of Churches, founded in 1993, represents Black Majority Churches in West Yorkshire and affiliated churches in South Yorkshire, promoting good communication and understanding.[46] The fact that Bishop Joe Aldred of the Church of God of Prophecy has been able to widen his remit, from directing the Centre for Black and White Christian Partnership in Birmingham and chairing the Council of Black-led Churches, to serving as Secretary for Minority Ethnic Christian Affairs with Churches Together in England has made a positive contribution to Black Majority Church unity and co-ordination.[47]

Collaboration has played an important part in the rise of Black Majority Churches. It has opened doors evangelistically and, as further consideration will show, has continued to open doors politically. Before examining this, the pattern of church-planting that has contributed most to this second wave of Black Majority Church growth has to be highlighted, as does the church-planting pattern that reached its high point in the late 1980s and early 1990s – planting by those who came to Britain to train.

---

[44] I remained on the steering team as one of the original three.

[45] http://www.cblcuk.com accessed 20 March 2011.

[46] http://www.wyaccc,org accessed 20 March 2011.

[47] http://www.churches-together.net/Groups/42999/Churches_Together_in/Working_Together/Minority_Ethnic_Christian/Minority_Ethnic_Christian.aspx accessed 20 March 2011.

Trained to Plant

Despite the fact that by 1980 there were long-established Bible colleges in Britain, welcoming a steady flow of African and Caribbean students, and that since 1963 a full-time Bible college in Birmingham had served The New Testament Church of God, many Africans arriving in Britain from the mid-1980s onwards were only aware of the Bible colleges attached to two London churches: Kensington Temple in Notting Hill Gate and Victory Church in Hampstead.[48] Both churches had nurtured a high profile in Africa through regular staff travel to participate in missions and conferences.[49]

Hampstead Bible School of Faith began in 1983, with Victory Church, Hampstead starting shortly afterwards. Both entities were founded by Michael Bassett, an Englishman who moved to America from Britain in the 1970s and made a commitment to Christianity after watching an end-time prophecy programme on an American Christian television channel. Subsequently he became involved, along with his American wife, in Faith Christian Fellowship in Tulsa, a church then led by Buddy Harrison, the son-in-law of Kenneth Hagin who is regarded as the father of the Word of Faith movement. On his return to Britain in 1978 Bassett, under Harrison's guidance, set up Faith Christian Fellowship, Bath before refocusing in 1982 on the possibility of a London-based Word of Faith Church and Bible College.[50]

Hampstead Bible School of Faith and Victory Church, Hampstead began as white, predominantly English, upper middle-class establishments, reflecting the then locus of Word of Faith interest in Britain. By the mid-1980s, however, it was clear that the Word of Faith message was proving more popular in Africa than in Britain and, by the end of the decade, the church and Bible college in Hampstead had completely changed with African preachers, such as the Ghanaian Nicholas Duncan-Williams and the Nigerian Benson Idahosa, becoming regular guests at the pulpit and visiting African church leaders sitting contentedly in conferences, listening to preachers such as South Africa's Ray Macaulay and Kenneth Copeland's associate, Jerry Savelle.[51] For the college, the change came when Duncan-Williams encouraged his church members in Ghana to register with Hampstead and reports spread that Victory Church, with its American-style ministry and Word of Faith message, was a good location for upwardly mobile West African students seeking Bible college training in Britain.

The visa situation in the late 1980s helped as it was possible to obtain a visa for Britain to attend a full-time Bible college course and to apply for a change of visa without leaving the country. Students who had arrived to study English, for

---

[48]   Osgood, '*African*', p. 118.

[49]   KT's Colin Dye accompanied Reinhard Bonnke in Burundi early in 1989.

[50]   H. Osgood, '*African*', pp. 119–27.

[51]   N. Duncan-Williams leads Action Faith Ministries, Ghana. The late Benson Idahosa led the Church of God Mission, Nigeria. Jerry Savelle is from Dallas-Fort Worth.

example, could transfer to Bible College and then change from a student visa to a work visa so as to stay on to church-plant. In the late 1980s most Hampstead students were African, with ethnic diversity provided by the quarter of students who were second generation Caribbean British residents. In the early 1990s Brazilians also began to attend the Bible College.

Victory never kept track of its students or of the churches they planted. Graduating students were expected to fend for themselves. There has never been a Victory-linked churches' network and, for much of the time, there was no alumni association. Given that over 1,000 students passed through the college a claim that, in London alone, over 100 congregations were planted by graduates seems reasonable.[52] The Bible College closed soon after the church had a change of leadership in 1995.

By contrast, whilst Victory in the early 1990s was known for its American Word of Faith roots and its predominantly African congregation, Kensington Temple (KT) over the same period was known for its size, location and overseas mission engagement. When the Elim denomination appointed Wynne Lewis as KT's minister in 1980, the church membership stood at about 500. By 1986 it had more than trebled.[53] The Notting Hill area of London where KT has its premises is renowned for its multi-cultural mix; throughout the 1980s this was increasingly reflected in the composition of the church's congregation. Lewis had a significant overseas ministry and KT under his leadership became known world-wide. When Dye founded the church's Bible College, the International Bible Institute of London (IBIOL), in 1986 it was this backdrop that guaranteed the college an international student body from the outset. Although a denominational college with a deliberately academic staff, IBIOL taught a syllabus very similar to that of Hampstead (without the Word of Faith emphasis). Again the main focus was on equipping church-planters. However KT, unlike Victory, had a church-planting policy and throughout the 1990s Dye developed this, conceiving the London City Church which offered roles for all the would-be church-planters emerging from IBIOL. Whilst this seemed constructive, it had its complications because of the denominational claims it placed upon the church-planters given KT's standing within the Elim denomination.

The era of bringing students from Africa to train to plant, which was so important in the late 1980s and early 1990s, had ceased to become a dominant means of African church growth by the turn of the millennium.[54] A number of the larger African churches had established their own part-time Bible colleges to help their resident members acquire ministry skills and develop their Bible knowledge. However, when these churches have started branches, much of the training has been given through apprenticeship techniques, with potential ministers serving in supervised roles of

---

[52]   Information from Hampstead's former Dean of Students.

[53]   J. Hywel-Davies, *The Kensington Temple Story* (Crowborough: Monarch Books, 1998), pp. 84–94.

[54]   IBIOL saw a mid-1990s shift towards Latin American students. Dye built relationships in Brazil during the early 1990s.

increasing importance within the main church before being given responsibility for a church-plant. KICC has developed a number of its own church-plants in this way and Glory House (formerly Glory Bible Church) for several years operated a Bible college on the lines described, at times advertising extensively on Premier radio to bring in students from outside its own congregation.

Called to Plant

The final pattern of church-planting to be illustrated has been the most entrepreneurial. It involves people who have 'stepped out in faith' in response to the 'call of God' without persuasion from fellow nationals, commissioning by a sending denomination or training at a Bible college. They have not come on missionary visas, invited by *bona fide* churches impressed by their ministry experience in their country of origin, but have arrived in Britain with the intention of fulfilling some form of secular employment and then had a change of direction. In certain cases the change of direction has been partly prompted by employment frustrations. When facing revalidation requirements or other employment difficulties in Britain, some have considered ministry possibilities rather than take lower grade posts. Christians who have trained as teachers, academics, solicitors or medical doctors in their homeland have gone on to become church planters, seeking to be a blessing rather than a burden on Britain. They call on their past experiences of church life in Africa to equip them for their newly selected roles. They then put themselves through a personal preparation programme of reading, praying, seeking advice and assimilating ministry material through conferences, television, videos and tapes before gathering friends and family to help found their ministry, usually in a hired hall with some sacrificially acquired musical instruments and a portable public address system. Theological qualifications often follow later.

For others however there are no employment frustrations, just a sense that they should be working in some form of Christian ministry. These people then go through much the same preparatory process but often combine their early days in ministry with a full-time secular post. Although African churches do accord their pastors a degree of status as a 'Man of God', prestige and finance are rarely the motivation. In African churches congregational members receive a regular diet of motivational preaching, where personal progress is the goal and 'blessing the preacher financially' is presented as a key to success, yet this has to be balanced against a tendency to set the spiritual qualifications of 'the Minister' at a level that seems almost unattainable to the average congregation member. There is a conviction that the real qualifications for ministry lie in God-given giftings and spiritual anointings that cannot be acquired by means other than divine intervention or considerable periods of extensive association with those already so gifted and anointed. Those who see themselves as called to church-plant have generally concluded that they have come to possess such giftings and anointings that mark them out from their fellow congregation members, often speaking of divine visitations or significant specific personal contacts.

An added pressure for most Africans in Britain is the need to send money back to their families. Family members who come to Britain are considered to be privileged and, given the nature of corporate family consciousness in Africa, there will often be a sense that, as the whole family contributed in some way to their going, everyone deserves to be blessed. The need for gainful employment therefore has increased significance. Proud though families might be of their doctor, lawyer, teacher or accountant son or daughter moving to Britain, there is equal, if not greater, pride in learning that he or she has now been 'called' to the ministry. There is a tendency for families to think of success and to look at the ministers around them in Africa who have both status and finance. Indeed, when church-plants with African congregations in Britain are successful they can provide good levels of remuneration but there is a counterbalance to this in that, during the pioneering phase of church-planting, overheads tend to exceed income considerably. Whilst those who are 'called to plant' have to show a high level of entrepreneurial ability in terms of taking initiatives and assessing risks, they also have to be prepared to make considerable personal sacrifices. The degree of willingness to make personal sacrifice can separate the church-planter with self-seeking motives from the church-planter with altruistic intentions. The same is true of the readiness to endure the time-consuming process of putting in place proper structures of finance and governance accountability, with the need for trustee appointments, accurate bookkeeping, dependable audits and appropriately drafted documents for charity registration.

This entrepreneurial church-planting phase has been extremely significant for independent church growth in Britain, yet those who have opted for it have quickly discovered that they have not chosen an easy route. Church-planting has a significant impact on their lifestyles, proving demanding in terms of time, patience, energy and finance. The church-planter's family home often has to serve as a store for equipment and a venue for meetings, while the family car becomes a cross between a transit van and a taxi.[55] As such realities take hold, convictions concerning calling can be strongly tested. In situations as challenging as these, entrepreneurial church-planters do value each other's affirmation. Being invited by a host pastor to sit in specially reserved seating at the front may seem trivial but, for some church-planting pastors, it is the mutual recognition that helps keep alive their sense of divine calling.

External Relations

When Edwards looked back to the period between 1960 and 1975 and saw that, within the Black Majority Churches of the time, 'a keen interest in social and political issues began to develop' he could never have anticipated where it might

---

[55] Ashimolowo recalls taxiing members. Unattributed, *'London Calling'* (March 2002), p. 5.

lead.[56] The rise of Black Majority Churches has not just been a numerical rise but a rise in political profile. When the Black Majority Churches held a national conference in 2000, both the Prime Minister and the Leader of the Opposition were present to speak.

At the official launch of the Faith in the Future conference on 11 November 1999, Mark Sturge, the then General Director of ACEA, had raised the possibility of the British education system having failed black children, saying that '[m]any within the Black Majority Churches were so concerned by the current situation that serious thought should be given to the need for BMCs to establish church-based schools for Black children.'[57] Tony Blair and William Hague attended the conference to contribute to the 'black education' debate with Blair explaining, to an enthusiastic response, that he wanted to 'make this a country where success in education leads to a good job; where hard work gets its just reward; where what matters is who you are, not where you're from', backing up his words by encouraging Britain's black youth to venture into politics.[58] The similarities in Hague's speech the next day were remarkable. Hague emphasized his conviction that the Black Majority Churches had much to offer in the area of 'faith-based welfare' and concluded with a reference to a future black Prime Minister.[59] Despite the 2001 General Election not establishing a black Prime Minister, the door to Number 10 did open quite frequently to Black Majority Church leaders and notably to key activists such as Nims Obunge, the Nigerian, Tottenham based pastor who founded the Peace Alliance, who were able to contribute on aspects of societal transformation in the light of minority ethnic sensitivities.[60] In 2010, with a new government, the pattern continued and by October the Prime Minister and the Work and Pensions Minister were again meeting with Black Majority Church leaders.[61]

Political openness to Black Majority Churches has not always translated into positiveness in the press. Child deliverance issues have on several occasions caused the press to question African Pentecostalism, as has the inevitably large income of some Black Majority mega-churches.[62] Technical issues that arose with the Charity Commission have also been reported sensationally and

---

[56] J. Edwards, 'Afro-Caribbean', p. 109.

[57] Unattributed, 'When ACEA speaks …', *Focus* (February-April 2000), p. 13.

[58] Ibid.

[59] Ibid.

[60] Sarah Kinson, '*London People; Rev Nims Obunge*', http://www.bbc.co.uk/london/content/articles/2008/12/05/londonpeople_nims_obunge.shtml, accessed 22 March 2011.

[61] http://www.centreforsocialjustice.org.uk/default.asp?pageRef=153, accessed 22 March 2011.

[62] J. Westhead, 'Abuse Case Sparks New Fears', 3 June 2005, http://news.bbc.co.uk/1/hi/uk/4602543.stm, accessed 22 March 2011; R. Gledhill, 'Poor Christians Are Deluded By "Grab It" Gospel', *Times* (17 March 2003), p. 4.

Mission to London struggled to receive a positive press.[63] Whereas those on the inside of Black Majority Churches have known how to set these reports in context, it has been harder for those of us who are white and live on the fringes of Black Majority Church life. Nonetheless, there have been examples where the wider church has risen above occasional negative press opinion and demonstrated a high level of commitment. In London, one such instance relates to KICC's premises challenges.[64] The Global Day of Prayer, London and the Street Pastors project also provide strong examples of inter-church co-operation.[65]

In 2005 the problems KICC faced over the proposed compulsory purchase of its Hackney site in readiness for the 2012 Olympics began to come to the fore. The agreement eventually entered into opened the possibility of relocating the church to Rainham and KICC moved temporarily into a Walthamstow theatre it had purchased whilst planning permission for the new development was being sought from the local authority. When local residents objected to KICC's move, citing amongst other things the size of the proposed facility and questioning the need for such a large congregation, London church leaders from all denominations wrote stating their conviction that large churches, as well as local community churches, were relevant for the capital's spiritual health. This collaboration was much appreciated by KICC although it did not carry sufficient weight with the Secretary of State for Communities and Local Government to win the day at appeal. At the time of writing KICC still awaits a permanent home.[66]

The Global Day of Prayer in London has proved to be a remarkable cross-cultural event and the Street Pastors programme, which began in some of London's inner city boroughs with members of the capital's Black Majority Churches among the initiators and early participants, is growing into an international movement. The success of these projects in bringing together the diversity of the wider church can be attributed to the cross-cultural skills of the Black Majority Church leaders who head them – Dr. Jonathan Oloyede for Global Day of Prayer, London and the Revd Les Isaac for Street Pastors. The contribution of such 'bridge-builders' to the rise in profile of Black Majority Churches should not be under-estimated. If Black Majority Churches were to arise without such linkages the wider church in Britain would be the poorer and the Christianity presented to society would be so diverse as to lack coherence and commonality of purpose.

---

[63]   R. Gledhill, 'Charity Law to End Fraud in Black Churches', *Times* (6 October 2004), p. 3. T. Pain and C. Manning, *Miracles are Impossible: You Decide* (Robertsbridge: Battle Books, 1993), p. 13.

[64]   'Report on King's Ministries' para: 28. *'Friends of KICC'*, 1 (February 2006), pp. 2–3.

[65]   http://www.gdoplondon.com and www.streetpastors.co.uk, accessed 22 March 2011.

[66]   Unattributed, 'Mega church plans turned down', http://news.bbc.co.uk/2/hi/uk_news/england/london/7244798.stm, accessed 22 March 2011.

The Rise Continues

There are clear signs that certain aspects of multiplication will continue in Britain's Black Majority Churches. Even if the overall number of people attending Black Majority Churches was to remain static or decrease, the number of churches would grow as a result of outward movement from Britain's major cities. Already, as African families relocate eastwards from London into Essex and Kent, Black Majority Churches are increasing in those counties' provincial centres. This pattern is holding true in every direction from every metropolitan hub. Such expansion is helped by the fact that church-planting is so strongly in the mind-set of African church members that even in a relatively small congregation there will be one or two married couples (and maybe single men and women) weighing up the possibility of starting a church. It is true that the ultimate size of some of these church plants may not be particularly large; some may never need accommodation beyond the local school or community hall and some in time may merge or close.

This, though, is only part of the story. For everyone who senses a calling to plant a church there are others who are equally convinced that their spiritual destiny lies in joining the largest church they can find. The mega-church membership mind-set is at least as strong as the church-planting mind-set, so a second aspect of multiplication will be the development of yet more churches with a membership of 1,000 or more. Of course, between these two opposites are many who are simply happy to serve where they are, maintaining their loyalty to their local church, or to the 'mother-church' or denominational grouping that has birthed it.

In time there will almost certainly be personnel shifts amongst the second generation members of the African diaspora, as proved to be the case for the Caribbean denominations in the 1970s. In some cases this could involve a move across to white majority churches, not as a product of disillusionment but as a result of greater integration. Of course, many members of the African diaspora already worship in white majority churches, sometimes because of denominational loyalties but sometimes out of preferred identification.[67] It is important to remember that many Africans who came here in the 1980s and 1990s were already British citizens, born to parents who came to Britain on professional placements in the 1960s and 1970s.[68] Some of these returned with a strong Christian faith, activated in Africa's spiritual revival. Others are seen by the Black Majority Churches as part of the community they are seeking to reach. That said, no Black Majority Church in Britain is seeking to be a 'Black Totality Church' and every church has high hopes of finding a way of engaging in effective cross-cultural evangelism. Indeed, it could still turn out to be the case that Black Majority Churches will

---

[67]   Denominational figures from P. Brierley, *The Tide is Running Out: What the English Church Attendance Survey Reveals* (Eltham: Christian Research, 2000), pp. 135–6.

[68]   For excellent analysis of Britain's Nigerian diaspora see I. Emmanuel, *The Shift of a Lifetime: Moving a Generation from Survival to Significance* (Croydon: Sophos Books, 2010).

have more evangelistic success than their white counterparts in terms of reaching their white neighbours. After all, there is sufficient socio-economic breadth across the range of Black Majority Churches to facilitate intra-community relations. By 2010 white middle-class churches were forming bonds with middle-class Black Majority Churches, proving that common social and spiritual ground can transcend differences in cultural style.[69]

As Black Majority Church members find common social ground with their unchurched neighbours, the rise in Black Majority Churches may yet have an even greater impact on British church growth.

---

[69] The relationship between Holy Trinity Brompton and Jesus House (an RCCG congregation) is probably an example.

Chapter 8

African Pentecostal Growth: The Redeemed Christian Church of God in Britain[1]

Richard Burgess

African-initiated Pentecostal churches represent an increasingly important addition to the British religious landscape, especially in London. The 2005 *English Church Census*[2] showed a steady decline in British church attendance over the previous seven years and the widespread closure of churches from the historic denominations. At the same time over 1,000 new churches were opened, a large proportion started by denominations or individuals from Africa. There are close to 300 African-initiated congregations and denominations listed in the Black Majority Churches UK Directory (2003/4). Most are Pentecostal churches and over half are founded or led by Nigerians. Some are part of transnational networks; others are independent churches with no formal links outside Britain. Of Britain's 10 largest mega-churches, five are led by Nigerians.

This chapter focuses on one particular Nigerian (Yoruba)-led denomination, the Redeemed Christian Church of God (RCCG), founded in 1952 by Josiah Akindayomi. In 1981, Enoch Adejare Adeboye, a former university lecturer, became the General Overseer following the death of the founder. This leadership transition is often considered the major event in the history of the RCCG, propelling the church into a period of rapid expansion. From a small, localised Pentecostal denomination in South-Western Nigeria, it has become a movement of global significance with over 14,000 branches nationwide and with branches in over 140 nations,[3] making it one of the fastest growing Pentecostal churches in the world. This study is based on participant observation in RCCG congregations, interviews with church pastors, a congregational questionnaire survey and content analysis of RCCG literature.[4]

---

[1] Fieldwork for this chapter was conducted as part of the research project, entitled 'Transnational Nigerian-initiated Pentecostal churches, networks and believers in three Northern countries: migrant churches as a potential and potent social force,' funded by NORFACE. See http://www.relemerge.org/project_09 accessed 20 July 2011.

[2] See http://www.eauk.org/resources/info/statistics/2005englishchurchcensus.cfm, accessed 2 March 2010.

[3] National Chairman of the Central Missions Board (RCCG), interview, 25 April 2009.

[4] The questionnaire survey was conducted during 2008 and led to 925 usable questionnaires.

I begin with a historical overview of African-led churches in Britain before discussing the factors behind the RCCG's popularity and growth. Some social scientific explanations of African churches in Europe focus on their social function, for example as a means of survival and empowerment and of reinforcing or constructing identity in a context of social marginalization, racial discrimination and socio-economic and cultural deprivation.[5] This chapter follows those studies that adopt a more holistic approach by taking account of sociological, theological and missiological factors behind their emergence and growth.[6] By doing so, it provides a glimpse into the life of one of the most dynamic churches in Britain.

African-led Churches in Britain

The spread of African-led churches to Britain must be understood within the context of social and religious developments in home and host countries.[7] The first wave of African church planting was directly linked to the increase in immigration from the 1960s. It consisted of mainly Aladura-type churches from Nigeria, transplanted to cater for the social and spiritual needs of their members in the diaspora.[8] A relatively liberal British migration policy, combined with poor governance and a decline in educational standards at home, resulted in a growing African migrant community, especially from former British colonies such as Nigeria and Ghana. The impulse behind migration was linked to upwardly-mobile aspirations as students arrived with the intention of returning to their homelands, following their studies, to join the middle ranks of the educated elite. Like their Caribbean counterparts a decade earlier,[9] African migrants encountered discrimination, cultural differences and unfamiliar church styles in British churches. Some opted to leave the Christian church altogether. Others chose to persevere and remain

---

[5]   For example, P. Kalilombe, 'Black Christianity in Britain,' in G. ter Haar (ed.), *Strangers and Sojourners: Religious communities in the Diaspora* (Leuven: Peeters, 1998), pp. 173–93; S. Hunt, 'Neither here nor there: The construction of identities and boundary maintenance of West African Pentecostals,' *Sociology*, 36.1 (2002), pp. 147–69.

[6]   See G. ter Haar, *Halfway to Paradise: African Christians in Europe* (Cardiff: Cardiff Academic Press, 1998); J. Kwabena Asamoah-Gyadu, 'An African Pentecostal on mission in Eastern Europe: the Church of the "Embassy of God" in the Ukraine,' *Pneuma*, 27.2 (Autumn 2005), pp. 297–321; O. Kalu, *African Pentecostalism: An Introduction* (Oxford: Oxford University Press, 2008), pp. 271–91.

[7]   For a history of African-led churches in Britain set within the wider context of the 'black majority church' movement, see Chapter 7, Osgood, *Rise of Black Churches*.

[8]   J. Jehu-Appiah, 'Models of mission and ministry: the Council of African and Caribbean Churches (UK),' *International Review of Mission*, 89.354 (2000), pp. 442–4; H. Harris, *Yoruba in Diaspora: An African church in London* (New York: Palgrave Macmillan, 2006).

[9]   P. Kalilombe, 'Black Christianity in Britain,' *Ethnic and Racial Studies*, 20.2 (1997), pp. 308–15.

within the historic denominations they belonged to in Africa. The most common response however was the formation of African-initiated churches.[10]

The second wave of African church-planting involved mainly African neo-Pentecostals from Nigeria and Ghana.[11] It began in the 1980s, again as a means of catering for the growing number of members who had migrated to Britain in pursuit of education and employment at a time of economic decline at home. Here we see the dynamics of migrant religious behaviour being influenced by developments at home, where neo-Pentecostal expressions of Christianity, associated especially with university graduates and students, were beginning to dominate the religious terrain. Most of the earliest churches were transplants from Nigeria, such as the Deeper Life Bible Church (1985), Foursquare Gospel Church (1985), New Covenant Church (1986), and the Redeemed Christian Church of God (1988). An early Ghanaian initiative was the Universal Prayer Group Ministries (UPG), founded in 1985, which opened its first church, Edmonton Temple, in 1988.[12]

A new phase occurred in the early 1990s when some African church planters left their denominations to establish independent congregations, partly due to frustrations over their inability to integrate into the British religious landscape because of denominational constraints. This coincided with an 87% increase in the number of Nigerian migrants in Britain during the 1990s, from 47,201 in 1991 to 88,380 in 2001, with about 80% resident in London.[13] The most significant transfer occurred with Matthew Ashimolowo leaving Foursquare to start Kingsway International Christian Centre in 1992. KICC has grown to become the largest single congregation in Western Europe. Another development saw individual Africans, who had migrated for secular employment or to further their education, setting up their own independent congregations with no formal links to a sending denomination at home or in Britain. The majority were started by Nigerians or Ghanaians and most were located in London.

African Pentecostal transplants, such as the Redeemed Christian Church of God (RCCG), have also continued to grow. The RCCG began in Britain in 1988 as a London-based house fellowship, later named Angel Parish following its relocation to the Angel, Islington. The planting of its flagship congregation, Jesus House, in 1994 ushered in a period of rapid expansion, especially among London's large Nigerian community. By April 2004, there were 161 parishes in

---

[10]   Ibid., pp. 313–4.

[11]   This overview is based on H. Osgood, '*African neo-Pentecostal churches and British Evangelicalism 1985–2005: Balancing Principles and Practicalities*,' (PhD, School of Oriental and African Studies, London, 2006) and on oral interviews with African pastors.

[12]   For a study of a second church started by the UPG, Freedom Centre International, see Chapter 9, A. Duffuor, Moving Up and Moving Out.

[13]   http://www.migrationinformation.org, accessed 9 January 2009. This does not take account of the large number of illegal immigrants and asylum-seekers.

Britain (125 located in London) with a total membership of 45,377.[14] By 2010, this had increased to over 440 parishes, with approximately 85,000 members.[15]

Migrant Churches: Social Capital and Holistic Salvation

One reason for the RCCG's growth and popularity in Britain is the way its social and religious support networks assist African Pentecostals to negotiate the migration process and become incorporated into British society. This is important in migrant contexts where people are separated from traditional extended family networks. While they hope for a better life in Britain, African Pentecostals often encounter difficulties, ranging from financial problems and unemployment to immigration difficulties and racial discrimination. In the case of Nigerian Pentecostals they also have to contend with a perception of Nigerians by white Europeans as prone to corruption and criminality.

In the literature, African churches in diaspora are often referred to as 'migrant' or 'immigrant' churches due to their capacity to cater for the needs of African immigrants.[16] According to Gerrie Ter Haar, they 'contribute significantly to the material and immaterial well-being of African migrants', especially those living in the large urbanized and industrialized areas of Western Europe.[17] One pastor explained why the RCCG is popular with Nigerian immigrants in Britain:

> [T]he reason for that may be where we are coming from and what we've gone through and why we've had to come closer to Christ ... It's almost like a home away from home, like a community away from home. Because once you find yourself here you don't have the support network that you once knew back at home. Therefore the church becomes a form of support network.

---

[14]   A. Ukah, 'Reverse mission or Asylum Christianity? A Nigerian Church in Europe,' in T. Falola and A. Agwuele (eds), *Africans and the Politics of Popular Cultures* (Rochester, NY: University of Rochester Press, 2009), pp. 104–32.

[15]   *The Redeemed Christian Church of God United Kingdom Directory of Parishes 2010* (London: The Redeemed Christian Church of God UK, 2010); B. Adedibu, '*The urban explosion of black majority churches: Their origin, growth, distinctives and contribution to British Christianity*' (PhD, North-West University, South Africa, 2011).

[16]   See O. Kalu, 'African Pentecostalism in Diaspora,' *PentecoStudies*, 9.1 (2010), pp. 9–34; J. Hanciles, *Beyond Christendom: Globalization, African Migration, and the Transformation of the West* (Maryknoll, N.Y.: Orbis Books, 2008); C. Währisch-Oblau, *The Missionary Self-Perception of Pentecostal/Charismatic Church Leaders from the Global South in Europe: Bringing Back the Gospel* (Global Pentecostal and Charismatic Studies 2; Leiden: Brill, 2009).

[17]   G. Ter Haar, *Halfway to Paradise*, p. 43.

In contrast to current religious trends in Britain, where there has been a marked decline in church attendance, congregational life remains an important expression of African Christian faith in the diaspora, a means of offsetting the pressures of individualization and fragmentation in Western society. Thus, Grace Davie's portrayal of religious trends in Britain in terms of a persistence of religious belief over against a decline in religious belonging does not apply to the African Christian diaspora where believing and belonging generally go hand in hand.[18] My own research suggests that the presence of RCCG congregations has increased the level of religious participation among Nigerian immigrants. For example, in the survey 86% stated that since joining the RCCG they attend church more often, 87% stated that they pray more often and 48% said they evangelize more often. Certainly, the level of commitment in terms of church attendance and lay ministry is high compared to many white-led churches.

The function of churches as social support mechanisms is often linked to theories of social capital and to discussions about the relationship between the state and religious groups in the West. The concept of 'social capital', first introduced by Pierre Bourdieu,[19] has been an influential component of UK public policy debates. It refers to the values and resources that 'both result in, and are the product of, socially negotiated ties and relationships'.[20] Robert Putnam argues that social capital built through voluntary associations encourages social cohesion.[21] The 'communitarian turn' in British politics since the early 1990s has emphasized the need to strengthen participation in civil society and balance rights with responsibilities.[22] As a consequence, the British government has begun to recognize the potential of 'faith communities' to contribute to social capital and social welfare provision, especially in urban contexts. It is felt that, with their existing neighbourhood involvement and local networks, they may be the most suitable organizations to promote social cohesion.[23] In 2006, the Commission on Urban Life and Faith published a joint document produced by the Anglican and Methodist churches and intended as a call for Christians to engage more effectively with Britain's urban centres. The authors use the term 'faithful capital' to describe the distinctive contributions the church and individual Christians in

---

[18]   G. Davie, *Religion in Britain since 1945: Believing without Belonging* (Oxford: Blackwell, 1994).

[19]   P. Bourdieu, 'Le Capital Social: Notes Provisoires,' *Actes Rech. Sci. Soc.*, 31 (1980), pp. 2–3.

[20]   P. Cheong, R. Edwards, H. Goulbourne and J. Solomos, 'Immigration, social cohesion and social capital: a critical review,' *Critical Social Policy*, 27.1 (2007), p. 4.

[21]   R. Putnam, *Bowling Alone: The Collapse and Revival of the American Community* (New York: Simon and Schuster, 2000).

[22]   L. Bretherton, *Christianity and Contemporary Politics* (Chichester: Wiley-Blackwell, 2010), p. 32.

[23]   R. Furbey and M. Macey, 'Religion and Urban Regeneration: a Place for Faith?', *Policy and Politics*, 33.1 (2005), pp. 96–7.

local communities can make to wider social capital through corporate worship, caring for others and commitment to human dignity and social justice. They argue that 'faithful capital,' found in abundance in communities of faith, is crucial for the survival and sustenance of urban life.[24]

One way the RCCG contributes to 'faithful capital' is through its congregational welfare departments which assist members in financial difficulty. Churches also organize seminars on such topics as business management, investment, immigration issues, marriage and health awareness. RCCG's Royal Connections parish, located in the ethnically-diverse London borough of Newham, has an 'integration team', run by volunteers, to assist migrants to settle. Above all, churches provide access to social and spiritual resources for new migrants by providing contexts for communal worship, prayer and Christian fellowship, thus contributing to the stocks of social capital necessary for successful integration. Prayer in particular is considered an important resource for dealing with obstacles to successful integration. Every parish has a regular prayer meeting and most worship services provide opportunities for people to receive prayer for particular needs, whether these are immigration issues, financial and health problems or family relationships. Many congregations have house fellowships to provide pastoral care for members. They also have a variety of single interest groups to support different categories of people, including youth, women, men, lone parents, childless couples and business people.

Another reason for the RCCG's popularity among African immigrants is its holistic concept of salvation, which includes not only holiness but healing, deliverance and prosperity. The appeal of these theologies is obvious in a hostile economic environment like Africa, where access to medical facilities and to state funds is severely restricted and adverse circumstances are often blamed on the activities of malevolent spirits. However, they are also popular in Britain among African migrants, who sometimes find it difficult to support their families, especially if they are students or low-paid workers without recourse to public funds. As Ogbu Kalu reminds us, immigrants retain the spiritual worldview of their indigenous cultures and find Pentecostal churches 'attentive to their deeply felt needs.'[25] In the survey, 85% of RCCG members said they were attracted to the church because of its problem-solving approach, while 33% said they had experienced divine healing and 41% deliverance since attending the church. Success-oriented theologies which link faith and prayer with the expectation of material prosperity and success, are especially attractive and reflect the preoccupation with individual progress among Nigerian Pentecostals. One RCCG pastor put it like this:

---

[24]   Commission on Urban Life and Faith, *Faithful Cities: A Call for Celebration, Vision and Justice* (London: Methodist Publishing House/Church House Publishing, 2006), pp. 3, 1.

[25]   O. Kalu, *African Pentecostalism*, p. 288.

We preach the whole gospel ... But at times African-based churches tend to sway towards success and prosperity because of our background ... maybe because we have been disadvantaged before; maybe because we have been poor before ... And then when you look at our congregations in the Western world, in Europe, you discover the majority are migrants. So right now they are struggling, so they need faith for them to come up.

Perhaps more surprising is the continuing appeal of deliverance theology. However, despite the influence of secularization, issues such as witchcraft and ancestral covenants continue to be a reality for Africans in the diaspora. Deliverance theology is popular because it is practical and progressive in orientation, enabling Africans to make a break from past social and religious associations that are considered a hindrance to personal development. The RCCG holds regular programmes and conferences which provide ritual settings for the promotion of healing, deliverance and prosperity teaching. For example, Victory House in London has an annual 'Healing and Deliverance Week' and a monthly programme called 'Wealth Must Change Hands'. Often speakers from outside Britain are invited to these events, reflecting the transnational nature of African Pentecostal churches.

Pentecostalism's propensity to precipitate socio-economic mobility is particularly appealing to African migrants in Britain. Economic deprivation is recognized as a factor preventing successful integration and as a key underlying source of tension undermining community cohesion in Britain.[26] Participation in Pentecostal networks provide Africans in Britain with opportunities to prosper financially, whether as an outcome of 'faith' teaching, increased work ethic or business acumen. In the survey, 78% of members said their finances had improved and 67% said they had experienced job promotion since joining the RCCG. Many African Pentecostals in Britain are highly educated professionals with a strong motivation to succeed, which makes them especially drawn to success-oriented theologies. Stephen Hunt notes the way the RCCG in Britain has moved away from the sectarian and millenarian focus of traditional black Pentecostalism by inculcating some of the core values of western society, such as materialism, success, careerism and human potential.[27] While it still maintains a commitment to faith teaching, there is generally more of an emphasis on generating money through hard work and wise investment than in Africa, though these are often closely linked in Pentecostal imagination. Congregational in-house magazines contain articles on financial issues, careers advice and advertisements on behalf of financial advisors, mortgage advisors and property consultants. African Pentecostals often regard

---

[26]   Commission on Integration and Cohesion, *Themes, Messages and Challenges: A Summary of Key Themes from the Commission for Cohesion and Integration Consultation* (Wetherby, North Yorkshire: Communities and Local Government Publishers, June 2007), p. 6.

[27]   S. Hunt, 'Neither here nor there,' p. 165.

financial accumulation as a means to an end, a way of financing evangelistic and social projects or allowing more time for Christian ministry.

Mission Churches: Empowering the Laity and Planting Churches

While the RCCG functions as a social and religious support network for African migrants, its rapid expansion has been driven by a global missionary agenda which is fuelled by the founder's vision, the church headquarters in Nigeria and the missionary ambitions of its British leaders. One of the church's strengths is its internal organization which is designed to empower and mobilize the laity to engage in ministry and mission.[28] This is exemplified by Royal Connections in Newham where the senior pastor is assisted by a cadre of lay ministers who share his vision. Most have come up through the ranks of the church and have either remained within Royal Connections or have become congregational pastors themselves. The RCCG's creation of a category of lay leaders, called 'workers,' is innovative in terms of African Pentecostal ecclesiology. 'Workers' in RCCG are members who have undergone a four-month period of training, enabling them to fulfil various practical roles in the church while continuing in their secular occupations.[29] Workers are also encouraged to receive Holy Spirit baptism, a key component of RCCG spirituality and closely aligned to power for service. In the survey, 95% of respondents said they had experienced Holy Spirit baptism.

The RCCG's growth in Britain is also facilitated by its capacity to empower women and young people. While the majority of pastors are male, there are also a number of senior and influential women, including Modupe Afolabi, the UK Executive Administrator, and Adewunmi Oladunjoye, senior pastor of the Holy Ghost Zone, a network of about 10 congregations. The RCCG also appeals to young people who make up a large proportion of its membership. Most branches have strong youth fellowships which organize a variety of activities to attract and retain young people. This holds out promise for the future if the church is to maintain the same levels of growth among second and third generation migrants. Furthermore, young people, who have been brought up in Britain, are more likely to be able to create church communities suitable for a post-Christian context.

RCCG members regard the church as a significant social force with the potential to reverse the secularizing tendencies of British society. From their perspective, Nigeria is currently experiencing a Christian revival which they hope to introduce into Britain through a process of reverse mission. In the literature, the term 'reverse mission' refers to the purported historic shift in the direction of

---

[28] A. Ukah, 'Mobilities, migration and multiplication. The expansion of the religious field of the Redeemed Christian Church of God (RCCG), Nigeria,' in A. Adogame and C. Weisskoppel (eds), *Religion in the Context of African Migration* (Bayreuth: Bayreuth African Studies, 2005), p. 330.

[29] Ibid., p. 127.

mission.[30] Most commonly it is used to refer to the emergence of African, Asian and Latin American Pentecostal churches in the northern continents and their aspirations to re-evangelize the former heartlands of Christianity. The rhetoric of reverse mission adopted by Nigerian Pentecostals in Britain relies upon a particular self-representation and conception of the Other encountered in the host society. This often develops after their arrival in response to the perceived secularization and decline in indigenous British Christianity compared to the religious vitality at home. Studies of contemporary international migrations have shown that the overwhelming majority are economically driven.[31] This was born out in my research where I found that most RCCG members migrated either to study in order to improve their chances of gaining lucrative employment or to work, hoping to save money and improve their future prospects. Many of those who have migrated to Britain to find work or to study however, consider that God has given them a unique opportunity to bring the gospel back to those who originally provided it. Furthermore, a number of influential RCCG pastors, responsible for facilitating church growth, migrated specifically for missionary purposes.

Included within the RCCG's mission statement is the aim to 'plant churches within five minutes walking distance in every city and town of developing countries and within five minutes driving distance in every city and town of developed countries.'[32] According to Asonzeh Ukah, there were pragmatic reasons behind this strategy: to overcome the problem of transportation, considered a hindrance to church attendance, and to transform members into church-planters.[33] The RCCG encourages members to plant churches wherever they are, thus fulfilling the divine promise given to its founder that the church would spread around the world before the Second Advent of Christ. Ukah identifies three ways RCCG congregations are founded outside Nigeria. First, a rich congregation in Nigeria could sponsor the establishment of a branch in Britain. Second, a member of RCCG who has migrated either for work or study may start a church, which is then incorporated into the RCCG family once it becomes viable. Finally, a rich congregation in Britain can plant a church by commissioning one of its members. This is the most common means of planting new branches.[34] By 2009, the RCCG had planted churches in 68% of Britain's cities.[35] Not surprisingly, most churches are concentrated in places

---

[30]   R. Catto, 'Non-western Christian missionaries in England: Has mission been reversed?,' p. 109, in S. Spencer (ed.), *Mission and Migration*, (Calver: Cliff College, 2008), pp. 109–18; M. Ojo, 'Reverse Mission,' in J. Bonk (ed.), *Encyclopedia of Missions and Missionaries* (New York/London: Routledge, 2007), pp. 380–82. See also Chapter 6, R. Catto, Reverse Mission.

[31]   S. Castles and M. Miller, *The Age of Migration. International Population Movements in the Modern World* (Basingstoke: Palgrave Macmillan, 2003).

[32]   See http://rccgint.org/vm.html accessed 8 October 2009).

[33]   A. Ukah, 'Mobilities', p. 328.

[34]   A. Ukah, 'Reverse Mission,' pp. 117–8.

[35]   B. Adedibu, 'Urban explosion', p. 91.

where there are clusters of Nigerian immigrants such as London, Birmingham and Manchester, with by far the largest number in London.[36] Congregations occupy a variety of local spaces, ranging from former industrial warehouses, office spaces or business centres to school halls, cinemas and traditional church buildings.

While Jesus House is the RCCG flagship congregation, with over 2,500 members,[37] there are other churches that have made significant contributions in terms of church growth. One is Trinity Chapel, located in the London borough of Newham, which was started in 1996 as a church plant from Jesus House. Between 1999 and 2006 its annual average attendance level grew from 245 to 880 and it has planted out seven new churches.[38] Another example is House of Praise which has planted over 15 churches in Britain, Germany and Canada. The RCCG is able to generate considerable financial and human resources through its mandatory tithing system and workers-in-training programme, which have facilitated its church-planting activities. Allowing pastors to combine secular work with ministerial responsibilities to make ends meet also encourages lay leaders to become church planters. However, the majority of parishes are small which makes it difficult for them to engage in church-planting. In the survey, 39% of RCCG pastors reported a church attendance of less than 50, 66% less than 100 and 85% less than 200. Conversion rates are difficult to determine. In the survey, 55% of pastors reported fewer than 10 converts in their churches over the previous year. It seems likely that church growth is largely through transfer rather than conversion.[39] An exception is Trinity Chapel which recorded 165 new converts in 2010.[40]

One of the conditions for planting a new congregation is to find a suitable space to hold meetings. Acquiring a permanent place is often a significant step in the process of integration and growth. Many RCCG congregations have to move from place to place which seriously hampers their organizational structures, their numerical growth and their capacity for civic engagement. Often they have to rent space for their meetings which they share with others. This means that they are sometimes forced to hold their meetings at less convenient times, resulting in declining attendance levels. In the survey, 37% of parishes owned or leased a building, while 63% occupied rented space. Invariably, financial constraints and planning regulations are the main obstacles to obtaining a building of their own. Once they do so, congregations are often left with heavy debts and the added financial burden of renovation and refurbishment.

One church whose fortunes have fluctuated as a result of forced relocation is The Fountain, based in London. It began in 1998 with just 18 members meeting

---

[36]   According to the RCCG UK's *Directory of Parishes 2010*, out of 445 parishes 188 were located in London, 18 in Birmingham and 12 in Manchester.

[37]   Figure supplied by the senior pastor of Jesus House during the church's Annual Review, 26 April 2009.

[38]   Information supplied by the administrator of Trinity Chapel, 26 May 2011.

[39]   B. Adedibu, 'Urban Explosion,' p. 122.

[40]   Information supplied by the administrator of Trinity Chapel, 26 May 2011.

in a rented hall. It then had to relocate to a larger school hall but lost some of its members in the process. In 2004, it acquired its first permanent place of worship, which boosted the growth of the church. It was now able to respond more effectively to consumer demands by providing opportunities for social and religious engagement on a daily basis. Between 2001 and 2004 its membership was around 60 but, after it acquired a building of its own, membership grew rapidly so that, by 2008, it had about 650 members. The same year the London Borough of Barking and Dagenham served a Compulsory Purchase Order (CPO) and bought the property against the church's wishes. With the compensation money and other funds it was able to generate however, it has been able to purchase a £2.3 million building in North London.[41]

Community Churches: Conference Events and Civic Engagement

Studies of reverse mission sometimes measure success in terms of winning converts or adherents from indigenous communities and have consequently found migrant churches wanting.[42] Yet Nigerian Pentecostals in Britain often understand their mission in broader terms to include any activity that will change society for the better. This has driven some to embark on programmes of territorial expansion, not only through evangelism and planting churches but also by engaging in civic activity.[43] Pippa Norris and Ronald Inglehart have noted the relationship between religious participation and civic engagement. They link this to theories of social capital which suggest that regular church-going encourages belonging to faith-based organizations and joining community groups in civic society.[44]

In the case of the RCCG the turn to civic engagement has partly been a response to the difficulties it has encountered in a so-called post-Christian context like Britain, where people are increasingly unreceptive to traditional evangelistic techniques and reluctant to attend church. It is also a response to the Charitable Commission's public benefit test which requires religious institutions to engage in social action if they are to receive the tax benefits of charitable status. From the perspective of the members themselves civic action is an expression of the church's commitment to the biblical mandate to love one's neighbour by addressing the spiritual, physical and social needs of wider society. Thus Agu Irukwu, senior

---

[41] Pastor Thomas, interview, 25 April 2009; A. Adedoyin, 'RCCG acquires Fountain frontage on the A13 corridor approach,' *Festival News* (November 2008), p. 30.

[42] P. Freston, 'Reverse Mission: A Discourse in Search of Reality?,' *PentecoStudies*, 9.2 (2011), pp. 153–74; C. Währisch-Oblau, *Missionary*; J. Hanciles, *Christendom*; A. Ukah, 'Reverse Mission'.

[43] For the importance of civic engagement for African-led churches in Britain, see also Chapter 9, A. Duffuor, Moving Up and Moving Out.

[44] P. Norris and R. Inglehart, *Sacred and Secular: Religion and Politics Worldwide* (Cambridge/New York: Cambridge University Press, 2004), p. 22.

pastor of Jesus House, refers to the church's duty 'to show the love of God in a practical way' through prayer, charitable giving and participation in social welfare programmes.[45]

The focus on civic engagement is reflected in the RCCG's annual 'Christians in the Marketplace' conference in London. Workshops at the April 2008 conference included 'How to run your business from a Christian perspective,' 'Faith and Social Enterprise', 'Building Social Capital through community projects' and 'The role of Christians in politics'. A much larger event is the Festival of Life (FOL), which has helped to raise the RCCG's profile in the national public sphere. Held biannually in London's Excel Centre, the FOL attracts over 25,000, mainly African, participants during one night of praise, prayer and preaching. It also provides a platform for a variety of public figures, including prominent church leaders, Christian politicians and senior members of the Metropolitan Police Service, as well as space for different civic organizations to publicize their activities.

There are two main strands to the RCCG's social ethics. The first focuses on the provision of social services at the level of neighbourhoods. Some RCCG programmes fall within the category of relief and individual charity – for example, Royal Connections' 'Feed the Homeless' project and Croydon Tabernacle's 'Heart of Compassion,' both geared towards helping the poor in London. Other RCCG programmes fall within the category of development-oriented ministries. One example is the Novo Centre, a drop-in centre in north London set up to help combat the causes of youth-related offences by mentoring young people and providing an alternative social context for them in which to express themselves. For some RCCG congregations, engaging in social ministry has helped to overcome ethnic barriers, enabling them to make meaningful connections with local communities.

The second main strand of thought regarding social engagement focuses on changing society for the better by enabling lay members to become leaders in the arenas of politics, media, business and education. One congregation that has embraced this model is Trinity Chapel, whose social vision is reflected in its church motto: 'Developing Leaders. Influencing Society.' It implements this through an ancillary organization called 'Transformation Initiatives', which runs a number of projects and programmes ranging from feeding projects, drug rehabilitation programmes, youth mentoring programmes, sexual purity in teenagers and dance classes. Like other Pentecostal churches, the RCCG considers prayer an important means of political engagement and social transformation. This is reflected in the regular periods of prayer and fasting followed by all its branches in Britain and in its participation in the Global Day of Prayer, London, led by the Nigerian pastor Jonathan Oloyede. While the bulk of African Pentecostal prayer focuses on personal needs such as healing, deliverance, fertility and finances, some RCCG congregations organize programmes specifically to address national issues.

---

[45]   A. Irukwu, 'In the Crucible with Pastor Agu. Our Corporate Social Responsibility,' *Outflow* (October 2008), p. 5.

Charismatic Leadership and Cultural Orientation

There is considerable diversity in terms of congregational size, church-planting capacity and civic activity among RCCG congregations in Britain. In order to explain these differences, two further factors need to be taken into account. The first is church leadership. Several studies of Pentecostalism have found a positive correlation between charismatic leadership and church growth.[46] One of the reasons for the RCCG's popularity in Britain is the charismatic style and gifting of its leaders. This is exemplified in the life of Enoch Adeboye, the current General Overseer. In Weberian terms the process of institutionalization is normally associated with a decline in charismatic authority, which is then replaced by either legal-rational or traditional authority. However, as Ukah shows, the institutionalization of authority following Adeboye's succession resulted in the 'recharismatization' of the movement and the transformation of RCCG from a locally embedded, predominantly Yoruba church to a global, transnational phenomenon.[47] Adeboye is known nationally and globally for his personal integrity, charismatic gifts of healing and prophecy and teaching ability. One of the most respected church leaders in Nigeria, he travels the world, hosting conferences in the USA and Europe, ordaining pastors, and visiting parishes. He also rubs shoulders with politicians and presidents. This is important in a context where the status and prosperity of family and community heads is considered to reflect positively or negatively on the members. In January 2009, the magazine *Newsweek* listed Adeboye as one of the 50 Global Elites.

To some extent, Adeboye's charismatic style and gifting is replicated in the ministries of some of the more successful RCCG pastors in Britain. This is partly explained, from a participant point of view, by the transfer of charismatic authority through the ritual of ordination which is usually conducted by Adeboye himself. It is generally the case that larger parishes are led by men or women who possess charismatic healing and prophetic gifts, motivational skills, and evangelistic and preaching abilities. One example is Tony Rapu, former pastor of one of the largest RCCG congregations in Lagos, Nigeria. In 1994, Rapu planted Jesus House in Central London. The combination of charismatic and innovative leadership and the church's location, contemporary worship style and emphasis on 'excellence' contributed to its rapid growth so that, within a year of its inception, Jesus House was attracting around 400 people to its services.[48] Another example is Leke Sanusi, who started Victory House in 1997. Within 10 years, membership had grown to around 700 and Victory House had planted 10 new branches, including two in the USA. In 2007, it opened its new 1,000-seater auditorium, which it purchased for

---

[46]   W. Kay, *Pentecostals in Britain* (Carlisle: Paternoster, 2000); M. Poloma, *Assemblies of God at the Crossroads* (Knoxville, TN: University of Tennessee Press, 1989).

[47]   A. Ukah, *A New Paradigm of Pentecostal Power: A Study of the Redeemed Christian Church of God in Nigeria* (Trenton NJ: Africa World Press, 2008), pp. 83–4.

[48]   Pastor Agu Irukwu, interview, 30 October 2007.

£4.75 million. Sanusi's healing gifts are evident from the many testimonies that appear in the church's in-house magazine, *Prayer Works*. He is also noted for his preaching and teaching ability and is in much demand as a conference speaker.

In organizational studies a distinction is made between transactional and transformational or charismatic styles of leadership. Whereas transactional leaders cater for their followers' immediate self-interests by offering material incentives, transformational leaders cause their followers to become committed to the leader's mission and to make personal sacrifices on behalf of others.[49] RCCG pastors who have embraced the transformational model of leadership have tended to be more successful in terms of church growth and social influence. One example is Sola Fola-Alade, senior pastor of Trinity Chapel. In a recent magazine article he describes transformational leaders as 'change agents who are redefining the landscape, changing mindsets, and reforming communities, cities, nations and various decaying institutions such as the family, politics, business, media and education.'[50] Fola-Alade's social vision has been influenced by the popular Argentine Pentecostal, Ed Silvoso, Director of Harvest Evangelism and the International Transformation Network, who has held conferences at Trinity Chapel on 'marketplace transformation' and 'transformational leadership.'

Cultural orientation is a second important variable influencing church growth and social influence. Another reason for the RCCG's popularity has been its ability to reinvent itself in response to modernizing trends. Enoch Adeboye has been largely responsible for this 'religious rebranding' through his implementation of a series of innovative initiatives. The most significant transformation was a shift in the demographic composition of the RCCG as members of the educated elite were attracted to its ranks. This was a response to the prevailing Nigerian Pentecostal milieu, which was dominated by university graduates and students. Prior to this, RCCG culture was characterized by anti-materialistic lifestyles, strict dress codes and solemn worship services, mostly conducted in Yoruba. The most important initiative introduced by Adeboye was the model parish system which became a major source of growth as young professionals and members of the upper middle class entered the ranks of the church. In contrast to the 'classical' parishes, which had been the format established since the inauguration of the church, these parishes embraced modern technology, discarded dress code restrictions and used only English in services. They were usually headed by young professionals which commended them to the upper middle class strata of Nigerian society. More recently, some model parishes have emphasized prosperity teaching

---

[49]   B. Bass, 'Two Decades of Research and Development in Transformational Leadership,' *European Journal of Work and Organizational Psychology*, 8.1 (1999), pp. 9–32; B. Shamir, R. House, M. Arthur, 'The Motivational Effects of Charismatic Leadership: A Self-Concept Based Theory', *Organization Science*, 4.4 (November 1993), pp. 577–94.

[50]   S. Fola-Alade, 'Are you a Transformational leader?', *Leadership & Lifestyle Magazine* (Summer 2008), p. 5.

rather than the holiness message found in the classical parishes.[51] Many British-based RCCG pastors are products of the model parish system in Nigeria. Included within their ranks are lawyers, medical doctors, university lecturers, accountants and investment bankers. As well as supplying potential missionaries for Western contexts, the model parish system has proved attractive to Africans in Britain, where it has become the dominant pattern for RCCG congregational life.

There remains considerable variation however in terms of cultural orientation within RCCG UK, which affects the growth of individual congregations and their ability to engage in civic activity. Those whose main focus is the African diaspora have made limited headway in terms of church growth and social engagement. Others such as Jesus House and Trinity Chapel, which are cosmopolitan in character and more oriented towards British culture, have fared better. Despite their multicultural aspirations, RCCG membership remains predominantly Nigerian. In the survey, 97% of respondents were Nigerian (77% Yoruba) and 2% from other African or Caribbean countries. Jesus House's cultural sensitivity has resulted in a higher number of non-Nigerian members, including those from Kenya, Zambia, the Congo, Ghana, Jamaica and Brazil, as well as a small number of indigenous British. However, in general it seems that the flexibility of the RCCG's Pentecostal spirituality is insufficient to break down the cultural barrier between African and indigenous British society. While parishes provide culturally relevant expressions of Christianity for African migrants and regard themselves as multicultural congregations, they are generally failing to adapt their message, strategies and styles to cater for a Western audience. Afe Adogame identifies a 'lack of cross-cultural appeal' and the tendency of African migrants to interact mainly with fellow Africans as the main barriers towards the realization of a multi-racial group.[52] Nigeria's global reputation for corruption and criminal activity and the perception of African churches by white Europeans as institutions obsessed with money and the activities of evil spirits are also barriers to the formation of cosmopolitan congregations. However, the reluctance of white indigenous British to join African-led churches compared to the willingness of Africans to join white-led ones suggests that the remnants of a colonial disposition persist within the fabric of British society.

Conclusion

African initiated Pentecostal churches in Britain are becoming increasingly visible in public space as they acquire their own buildings, plant new branches, organize conferences, initiate social welfare programmes and make use of the media. Some, it is true, have come and gone but others, such as the RCCG, have continued

---

[51]   A. Ukah, 'Mobilities', pp. 323–4.

[52]   A. Adogame, 'African Communities in Diaspora', in O. Kalu (ed.), *African Christianity: An African Story* (Pretoria: University of Pretoria, 2005), p. 508.

to grow at a time when British church attendance is generally in decline. From the 1960s poor governance and economic decline at home, combined with a relatively liberal immigration policy, resulted in a large African Christian migrant community. Encountering racism in the workplace and discrimination and cultural differences in existing British churches, they soon formed churches of their own. Subsequently, denominations in Africa began to set up branches in Britain to cater for the social and spiritual needs of their members in the diaspora. They have been joined by African entrepreneurs who have left their secular employment to become independent church planters. While these churches have continued to provide social and religious capital for migrant communities, their growth has been stimulated by a conscious missionary agenda. This is especially the case with the RCCG, whose aggressive church-planting strategy has been sustained by its ability to generate considerable financial and human resources. As I have shown, for some RCCG congregations, this missionary agenda has also included a strong emphasis on civic engagement, aimed at changing society for the better.

The RCCG's predominantly youthful membership holds out promise for the future in terms of maintaining levels of participation among second and third generation migrants. However, the church is facing a critical moment in its history, similar to the one faced by the Caribbean churches in the 1980s and early 1990s when they lost a whole generation of young people who either migrated to white majority churches, left to start new churches, or abandoned the church altogether.[53] The moral relativism and anti-authoritarian ethic of late modern British society presents serious challenges to young African Christians whose identity is traditionally shaped by communal ties and constrained by social pressures to conform.[54] There are also the tensions caused by encounter with the secular worldview prevalent in institutions of higher learning, the media and among peers. Second-generation African Christians who have grown up in such a climate are unlikely to remain unaffected by this 'cosmological secularization'[55] and the tendency to treat religion as just another compartment of life. Much will depend upon the church's response to this new phase in its history. The RCCG will also need to respond to proposed changes in the UK's immigration policy. While many pastors and members are now British citizens who intend to remain in their adopted country, increased immigration restrictions make it important that the church find ways of attracting indigenous British clientele and nurturing indigenous leaders if it is to sustain its current growth rates and fulfil its multicultural ambitions. To do so, individual congregations may need to be open to learn from those they encounter, not least the existing British churches. Interestingly, some congregations and pastors are beginning to move in this direction by adopting a more self-critical and ecumenical approach to mission. For example, in an article

---

[53] M. Sturge, *Look What the Lord has Done! An Exploration of Black Christian Faith in Britain* (London: Scripture Union, 2005), p. 220.

[54] H. Harris, *Yoruba in Diaspora*, p. 229.

[55] H. Harris, *Yoruba in Diaspora*, p. 238.

entitled 'Get me out of here! I'm White,' RCCG pastor Yemi Adedeji encourages his fellow Africans to be sensitive to British culture in their presentation of the gospel, not to appear arrogant but to present themselves as learners, not teachers.[56] A significant development is the close relationship between Jesus House and Holy Trinity Brompton, one of the largest Anglican churches in London. The RCCG has also established a mission partnership with the Anglican Church Mission Society (CMS), signalling the beginnings, perhaps, of a 'common mission' involving both African and indigenous British churches.

---

[56] Y. Adedeji, 'Get me out of here! I'm White', *Festival News* (March 2008), pp. 14–5.

Chapter 9

Moving Up and Moving Out?: The Expansion of a London-based 'African Pentecostal' Church

Amy Duffuor

This chapter is the result of my examination of the role of locality, spirituality and identity in the civic engagement of an 'African Pentecostal'[1] church in Peckham, London.[2] The case study was Freedom Centre International (FCI or FCI-Peckham), a multi-ethnic church with a predominantly African migrant congregation. The ethnographic fieldwork was conducted mainly within the church from July 2010 to September 2010 and culminated in 50 semi-structured interviews and extensive participant observation. In order to protect the confidentiality of informants I have anonymized all names in this chapter. Essentially, this chapter reflects a grassroots study of how the Pentecostal project affects the understandings and manifestations of civic engagement[3] among African migrants in London.

Pentecostalism is a global, international and transnational religion that emphasizes the 'experience' of the worshipper; Pentecostals generally believe in the following: faith healing, miracles, being 'touched' by the Holy Spirit and oral liturgy.[4] One of the most important tenets of many Pentecostal churches is the prosperity gospel, which puts forth that the spiritual and material fortunes of

---

[1] Most congregants in this case study did not conceive of their church as being defined by ethnic boundaries. Therefore, all mentions of 'African Pentecostal' or 'Black Pentecostal' churches were put in quotation marks in order to underscore and implicitly critique the academic and evaluative discourse that dominated this area of study.

[2] A. Duffuor, 'Fusing faith and place: The role of locality, spirituality and identity in the civic engagement of an "African Pentecostal" church in London' (MPhil: University of Oxford, 2011).

[3] I utilize Ehrlich's definition of civic engagement, which stresses both political and non-political processes. For a complete definition, see T. Ehrlich (ed.), *Civic Responsibility and Higher Education* (Westport: The American Council on Education/The Oryx Press, 2000), pp. vi.

[4] J. Robbins, 'The Globalization of Pentecostal and Charismatic Christianity', *Annual Review of Anthropology*, 33 (October 2004), pp. 117–3; R. Marshall, 'Power in the Name of Jesus', *Review of African Political Economy*, 52 (November 1991), pp. 21–37; S. Coleman, 'Textuality and Embodiment among Charismatic Christians' in E. Arweck and P. Collins (eds), *Reading Religion in Text and Context: An Introduction* (Aldershot: Ashgate, 2006),

a worshipper are dependent on how much they 'give' to God, who will reward them by 'prospering' them.[5] One way to 'give' to God is through the church and Pentecostals are often expected to give money and time to the institution. Pentecostalism also lacks an explicit overarching theology and consequently the movement has broad appeal.[6] For example, there are an estimated 500 million Pentecostal and Charismatic Christians worldwide[7] and, according to the Directory of Black Majority Churches UK,[8] there are 500,000 Black Christians in the United Kingdom, a large number of whom are Pentecostals, with the overwhelming majority in London. As a result, it has been suggested that the global Pentecostal movement plays a significant role in the ways in which its worshippers understand and engage with the world.[9] This is especially salient for Britain, as Black-led churches have been recognized as important welfare providers for local populations.[10] And, given the country's recent public sector cuts, it is particularly

---

pp. 157–68; G. Ter Haar, *Halfway to Paradise: African Christians in Europe* (Cardiff: Academic Press, 1998).

[5] R. Marshall, 'Power in the Name of Jesus', *Review of African Political Economy*, 52 (November 1991), p. 22.

[6] A. Adogame, 'Pentecostal and Charismatic Movements in a Global Perspective' in B. Turner (ed.), *The New Blackwell Companion to the Sociology of Religion* (Oxford: Blackwell Publishing, 2010), pp. 498–518; N. Toulis, *Believing Identity: Pentecostalism and the Mediation of Jamaican Ethnicity and Gender in England* (Oxford: Berg, 1997); J. Robbins, 'The Globalization of Pentecostal and Charismatic Christianity', *Annual Review of Anthropology* 33 (October 2004), pp. 117–43; R. Marshall, 'Power in the Name of Jesus', *Review of African Political Economy*, 52 (November 1991), pp. 21–37; P. Gifford, *African Christianity: Its Public Role* (London: Hurst & Co, 1998).

[7] A. Adogame, 'Pentecostal and Charismatic Movements in a Global Perspective' in B. Turner (ed.), *The New Blackwell Companion to the Sociology of Religion* (Oxford: Blackwell Publishing, 2010), p. 498.

[8] http://www.bmcdirectory.co.uk, accessed 21 April 2011.

[9] S. Coleman, *The Globalization of Charismatic Christianity* (Cambridge: Cambridge University Press, 2000); R. Marshall, 'God is not a democrat: Pentecostalism and Democratisation in Nigeria' in P. Gifford (ed.), *The Christian Churches and the Democratisation of Africa* (Leiden: Brill Publishers, 1995), pp. 239–60; A. Adogame, 'From House Cells to Warehouse Churches: Place-making Processes in a Transnational African Church' in G. Hüwelmeier and K. Krause (eds), *Traveling Spirits: Migrants, Markets, and Mobilities* (London: Routledge, 2010), pp. 165–84; N. Glick Schiller and A. Çağlar, 'Introduction: Migrants and Cities' in N. Glick Schiller and A. Çağlar (eds), *Locating Migration: Rescaling Cities and Migrants* (Ithaca: Cornell University, 2011), pp. 1–22; R. van Dijk, 'Cities and the Social Construction of Hot Spots: Rescaling, Ghanaian migrants and the Fragmentation of Urban Spaces' in N. Glick Schiller and A. Çağlar (eds), *Locating Migration: Rescaling Cities and Migrants* (Ithaca: Cornell University, 2011), pp. 104–22; O. Kalu, *African Pentecostalism: An Introduction* (Oxford: Oxford University Press, 2008).

[10] N. Toulis, *Believing Identity: Pentecostalism and the Mediation of Jamaican Ethnicity and Gender in England* (Oxford: Berg, 1997); G. Ter Haar, *Halfway to Paradise: African Christians in Europe* (Cardiff: Academic Press, 1998).

relevant to understand the ways in which British-based 'African Pentecostal' churches engage with their local communities.

FCI-Peckham serves as a fascinating case study in this regard as it is a self-proclaimed 'community-based' church. FCI-Peckham is a church within the Universal Prayer Group Ministries (UPG), a Christian organization and registered charity that was founded by Revd Dr. S.K. Boafo in 1985.[11] The first UPG church opened in North London in 1988 and eventually expanded to South London in 1998. The church ultimately settled in Peckham, a neighbourhood in the borough of Southwark, which is home to a large black community. Black Africans constitute the largest ethnic group at 34% of the population[12] and Peckham is a multicultural melting pot. However, the area experiences a high level of income and employment deprivation and, interestingly, its public perception as a place of high crime, gang activity and dilapidated council housing is precisely what attracted FCI-Peckham to the area.

At FCI-Peckham both head pastors, Nelson and Elizabeth, are Ghanaians. The church has a primarily Ghanaian congregation (around 60%), but also includes congregants from other African countries, the Caribbean and the Czech Republic. In spite of the overwhelmingly African migrant background of the congregation, congregation members assert that their primary identity is not one of race, class, gender, or ethnicity, but is as 'children of God,' 'Christians,' or 'followers of Christ.' I label the congregation's assertion of their Christian identity as 'Christian cosmopolitanism', as other scholars have called it.[13] It is however important to note that congregants' Christian cosmopolitan identity is shifting and contextual and this fluidity produces tensions within FCI-Peckham's Christian cosmopolitan project. This Christian cosmopolitan project informs congregants' conceptualization

---

[11] For a comprehensive history of Freedom Centre International, see Chapter 7, H. Osgood, Rise of Black Churches.

[12] Southwark Analytical Hub, *Peckham Community Council's Population: Now and the Future* (London: Southwark Analytical Hub – Southwark Council and PCT Data Sharing Partnership, 2008), http://www.southwark.gov.uk/downloads/download/308/population_and_migration, accessed 20 July 2010.

[13] A. Adogame, 'Globalization and African New Religious Movements in Europe' in O. Kalu (ed.), *Interpreting Contemporary Christianity: Global Processes and Local Identities* (Grand Rapids: Eerdmans Publishing, 2008), pp. 296–318; N. Glick Schiller, A. Çağlar and T. Guldbrandsen, 'Beyond the Ethnic Lens: Locality, Globality and Born-Again Incorporation', *American Ethnologist*, 33.4 (November 2006), pp. 612–33; N. Glick Schiller and A. Çağlar, 'Introduction: Migrants and Cities' in N. Glick Schiller and A. Çağlar (eds), *Locating Migration: Rescaling Cities and Migrants* (Ithaca: Cornell University, 2011), pp. 1–22; P. Kalilombe, 'Black Christianity in Britain', *Ethnic and Racial Studies*, 20.2 (1997), pp. 306–24; K. Krause, 'Cosmopolitan Charismatics? Transnational ways of belonging and cosmopolitan moments in the religious practice of New Mission Churches', *Ethnic and Racial Studies*, 34.3 (2011), pp. 419–35; J. Robbins, 'The Globalization of Pentecostal and Charismatic Christianity', *Annual Review of Anthropology*, 33 (October 2004), pp. 117–43.

and actualization of civic engagement and is particularly evident in the church's current expansion from Peckham, London to Welling, Greater London.

In this chapter, I explore the cosmopolitan and class narratives embedded in FCI-Peckham's expansion to Welling, a London suburb, which is a 40 minute train commute from Peckham. I argue that 'the Welling project' is a distinct practice of FCI-Peckham's paradigm of civic engagement, one that is informed by locality and a cosmopolitan, Pentecostal agenda. Ultimately, I question whether the church's expansion to Welling signifies that it is 'moving up and moving out' of Peckham and what this means for FCI-Peckham's role as a continuing welfare provider for Peckham's low-income black community.

The 'Shifting' Process of Expansion

FCI-Peckham's expansion to Welling is perceived to be an important act of civic engagement, as it allows the church to fulfil its global mission by making the love of God known to a new community. FCI-Welling opened its doors on 6 February 2011 and FCI-Peckham members have elatedly exclaimed that 'the church is a blessing from God' and 'an example of God taking FCI to the next level!' Daniel, a 30 year-old Ghanaian migrant who is a worship leader at both FCI-Peckham and FCI-Welling, has happily stated, 'the whole set-up in Welling is God's promotion ... I'm glad because it's the vision of the church and it's come to pass. I'm glad because I am a part of what God is doing.' Daniel's words highlight that FCI-Peckham is fulfilling spiritual aspirations by expanding to Welling and that congregation members play a significant part in achieving this goal. Similarly Elizabeth, the British-Ghanaian co-pastor of FCI who also runs the women's ministry, explains 'for us, Welling is very exciting. It's just like we've been re-born.' Elizabeth's use of 'rebirth' underscores biblical scriptures and the way in which FCI-Welling represents a positive and welcome change to the ministry. Both Elizabeth and Daniel underscore the potential of FCI-Welling regarding civic engagement in both spiritual and physical ways.

FCI-Welling's latent use of this-worldly and otherworldly plans of civic engagement is also evident in a flyer for the opening, which describes the event as 'The Grand Opening of FCI Welling Church and Community Facility.' It is noteworthy that the flyer accentuates both 'church' and 'community facility', and FCI-Welling clearly presents itself as a religious and public space for the surrounding community. Additionally Val Clark, the Mayor of Bexley, and Professor Kwaku Danso-Boafo, Ghana's High Commissioner to the United Kingdom, attended the commencement of the church. The presence of these two politicians signifies the simultaneously local and transnational dimension of the church opening, particularly the way in which FCI-Peckham's Christian cosmopolitan identity is still rooted in a sense of 'home,' which is Ghana for the largely Ghanaian congregation.[14]

The edifice of FCI-Welling is located in a large, refurbished bingo hall that seats 1,000 people. The front of the building spells Freedom Centre International in big blue letters, along with the official website and Pastor Nelson's title. The interior is equally impressive with a bi-level stage displaying the words 'free to prosper,' plush stadium seating and designated rooms for church ministries. The impressive edifice of FCI-Welling is a clear statement of identity politics and presence as the church demonstrates its 'prosperity', 'arrival,' and 'next level status' through the building's aesthetics.

One reason for the expansion of FCI-Peckham to Welling is the growing size of the congregation. FCI-Peckham comfortably seats around 500 people, but often has 600-700 attendees. However, Matthew, the Ghanaian project manager of FCI, who has been attending since the late 90s, explains that Peckham has always been a temporary church:

> Right from the time we moved into Peckham we realized it was a place in transition. The facilities were not conducive to the things we wanted to do. Also, the sort of work that we wanted to do we knew this wasn't the right place. So as soon we moved into Peckham eleven years ago we started talking about the need to move into a bigger place, a purpose built facility that will be able to accommodate what we need to do.

I would like to draw attention to the word *transition* within Matthew's quote. FCI-Peckham conceives of itself as a church in transition – shifting narratives are not only embedded in the physical expansion to Welling but also in the paradigm and discourse of civic engagement. In particular, FCI-Peckham propagates a discourse that includes 'faith', 'community' and 'impact', and consciously interpolates different narratives and identities within that dialogue. Scholars such as Rhodes and Brown posit that narratives are the style and substance of life through which identities, moral orders and relational patterns are constructed[15] and FCI-Peckham constructs particular narratives for the congregation which inform their paradigm and practice of civic engagement. Therefore, it is important to examine FCI's 'shifting narratives,' such as its expansion to Welling, and the way in which they reinforce or alter the paradigm of civic engagement for the congregation.

One 'shifting narrative' that reinforces FCI's cosmopolitan, Pentecostal agenda is the expansion process from Peckham to Welling. It is noteworthy that Pastor Nelson and the church leadership in actuality decided to expand to

---

[14]   For a good overview of 'rooted cosmopolitanism,' see K. Appiah, 'Cosmopolitan Patriots' in P. Cheah and B. Robbins (eds), *Cosmopolitics: Thinking and Feeling Beyond the Nation* (Minneapolis: University of Minnesota Press, 1998), pp. 91–116.

[15]   C. Rhodes and A. Brown, 'Narrative, Organizations and Research', *International Journal of Management Reviews*, 7.3 (December 2005), pp. 169–70.

another location. In 2009, the church tried to acquire two different properties in Camberwell, the ward neighbouring Peckham, which has a similar ethnic and class demographic. Both times these acquisitions were unsuccessful and, as a result, church leadership shifted its attention to Welling. Welling appears to be an unlikely choice for expansion as it contains a predominantly white demographic in the Greater London Area. However Pastor Nelson, the head pastor of FCI, justifies his choice to the congregation with a prophecy which reveals an FCI church with white and black people worshipping the same God. Pastor Kwabena, the younger brother of Elizabeth, who leads the music and youth ministry, explains 'there is a prophecy in this church, that this church is a multicultural church. So if it is multicultural, then whites, blacks, Asians, indigos whatever culture will come into this house.'

Pastor Kwabena's use of the word 'indigos' ruptures the idea of ethnic boundaries, and his use of the word 'multicultural' reverts to the church's Christian cosmopolitan identity. Pastor Kwabena's rhetoric not only illustrates the entrenchment of a cosmopolitan agenda within FCI's paradigm of civic engagement but also demonstrates that the demographics of Welling are ideal for its cosmopolitan project. Janice, a Ghanaian member of FCI-Peckham who came to the UK in 1993, also underscores Welling's suitability for a cosmopolitan agenda:

> If he's [God] taking us to Welling it's because they need a church like FCI. And I think it's all connected to where he already said he's taking us. If you are bringing freedom to people, it doesn't have to be a particular set of people. Freedom is for everyone. Maybe it's time for FCI to become a multiracial church.

Both Janice and Pastor Kwabena highlight that Welling represents a particular market for cultural and political capital as the area has fewer African-Independent Churches (AICs) than Peckham. In this way, FCI operates as a rational economic actor that tries to maximize utility by capitalizing on emerging markets. However, FCI-Welling is an enormously expensive project that cost over £2,000,000, and Kweku, a 41 year-old Ghanaian migrant who is part of the finance team, talks about the crucial contribution of FCI-Peckham congregants. He states 'even though we took a mortgage on FCI-Welling, we [the congregation] raised over half a million pounds for the project.' Kweku goes on to describe that the money mostly came from tithes and special projects such as engraved plaques or chairs. Basically, these plaques and chairs represented the congregation's 'spatial inscription' in Welling. It is also noteworthy that FCI owns not only the physical building of FCI-Welling but also two adjacent properties that it rents to Welling residents. Although it is difficult explicitly to map out FCI's financial situation, due to the sensitive nature of the subject, it is clear that the church has a large annual revenue.

Initially, FCI leadership had planned to close FCI-Peckham after it had acquired the Welling property. However members had expressed concern over the closing of the Peckham branch and had argued that Welling was too far and inconvenient for the elderly and families without cars. Consequently Pastor Nelson, the head pastor of FCI, has decided to keep FCI-Peckham open and has appointed his brother-in-law, Pastor Kwabena, as the resident pastor of FCI-Peckham. To accommodate the potential rift in the congregation Pastor Nelson has designated members of the pastoral ministry and heads of department to be posted at either Peckham or Welling. Essentially, FCI-Peckham has become one church in two locations.

Pastor Yaw, the head of FCI-Peckham's outreach ministry, assures me that FCI's involvement with Peckham will not change as a result of the expansion. He explains 'the community will not see that we move because we are still involved in the meetings and everything in Peckham ... We will still show the reason that God brought us to Peckham.' Pastor Yaw's words underscore a post-factum shift in the rhetoric of civic engagement as he acknowledges that FCI has made an impact in Peckham, but is careful to highlight that the church will continue to make an impact. Thus, Pastor Yaw demonstrates that 'God's work is never done' and his words draw attention to the 'shifting narrative' within FCI-Peckham, particularly a discourse of civic engagement that is both continuous and evolving. Similarly, Pastor Kwabena elucidates:

> We aren't going to give up Peckham because it's a prime area. There are a lot
> of souls on the street you can reach out to. So, we are going to use Peckham to
> set up a branch and we are looking at doing three or four services in Peckham in
> different languages like Twi,[16] Yoruba[17] and French.

It is important to note Pastor Kwabena's desire to conduct Peckham services in languages commonly found in Africa, which demonstrates that FCI-Peckham will 'shift' and cater to the local African community. I suspect that these 'ethnic' services at FCI-Peckham will be used to expand further the base amongst Peckham's Africans and to re-create the congregation post the Welling exodus. Therefore, while FCI leadership aspires to retain FCI-Peckham's 'ethnic' identity, in contrast they aspire for FCI-Welling to be a post-racial, ethnically-mixed church.

The next section explores the reasons behind FCI's desire to engage with the Welling community and how these reasons fit into a localized, cosmopolitan, and Pentecostal paradigm of civic engagement.

Welling: A Distinct Place

Welling is a district in the London Borough of Bexley which is located in South East London. Welling[18] is a commuter town, of which 93.8% of the population

---

[16]   Twi is a Ghanaian dialect.

[17]   Yoruba is a Nigerian language.

[18]   Official statistics for the district comprise both Falconwood and Welling, but nevertheless will be used to provide a demographic overview of the area.

is white.[19] In addition to being an overwhelmingly white area, it is also overwhelmingly English with 91.4% of the population born in England; moreover, 53% of the population is married and 74% of residents religiously identify as Christian.[20] Lastly, Welling is also economically stable with a total unemployment rate of 2.1%.[21] As the statistics show, Welling is a predominantly white English, Christian, family-oriented and middle-class area. However, its demographics *and* history of race relations make it a desirable place for FCI-Peckham to expand.

In 1989 Welling became the national headquarters for the British National Party (BNP), a radical-right political party perceived to be a racist, fascist, and homophobic organization. According to the Youth Against Racism in Europe organization,[22] the presence of the party in Welling sparked a rise in racist attacks and three young black and minority ethnic men (Rolan Adams, Stephen Lawrence and Rohit Duggal) were murdered in the area between February 1991 and April 1993. Consequently, Welling became the site of numerous protests against the BNP regarding their use of violence and racist campaign platforms.[23] In 1995 Welling Council shut down the BNP headquarters but the group has continued to have a presence in the area. For instance, Pastor Nelson has encountered resistance from BNP members during FCI's acquisition of the Welling property. This prompted Pastor Nelson to see another utility of FCI's presence in Welling – integration and 'community cohesion'. He postulates, 'we have discovered that FCI can be effective regarding social cohesiveness in Welling. This area has very strong BNP members who give us a lot of opposition. However, they are beginning to realize that we are not bringing any trouble for them and we want to engage with them.'

The desire of FCI to attract Welling locals, who are predominantly white and have a history of distrust of minorities, underscores FCI's 'reverse mission' and its objective of portraying a visibly international church. One strand of the reverse mission discourse posits that African pastors want to attract European 'natives' to their churches in order to save and convert them.[24] Europeans are perceived to need saving as a result of their penchant for homosexuality, drug use, pre-marital sex, etc. Although the term is problematic due to its normative assumptions

---

[19] Office for National Statistics, 'Neighbourhood Statistics Area: Falconwood and Welling (Ward)', Crown Copyright 2001, http://www.neighbourhood.statistics.gov.uk/dissemination/LeadDatasetList.do?a=7&b=6173582&c=Falconwood+and+Welling&d=14&g=327257&i=1001x1003&m=0&r=1&s=1304727907328&enc=1&domainId=16, accessed 18 February 2011.

[20] Ibid.

[21] Ibid.

[22] http://www.yre.org.uk/towerhamlets.html, accessed 8 March 2011.

[23] D. Renton, 'Memories from Welling', (2005), http://www.dkrenton.co.uk/welling.html, accessed 8 March 2011.

[24] D. Koning, 'Place, Space and Authority: The Mission and Reversed Mission of the Ghanaian Seventh-day Adventist Church in Amsterdam', *African Diaspora*, 2.2 (2009), pp. 203–26.

of a standard path of mission that can be reversed,[25] the idea does put forth a commentary of the FCI-Peckham case study.[26] For example, Pastor Elijah, a middle-aged Ghanaian migrant in charge of setting up FCI's East London branch, asserts his eagerness for reaching out to Welling 'natives':

> I am excited about the Welling project because we are fulfilling the calling of the ministry. The main calling is to expand and affect different communities … The people in Welling are going to be affected by the gospel of Christ … It's about going to Welling and really affecting the natives. For the natives, we are making every effort to reach out to them and see how best integration can work out.

Pastor Elijah's rhetoric of reverse mission and integration signifies the appropriation of a new position for African Christians, who are usually situated at the receiving end of the global power geometry.[27] FCI's re-negotiation of the global power dynamic aligns with the global and transnational nature of Pentecostalism, which also seeks to reposition itself within greater Christendom. However, Koning explains how difficult it is for 'African Pentecostal' churches to overcome ethnic boundaries in attracting new converts.[28] Therefore it is not the expansion of FCI that is unique, but the locality that FCI chose to expand to and, revisiting Koning's point, how the church will grapple with these 'ethnic obstacles.'

In spite of this, FCI is no stranger to addressing issues in the local community and there are important parallels between the church's choice of Peckham and Welling as distinct localities that warrant FCI's attention. The parallels comprise Peckham's reputation as an area that is home to violent crime, anti-social behaviour and gangs and Welling's reputation as an area that is home to violent crime, racial tensions and the BNP. The main difference between the two is Welling's overwhelmingly white demographic and higher-class status. In many ways the narrative of Welling seeks to represent traditional British culture while, coincidentally, FCI seeks religiously to re-appropriate British culture. Given this, Pastor Nelson's choice of Welling's 'Old Mecca' bingo hall, as the future site of FCI-Welling, is particularly telling. In essence, FCI's move to a bingo hall signifies a symbolic and spatial reclamation of a secular site of mainstream working-class British culture.

---

[25] Ibid., p. 203.

[26] For an excellent commentary on reverse mission among mainline churches, see also Chapter 6, R. Catto, Reverse Mission.

[27] K. Krause, 'Cosmopolitan Charismatics? Transnational Ways of Belonging and Cosmopolitan Moments in the Religious Practice of New Mission Churches', *Ethnic and Racial Studies*, 34.3 (2011), p. 423.

[28] D. Koning, 'Place, Space and Authority: The Mission and Reversed Mission of the Ghanaian Seventh-day Adventist Church in Amsterdam', *African Diaspora*, 2.2 (2009), pp. 203–26.

Bingo halls are a symbol of white British working-class leisure activities and also function as local centres for communities. They provide a 'home away from home,' companionship, an opportunity to celebrate traditional working-class values and a refuge from bleak personal situations.[29] However, many bingo halls have become vacant and their numerous rooms, grand foyers and large seating capacities make them an ideal space to transform into a church. 'African Pentecostal' churches frequently convert these allegedly 'immoral' spaces, which has prompted tensions between religious and community actors. For example, tensions have been mounting in Camberwell, London over the Nigerian-led Redeemed Christian Church of God's (RCCG) purchase of a former bingo hall, in the face of a large petition from the local community.[30] The fight for public space draws attention to secular actors who feel that churches impose their way of life on certain communities and, in particular, fosters local opposition to 'African Pentecostal' churches which not only touches on anti-religious sentiments, but also on anti-ethnic sentiments. In this instance, secularism intersects with a certain notion of working-class British culture in order to protect a specific form of 'history-constructed' nostalgia.

In order to re-appropriate symbols of British nostalgia, FCI's first act of civic engagement in Welling has been the reclamation and reconstitution of the 'Old Mecca' bingo hall. It is noteworthy that the 'Old Mecca' bingo hall was originally a 'mecca' for the working class, a secular site of pilgrimage that is now sought after as a 'mecca' for FCI's religious community. FCI employs onsite and offsite prayers, fasts and all-night vigils in order to facilitate a new 'symbolic geography of the sacred'[31] of the former secular space. FCI is not only committed to transforming the physical and spiritual dimensions of the church site but also to restructuring and rebranding the Welling community. Glick Schiller and Çağlar assert that migrants can become active agents in the transformation of neighbourhoods by offering alternative visions.[32] FCI's vision of Welling however, as an inclusive, multicultural space, appears to be guided not only by the distinct locality and a

---

[29]   R. Dixey, 'Bingo in Britain: An Analysis of Gender and Class' in J. McMillen (ed.) *Gambling Cultures* (London: Routledge, 1996), p. 149.

[30]   J. Prendergast, 'Residents Want Cinema Over Church Plan for Old Bingo Hall', 8 March 2010, http://www.southwarknews.co.uk/00,news,17643,185,00.htm, accessed 8 March 2011.

[31]   For a good overview on symbolic geographies of the sacred, see D. Garbin, 'Symbolic Geographies of the Sacred: Diasporic Territorialisation and Charismatic Power in a Transnational Congolese Prophetic Church' in G. Hüwelmeier and K. Krause (eds), *Traveling Spirits: Migrants, Markets, and Mobilities* (London: Routledge, 2010), pp. 145–64.

[32]   N. Glick Schiller and A. Çağlar, 'Introduction: Migrants and Cities' in N. Glick Schiller and A. Çağlar (eds), *Locating Migration: Rescaling Cities and Migrants* (Ithaca: Cornell University, 2011), pp. 1–22.

cosmopolitan, Pentecostal paradigm of civic engagement but also by underlying racial and class narratives.

Rebranding and Restructuring Welling: a Covert Racial and Class Narrative

It is worth stating that the racial and class narratives described in this section are postulations, since I was only privy to the beginning stages of FCI-Welling. Nonetheless, my focus on four informants' plans for civic engagement in Welling illustrates that FCI's cosmopolitan, Pentecostal paradigm is embedded within narratives of race and class which can be problematic. The four informants I highlight are: Pastor Nelson, the head pastor of FCI; Elizabeth, the co-pastor of FCI and the leader of the women's ministry; Pastor Kwabena, the former youth pastor of FCI-Peckham and newly-appointed resident pastor of FCI-Peckham; and, Irene, the youth leader of FCI-Peckham and FCI-Welling.

First, Pastor Nelson describes the new church as a multi-purpose healing centre. He explains, 'I want FCI-Welling to have a GP, youth community centre and legal centre. I want to make FCI-Welling a one-stop shop!' Pastor Nelson's drive to have a GP and legal centre touch on important cross-narratives regarding health and immigration. Issues of health and documentation are especially salient for FCI-Peckham congregants who utilize prayer as an important act of civic engagement to address these problems. Yet Pastor Nelson capitalizes on FCI's move to Welling to provide new physical solutions in addition to former spiritual solutions. Pastor Nelson's desires convey a sense of dual legitimacy, both in this-worldly and otherworldly realms, which can appeal beyond religion and 'African' boundaries. This shift is important for attracting potential Welling converts who may not understand or accept prayer as a legitimate resolution to material problems. It is evident that FCI operates a conscious evangelistic strategy, which suggests that former FCI-Peckham practices of civic engagement may not be suitable for the Welling demographic.

Similarly to Pastor Nelson, Elizabeth wants to create a women-focused health centre in FCI-Welling. She aspires to utilize the women's ministry to set up this centre which will address sexual health, blood pressure and other women's issues. She adds, 'the Women's Health Group will be for the community. It will start with members of the church and will be a walk-in thing. We will try and get nurses from the Welling community and also open it up to others in the community.' When I ask her why a similar initiative has not been started in Peckham, she replies, 'well, the big aim of the women's ministry at FCI-Peckham is for women to enjoy themselves. Among Africans, we tend to work, work, work and no play, so we've organized boat trips, theatre outings, and barbecues. We also hosted

Juanita Bynum[33] for Women's day last year, which was a big draw for the Peckham community.' It is noteworthy that FCI-Peckham women's activities are framed around leisure and a 'Black Pentecostal' identity, whereas plans for FCI-Welling's women's activities ignore ethnic identity politics and instead focus on gendered, Christian cosmopolitanism. The changing-identity registers between ethnic/racial and cosmopolitan identities can have important implications for civic engagement, such as Elizabeth's aforementioned desire to use a women's health centre to engage a wealthier, white locality, rather than a low-income, black locality that has a high rate of teenage pregnancy.

In order to publicize these initiatives to the Welling community, FCI creates networks with local authority figures to build social capital. Pastor Kwabena reveals:

> It all boils down to the relationships, you know? At the moment we have relationships with the police, with the councillors, we've already been doing the underground work and getting ourselves involved. You know what they said? They want us to let them know when the opening is because they want to invite people to be at the opening of our church. So you see? God is already doing his own work for us.

Pastor Kwabena's knowledge of local actors and their importance to the success of FCI-Welling has also been touched on in Monika Salzbrunn's work on Murids in Harlem, New York.[34] The Murids are a Senegalese Sufi brotherhood, and provide a great example of a religious group with a conscious strategy concerning interactions with the local community. Salzbrunn documents that Murids pay attention to the local geographic setting and political actors in order to understand and assess the opportunity structures of the area.[35] Similar to the strategy of the Murids in Harlem, FCI takes note of particular opportunity structures in its plans for civic engagement in Welling.

For example, Pastor Kwabena says that the music ministry will expand when the church moves to Welling. He explains:

> There is going to be an evening for the choir every other month where people come from all walks of life to come and enjoy the songs of God, praise God, and the worship we give to God. We might also try and put together Christian jazz concerts and see if we can also sell CDs.

---

[33]   Juanita Bynum is a popular African-American Pentecostal evangelist, author, actress and gospel singer.

[34]   M. Salzbrunn, 'Rescaling Processes in Two "Global" Cities: Festive Events as Pathways of Migrant Incorporation' in N. Glick Schiller and A. Çağlar (eds), *Locating Migration: Rescaling Cities and Migrants* (Ithaca: Cornell University, 2011), pp. 166–89.

[35]   Ibid., p. 174.

Pastor Kwabena's desire to sell Christian jazz CDs in Welling touches on customized leisure commodities. He is quite savvy about the Welling market and alters FCI's previous practice of selling African-inspired gospel music in Peckham to selling Christian jazz in Welling. The idea of using Welling as a space to have a jazz concert also underscores a class narrative. Although jazz originates from an African-American working-class background it has become a bourgeois pastime, regardless of race or ethnicity. And given that Welling is a middle-class area, it can be suggested that FCI church leadership is augmenting its approach to civic engagement that fits into a particular class structure.

Lastly, Irene discusses the new scope of youth activities as a result of the opening of Welling and she postulates different ways for youth group members to effect change, given the area's history. She states:

> I don't know how people in Welling are going to react to the fact that they have a lot of black people coming. Racism is still alive, especially in the UK ... In Welling, it's just our church and the Lidl. It's going to be a bit of a challenge but we in the youth will find a way. We are going to hand out free cakes and say come to our youth ministry and go to the shops and ask people to hand out stuff.

It is important to note Irene's characterization of Welling as a place of 'FCI-Welling and a Lidl,' which challenges the idea of Welling as a solely middle-class suburb. Lidls are budget supermarkets, often associated with the working-class and European migrants and thus this amalgamation of working and middle-class symbols underscores a 'shifting narrative' between the way people represent Welling and its actual dynamics. Furthermore, Irene's eagerness to go on the streets of Welling and not Peckham is surprising given that both areas have a history of violent crime. What differentiates the two is Welling's higher socio-economic class demographic, which I suspect plays a role in Irene's ease at engaging the Welling community, but not the Peckham community, on a 'street level'. Thus, class narratives are apparent in Irene's plans for civic engagement in Welling, but the question remains how pronounced they will be in practice. As of June 2011, none of the aforementioned activities suggested by Pastor Nelson, Elizabeth, Pastor Kwabena or Irene have come to fruition. This underscores the constant financial constraints of independent 'African Pentecostal' churches and a disconnect between church 'vision' and 'implementation.'

One unfortunate consequence of the Welling project is that many initiatives previously well supported at FCI-Peckham, such as the Bible College, day care and other church-based, social outreach activities, have been put on hold. Therefore, it may be appropriate to characterize FCI's expansion to Welling as 'moving up and moving out,' as FCI-Peckham operates in a limited capacity as a result of the move. The trend of 'African Pentecostal' churches relocating from inner-city urban areas to wealthier, suburban areas has been documented between East London and Essex[36] and this trend also aligns with the prosperity gospel, which argues that dutiful Pentecostal worshippers will receive spiritual and material blessings from God. With regards to FCI, the move to Welling is thus a concrete realization of the 'blessed nature' of the church, as FCI no longer operates exclusively in a working-class area, but is also present in a middle-class area that models the type of social mobility expected of members. It is important to remember that this class narrative is infused with a particular narrative of race as FCI desires to be a multiracial church and Welling is a predominantly white area. And ultimately, the church leadership's adept use of language, particularly the discourse of reverse mission and rebranding, substantiates its this-worldly and otherworldly Pentecostal agenda.

Conclusion

This chapter investigates the expansion of FCI from Peckham to Welling and has revealed the various reasons behind the church's distinctive choice of location. These reasons included a Pentecostal prophecy, reverse mission intentions and the attractiveness of the Welling demographic. In addition, FCI-Peckham was also attracted to Welling as a result of the area's tumultuous history with the BNP headquarters and therefore the church perceptively appropriated a discourse of reverse mission and integration to validate its cosmopolitan project. This cosmopolitan project advocated for church involvement in the rebranding and restructuring of Welling; these plans, however, appeared to be embedded in racial and class narratives, which had implications for civic engagement in Peckham. Ultimately, many of FCI-Peckham's activities were suspended or terminated as a result of the Welling Project, which led to some final questions: could FCI-Peckham be characterized as 'moving up and moving out'? And if so, what were the implications for its role as a welfare provider for Peckham's working-class black population?

In many ways I would argue that FCI-Peckham was indeed 'moving up and moving out' of Peckham. The unfortunate reality that many of FCI-Peckham's community outreach activities ceased, or were redirected to Welling, was a testament to the primacy of the Welling Project. For FCI-Peckham congregants, FCI-Welling represented a 'rebirth,' in aims, activities and, most importantly, congregational diversity. Consequently, FCI-Peckham understood its welfare role as shifting and contextual and did not believe that it had the responsibility to cater exclusively and permanently to low-income black populations. In essence, FCI-Peckham's expansion to Welling (and the Christian cosmopolitan project) was a challenge to critics who asserted that the responsibility of 'ethnic' churches was

---

[36]   R. Booth, 'Richer than St. Paul's: Church that Attracts 8,000 Congregation to a Disused Cinema', 11 April 2009, http://www.guardian.co.uk/world/2009/apr/11/kingsway-international-christian-centre, accessed 3 March 2011.

to uplift their local 'ethnic' communities. While the church should have the right to minister to whomever it wishes and, similarly, potential worshippers should not be constricted by race, ethnicity, or nationality, FCI-Peckham walked a fine line between contesting a notion of 'global blackness'[37] and advancing a problematic, racial and class-based Pentecostal agenda.

Furthermore, FCI-Peckham's Pentecostal agenda conveniently aligned with its Christian cosmopolitan project although, ironically, this project was limited to a black-white racial binary. However, this agenda demonstrated that the church leadership was adept at appropriating and employing different cosmopolitan registers in different contexts, which affected the congregation's understanding and actualization of civic engagement. Ultimately, this case study shed light on the vulnerable future of church growth in inner-city urban areas, as 'African Pentecostal' churches increasingly seek to take their 'faith to the suburbs.' It also remains to be seen how the black-white binary of reverse mission, subsumed under Christian cosmopolitanism, will evolve and whether these churches will constitute an accurate, inclusive representation of the Christian cosmopolitan project.

---

[37] For a good discussion on global blackness, see P. Gilroy, *Between Camps: Nations, Cultures, and the Allure of Race* (London: Allen Lane, 2000); S. Torres-Saillant, 'One and Divisible: Meditations on Global Blackness', *Small Axe*, 29.13 (2009), pp. 4–25.

Chapter 10

A History of Fresh Expressions and Church Planting in the Church of England

George Lings

New churches have arisen by the hundred outside of mainline denominations. New churches within the Anglican Church are the subject of this chapter. This chapter is a personal view in several ways. The first is that the account is shaded because the author has lived through it and the latest sections are the most conjectural as the swirls of the immediate past are still settling into the patterns people think they see. The danger of distortion grows in a second way when the author has been a direct part of the story being told. I admit to a sense of privilege and to an attendant disadvantage of being a participant observer of the Anglican church-planting scene since 1984. On the other hand I have been on the inside of conversations, conferences and report writing processes that have shaped that story. So this chapter has something of the nature of a private diary emerging in print and that may add to its interest.

Standing on the Shoulders of Others

1980 is inevitably an arbitrary year to choose. History does not work neatly with decades however much we like to characterize them. Despite this I am convinced, by reflection on the life of the wider church in England and interview with Anglican practitioners, that what later we came to call the 'church planting movement' had important antecedents. Without them it is hard to see how such a development could have taken place.

Anglicanism, not just the Church of England, has lived through not much short of a revolution since about 1960. Anglicanism then might be characterized as a Sunday gathering, conducted in a consecrated building, using the Book of Common Prayer (BCP), led by a full-time clergyman for people drawn from one parish, itself connected to a diocese and its bishop who was rather remote, appearing only at confirmations and institutions. These landmarks have virtually disappeared as essential components of being Anglican. A group, from a network of people, might meet on Wednesday, in a pub, with a part-time, woman, leader, drawing on many liturgical sources and yet still claim Anglican identity. It is as though a high tide has come in and washed away sand, seaweed and stones which we thought would always be there. Nowadays it can be semi-seriously said that an

Anglican is whatever a Bishop approves of and is accountable to him – and soon that might be her.

I believe there are six major changes across the decades prior to 1980 which could be seen as a prelude to, and preparation for, the emerging church planting movement. My view is that the growth of church planting in the Church of England since 1980 is no whim or fad, nor mere human invention. It is, for me, a discernible movement of the Spirit in our day, drawing on the previous changes but also drawing the others into this divine mission.

Firstly, since 1910 and its Edinburgh conference, the *Ecumenical* movement has recovered a sense of belonging to one another in the universal church. We have not been able to move beyond fraternal partnerships to meaningful satisfactory forms of ecclesiastical unity and energy for that has diminished. What it has increased, however, is the sense of the provisional nature of all our denominations. In recognizing other ways to do and be church, we could no longer think there was only one way. Here was a harbinger of untidy yet acceptable diversity.

The *small group* movement has roots in the 1950s rise of Base Ecclesial Communities and learning brought back by mission agencies such as the Church Mission Society. It brought more intimate and accountable relationships between church members. It introduced an emphasis on communal learning and discipleship, lived out beyond the exclusive control of the clergy. We now know that the beginning of most fresh expressions of Church starts small, with the sending of teams in order to begin being church. This planting dynamic was needed, but small groups also challenged the view that only a congregation can be church. Cell Church, coming to Britain in 1995 and, later, Clusters or Mid Sized Communities, have added weight to this change.

Since the 1960s, we have been swept along by the *Lay Leadership* movement. It has overlapped with both the small group movement and the Charismatic movement, making ministry in teams of laity and clergy more common, desirable and normal.[1] Planting both needed and fed this trend. In church planting many more lay leaders were discovered, largely out of necessity, as congregations multiplied.

The advent of the Church of England's *Charismatic* movement, datable to 1964,[2] brought a further recovery of what then was called 'body ministry'. It led to greater creativity and participation in church life, to wider use of the 'Gifts of the Spirit' in worship, healing, church guidance, speaking and, less often, in evangelism. It accelerated the argument that the realm of experience should be added to the older Anglican epistemological triad of Scripture, Tradition and Reason. It fed the 'don't tell me, show me' aspect of later mission to post-modernity. From 1985, when I started gathering statistics on church plants, around 40% of them included being Charismatic as part of the tradition they acknowledged.

---

[1]   See, for instance: J. Stott in *One People* (London: Falcon Books, 1969); J. Robinson *Layman's Church* (Lutterworth: Lutterworth Press, 1963).

[2]   The year of the founding of the Fountain Trust by Revd Michael Harper.

The 1960s also saw *Liturgical revision*. It moved us beyond individualism, recovering a sense of the corporate and participative in worship. Over the years it opened more culturally accessible styles and content. It has stirred locally tailored creativity in worship, running in tension with centrally devised, newly authorized rites; a progression away from the hegemony of centrally authorized texts, to advised shapes and, more recently, to values lying beneath shapes.[3] In the context of planting more churches, worship is put to the acid test of public use by the non-churched. Liturgically aware leaders are pressed into the creation of culturally tailored, yet theologically faithful, worship and cannot be content with providing simply what is liked by the old in-crowd or the planting team.

The *Church Growth* movement came to Britain from the USA through the Bible Society in 1975. Under the humorous and perceptive hand of Eddie Gibbs it was somewhat Anglicized. It provided tools to make more accurate assessment of the strategic, numerical and organic life of the church and its mission. It offered a change of paradigm from the institutional view of church in which maintenance and being unchanging were positive virtues. This movement made growth more 'thinkable' and so more attainable.

A pair of reports in 1974 and 1975 embodies a wide number of these strands. David Wasdell was employed by the Church of England to assess its urban parochial system. His first work showed that about 180 attendees marked the ceiling with which a single cleric could work; that it made no difference to this figure whether the parish contained 2,000 or 15,000 souls; and that once the attending percentage was small, the local church became invisible. He concluded the parish system made a self-limiting church.[4] His second report advocated a policy of subdividing parish areas through the ongoing multiplication of lay led smaller unit churches.[5] The reports, though not fully adopted by the wider church, had a significant influence on early Anglican church planters, such as Bob and Mary Hopkins who went on to found the influential charity Anglican Church Planting Initiatives.[6]

It remains a value judgment whether this series of changes represents a significant renewal of the life of, and missionary engagement by, one of the larger denominations in Britain, or is to be interpreted as the desperate arm waving of a drowning church, going down under successive waves in the sea of secularism.[7]

---

[3] S. Croft (ed.) *The Future of the Parish System* (London: Church House, 2006), p. 180.

[4] D. Wasdell, *Let My People Grow* (Urban Church Project Work paper No 1, October 1974).

[5] D. Wasdell, *Divide and Conquer* (Urban Church Project Work paper No 2, June 1975), p. 16.

[6] R. Hopkins, *Church Planting: 2 Some Experiences and Challenges* (Bramcote: Grove Evangelism No 8, 1989), p. 8.

[7] Evidence for either conclusion can be found in: P. Brierley *Prospects for the Eighties* (London: MARC Europe, 1980); P. Brierley, *Pulling out of the Nosedive: A Contemporary Picture of Churchgoing* (London: Christian Research, 2006).

My own view, formed through personal contacts with some of the leaders bringing in these changes, as well as being in local churches that adopted them, is that they sprang from hope and discovery, not from pessimism and desperation. The situation did contain both decline and growth. The former was significantly attributable to an unsurprisingly rising nominalism, not helped by those elements of the church that had lost confidence. The latter was rooted, however, in belief and experience that healthy outward looking churches were to be thought of as normal. These made an impact and grew in depth and numbers. All these streams filled out this basic conviction and contributed to it. They form one part of the case that the upsurge in spirituality, so curious to the secularists, is an enduring feature. The six strands also illustrate that this is not a recent knee-jerk response to decline but a much longer story of positive development.

Early Practitioners and Watchers – Before 1987

Elsewhere I have explained that there were wider movements behind the growth from 1980. It was also true that a few church plants had begun in the 1970s. How different were these from the daughter churches of the 1930s and 1950s – two decades which saw nearly 250 new Anglican church buildings?[8] A few distinguishing marks can be discerned. Daughter churches always served areas, while plants also began to address cultural differences. The former met in owned ecclesial venues while the latter also used rented secular ones. In retrospect, both were in danger of remaining subservient and secondary to parish churches and were only led by assistant clergy or licensed lay people, which could compromise their growth to ecclesial maturity.[9] A church created in 1969 on the deprived local authority estate called Kingsmead, in the Hackney area of London, was perhaps the first church plant. It is a value judgment to what extent these were different from existing daughter churches. The greater and conscious desire for enculturation is taken as diagnostic in this study.[10] Looking back now these were mainly isolated cases but some patterns do emerge. Some congregations began in response to large areas of new housing. A few resulted from pastoral re-organization by which a new minister plus a team were appointed for a fresh start. In these cases a parish, or even diocesan, boundary was crossed but with full consent.[11] The leading reason was a response to very large parishes and the recognition, just as Wasdell had

---

[8]   R. Walford, *The Growth of 'New London' in Suburban Middlesex and the response of the Church of England* (Lewiston, NY; Lampeter: Edward Mellen Press, 2007).

[9]   G. Lings, *Anglican Church Plants, Church Structures, Church Doctrine* pp. 100–01. via: http://www.churcharmy.org.uk/ms/sc/encounters/sfc_eote.aspx, accessed 20 July 2011.

[10]   T. Longman, *The Church on the Estate* (Rushden: CPAS Fellowship paper, no. 282–3, 1973).

[11]   R. Hopkins, *Church Planting: 1. Models for mission in the Church of England* (Bramcote: Grove Evangelism No 4 1988), pp. 9–10.

claimed, of significant areas that were unchurched for practical purposes, despite the parish system. The most publicized case was under successive Rectors of Chester le Street in Durham diocese, Patrick Blair and Ian Bunting. They planted eight area congregations between 1971 and 1984. The views of the successive Rectors offer fascinating comparisons and have been documented.[12] But up until 1982 I doubt that there was a meaningful national pattern or strategic connection between examples, with the average number of new church plants per year from 1971–1982 being 3.6.

Around 1983, something began to emerge, the causes of which are conjectural. The facts are that the number of starts in that year and in 1984 more than doubled to nine per year. Moreover, that number doubled again to an average of 17 a year across the next four years (1985–8). I note two features that may be more than co-incidence. Firstly Revd Bob Hopkins and his wife Mary, seeing themselves as cross cultural missionaries, went in 1983 to St Helens in Lancashire, in a team of five, to be part of a church plant. They had sensed a call to church planting since their conversion in the early 1970s, from hearing about vigorous church multiplication in village homes in Thailand and earlier watching it from afar when they lived in Brazil. Though they rooted their conviction in New Testament practice, Peter Sertin, their Chorleywood vicar, had not known what to make of them or this call and sent them to see the new church leader Gerald Coates, who listened and told them to stay in the Church of England, which they did. They became the first hub of a very loose network of early practitioners and began to develop training for this discipline, unknown in England at this time.

In retrospect I now realize it was the beginning of another change of paradigm, little of which was perceived at the time. If Church Growth, at least in the minds of some, had superseded the priority of Church as Institution, then Church Growth itself was being overtaken by something that had been aided by it but did not fit inside it, viz. Church Planting. The change of mindset from an emphasis on more people in church to creating more churches is a large one. It encompasses a shift from thinking in terms of addition to a mindset of multiplication. It involves a reversal of mission direction from inwards to outwards. It marks a shift from a managerial mindset to a horticultural awareness. It ushers in challenges to give away human and financial resources; it raises issues of power, control and unity and, in retrospect, it opened the door to creating diversity. Even then the typical plant of 25 people leaving to begin a process of engaging with an under-churched community, leading to meeting in a secular venue, was notably different from life in the parish church.

---

[12] *Ten Growing Churches*, Grove Evangelism Booklet, no 6.

Steps Towards an Informal Network, 1987 Onwards

In 1987 the Hopkins called the first Anglican church planting conference, held in the hall of Holy Trinity Brompton church, then under the leadership of Prebendary John Collins. In the years that followed Bob Hopkins wrote two studies of church planting. In the first study, Hopkins set out an emerging theory.[13] Planting was described as no longer an overseas phenomenon but the continuation of earlier national practice through Wesley, mission halls and the daughter church movement. It was set within a kingdom framework, the practice of St Paul and the creation pattern of growth via multiplication, including diversity. He argued for planting as both a goal and a tool of evangelism. The very term 'planting' suggested horticultural metaphors of multiplication and growth. The Chester le Street model had earlier used the analogy of strawberries that sent out runners, giving support while the new plant established at the end of the runner, with the link eventually becoming redundant. Horticultural analogies were thus coined for how it occurred, and they began using some early statistics from the second Anglican church planting conference in 1988 which had drawn 180 people. From the start many variables were acknowledged: in the varying relations to parish boundaries, the size of the team sent, pioneer and progression dynamics and different cultural groups reached.[14]

From the work of the Hopkins and a Youth With a Mission training school based in St Helen's, they developed the process of evolving theory and training that was influential for later forms of training in church planting. Hopkins' second study of church planting reflected on three stories they had met which were working well. These illustrated the variety argued for in the first booklet. The fourth story covered the frustrations arising from an anonymous example which had three times been refused permission to start. It highlighted that the Church of England is not structured to allow life to flow from life but operates organizationally. Its parish boundary system was both praised and critiqued. Patronage was isolated as tending to prevent the identification of, and attention to, mission areas. Canon law was seen to be too prescriptive over imposing centralized liturgy upon diverse cultures, hindering the growth of indigenous church. The booklet ended with various calls: for changes in training, finding pioneers, allowing the planted congregations to further reproduce unlimited by parochial thinking, partnerships between bishops and pioneering teams including use of the mission agencies, and the rise of self supporting ministers.[15] Many of these calls would have to wait for the impetus from the Church of England report, *Mission-shaped Church*, some 15 years later.

Readers today may wonder why it took so long. The factors looking back are varied and deep. This is in addition to resistance to some, or all, of the six

---

[13]   R. Hopkins, *Church Planting 1*, pp. 5–13.

[14]   Ibid., pp. 14–28.

[15]   Ibid., *Church Planting 2*, pp. 20–28.

supporting developments explored in the first section of this chapter. In addition the inheritance of Western Christendom tends to doubt that human beings need rescuing, saving and changing by Christ. It assumes all people are Christians already and operates both a belief and practice that mission happens abroad. It has been largely blind to seeing England as post-Christendom and in essence its own mission field.[16]

In addition Anglicanism in particular often finds both enthusiasm and evangelism disagreeable, not least if they are combined. Hence it is widely held not only that the Decade of Evangelism [1990–2000] was foisted on the Church of England by foreign bishops at Lambeth 1988 but also that the effect was only to make it possible to talk about the topic.[17] Virtually nothing happened. On the one hand there was parochial complacency that non-attending adults would come back to church after leaving as teenagers, together with rosy idealism that everyone can, or will, come to their local church. On the other hand was cultural blindness to cross-cultural dimensions among the white Anglo-Saxon population, let alone ethnic groups, as well as ignorance that the majority of those under 50 had little, if any, church background. 'Back to church' thinking is still popular and advocated as a major and sufficient strategy.

Some specific fears also surfaced. People joining a newly started church but crossing a parish boundary to do so were seen as 'stolen sheep' even if they had no previous history of attending anywhere. This could be allied to fears that the growing number of evangelical clergy was leading to a takeover and that this tradition was barely Anglican. In this period the morale of the clergy decreased while their workload, and the expectations of many congregations, increased. In fairness most clergy had received little or no training in either mission or the management of change. Thus change became more threatening and, at times, fears were expressed that church planting would destroy the parish system. Occasionally this was not helped by a few church plant leaders displaying dismissive or arrogant attitudes to the historic church, or failing to consult before taking action. On occasion, writers were heard as more radical than their actual words merited – for instance in the discussion of the reform of parish boundaries by David Pytches and Brian Skinner in 1991.[18] In both circumstances the media worked to maximize controversy over relatively few sensitive cases. Moreover the action of pioneers and early adopters does not carry very much weight with a large and historic institution. Its decision making processes are slow and hard to change. Furthermore it takes many years for those shaped by new thinking to become the new senior leaders who have

---

[16] Contrary analyses existed, but were often unheeded – for instance: *Towards the Conversion of England* (London: Church Assembly, 1945), pp. 2–3, 37; L. Newbigin, *The Household of God* (London: SCM, 1953), p. 1.

[17] R. Warren, *Signs of Life: How goes the Decade of Evangelism* (London: Church House, 1996), p. 42.

[18] R. Hopkins (ed.) *Planting New Churches: George Carey and Others* (Guildford: Eagle, 1991), pp. 209–25.

leverage and influence. In my view the later years of influence of Archbishops George, and now Rowan, are a case in point.

In this period of exploration and resistance annual Anglican church planting conferences were held in London. Speakers were invited from the wider church, including sympathetic bishops and theological college principals. Between each conference, the vast majority of planting activity happened at the grass roots level without any national co-ordination or strategy. The conferences were the major places to share local stories, tease out emerging theory, connect with wider thinking and discern trends. In most years I presented evolving national statistics. A summary of the conference is in print and marks reflection on three chapters of the evolving story.[19] To gain longitudinal comparisons I have taken seven year inclusive periods; 1978–84, 1985–91, 1992–8. I also made a subgroup out of the few pre-1978 occurrences back to 1967 but deeper data on them was hard to obtain.

One of the clearest statistical shifts from the beginning of gathering data to 1991 was the increasing number of cases per year. The period 1967–77 averaged two per year. The 1978–84 era saw that accelerate so that, by the end of the period, it was 10 a year. The 1985–91 period saw another rapid rise so that, by its zenith in 1991, 40 plants a year were beginning and this was without any central body to direct the movement or central funding to assist it. The comparison is by no means exact but this was the annual rate at the height of Victorian church building. It was also true that the most common congregation size among plants was in the 50–99 range.[20] This figure compared quite favourably with the size of longer established congregations. By 1991 at least 15,000 people were attending a UK Anglican church plant.[21] As the sheer weight of this evidence started to make itself known a few dioceses, like Salisbury, began to contain church planting advocacy within their overall policy.[22] In the southern province the most plants occurred in the larger dioceses, London, Oxford and Chelmsford. Within the Northern Province Southwell diocese had easily the most examples under the encouragement of its Bishop, Pat Harris, with his prior missionary experience.

Some headlines of practice are worth noting.[23] It became clear early on that church plants started in nearly every social context. They occurred slightly more in areas of traditional strength, like the suburbs and towns, than in tougher areas

---

[19]   Ibid., pp. 161–78.

[20]   Over the whole period 40% of plants grew to this size. Bob Jackson described planting as the Anglican church's single most effective missionary strategy: *Hope for the Church* (London: Church House, 2002), pp. 132–45.

[21]   By 1998 attendance was well over 23,000. This is equivalent to attendance across a fair sized diocese.

[22]   *Going with God – Together*; The report of the priorities of the diocesan consultation, 1988–9. p. 70.

[23]   I am working with not only the figures available to me in 1991, but also the more accurate ones available by 1998, as not all live examples were known at the time or sent in data promptly. The latter are unpublished.

like the urban priority areas, local authority estates and new towns.[24] At that time the least frequent context was rural. We tried to track the motives that led people to plant and, from experience, offered six possible reasons from which they could select. The most common throughout was that there were areas in the parishes that their existing church did not reach. As time moved on, planters also became more and more aware of 'unreached people groups', which was a cultural, rather than geographical, consideration.[25] To connect with those unfamiliar with church there was an accelerating shift away from using church buildings as venues. Whereas over half the earliest plants used an ecclesial venue, by the 1990s only one third did so. Many of the latter were either already redundant or under threat of closure. Over the same period the proportion of plants that were Local Ecumenical Projects steadily declined from one in seven to one in 20. They made sense on whole areas of new housing but their cumbersome procedures and internal preoccupations earned them a bad name among the planting fraternity.

For reasons driven by the media and the way bad news is remembered best, Anglican church planting is associated with an unhelpful crossing of parish boundaries. At times, some within the movement thought this potential conflict inevitable and valuable as the creation of more plants, with people travelling more to find a church that worked for them, stretched the parish concept and its boundary system. Yet the facts present the reverse of this. Of the cases in the 1978–84 cohort, one third crossed the parish boundary, all with full permission. The 1985–91 grouping contained only one quarter of cases. The 1992–99 selection had still fewer, down to one sixth. This middle period, however, did contain four examples out of 160 which crossed a parish boundary without permissions. In retrospect this ushered in the next chapter of the story.

The Glare of Publicity 1991–94

Positive and negative publicity grew in this period. George Carey became Archbishop of Canterbury in April 1991. He had, for some time, been booked to speak at the May 1991 Anglican Church Planting conference and the event was attended by 700 people. Its content led to the first published Anglican book on the topic.[26] The raised level of interest assisted the creation of a charity to assist the work of the Hopkins and Anglican Church Planting Initiatives (ACPI) formally started in 1991 and continuing 20 years later.[27] In retrospect, this publicity made church planting flavour of the month and dangerously endowed it with messianic

---

[24]   The percentages of 'easier' to 'tougher' social contexts varied over the periods: 52–48% in 1978–84; 59–41% in 1985–91 and 61–39% in 1992–8.

[25]   From being peripheral in 1978, the cultural motive was significant in 20% of cases in the 1992–8 examples.

[26]   R. Hopkins, *Planting New Churches*.

[27]   See www.acpi.org.uk, accessed 10 July 2011.

expectations. We now know that some plants were begun because of the sheer popularity of the topic, for clergy career advancement, not missional reasons. Unsurprisingly these spurious versions proved short-lived.

Co-incidentally, 1990–91 was also a potentially explosive time in the history of recent Church of England church plants. In that period four unauthorised cross-boundary ventures were launched; three were charismatic evangelical in style, one classic evangelical. Local 'invaded' incumbents voiced strong disapproval in injured tones.[28] The bishops concerned sought in vain for solutions that would satisfy all parties. The national newspapers carried articles on the events that further raised the temperature, with predictable press emphases on conflict within the Church and a threat to the future of the parochial system. Significantly this occurred at a time when the Church of England's cohesiveness and financial viability were being severely tested by the issues of ordination of women to the priesthood and the Church Commissioner's £800 million 'losses' on investments. A scenario of 'Flying Bishops',[29] rocketing quotas *and* piratical plants was an over-rich mixture. How could these high energy, but potentially destabilizing influences be helpfully channelled back into the life of the Church?

A working party was set up in 1992 by the House of Bishops. It was chaired by Bishop Pat Harris of Southwell and I was asked to serve on it. Its report came out in 1994 as *Breaking New Ground*. The first chapter of the report was entitled 'Church Planting – Opportunity or Danger?' The title reflected the worried context in the wider church. Its headlines were twofold. Firstly, it assured the General Synod that Church planting was not an erosion of being Anglican. Planting was described as 'a *supplementary* strategy which enhances the essential thrust of the parish principle.'[30] To supplement is to add something different, or to insert something missing; here is admission that church planting is not simply a new experiment in mission. It has begun to affect Anglican identity and our practice and the doctrine of the Church. The parish by itself is not complete or enough.

Secondly, it tracked how British life is changing. The subheading of the first chapter was 'a vision of territory, neighbourhood and network.'[31] Such terminology was an admission that working with purely territorial parishes was not enough. To be Anglican – in other words having a church for the nation – meant supporting traditional parishes. But it meant more as well. Practical developments in mission and experiences of what worked were prompting changes in ecclesiology.[32]

---

[28] See G. Lings, *Church Plants.*

[29] The popular term for Provincial Episcopal Visitors (PEV), invented to care for parishes that opted on principle not to have women clergy or Eucharistic presidents.

[30] P. Harris (ed.), *Breaking New Ground* (London: Church House, 1994), p. vi, (his italics).

[31] Ibid.

[32] G. Lings, *New Ground in Church Planting*: Grove Evangelism no. 27 (Nottingham: Grove Books, 1994), p. 23.

Between Two Reports: 1994–2004

There are records of 234 church plants begun from 1990–98. Yet this continued incoming tide was not just adding more of the same. We began to notice that there was an increase in the *diversity* of what we saw. In effect the term 'church plant' turned out to be too general. We realized we were watching the birth of different species, of different sizes, colours and habits.[33]

Our previous understanding of diversity had been limited to variety across terms like Runners, Grafts, Transplants and Seeds. These were subdivided into Pioneer and Progression categories.[34] Looking back these were only ways of measuring inner dynamics related to kinds of ecclesial partnership and were derived from one analysis of different types of mission challenge.[35] The vegetative varieties in the 1994 report could not cope with the different kinds of fresh expressions of Church that would arise because deeper and new questions were being asked, such as 'what is church?' As the millennium ebbed to a close we noticed even more radical differences had occurred. The 'Alt Worship' groups had been around for some time.[36] By 1999 there were some 50 Anglican examples of cell churches, challenging the idea that church must be congregational.[37] Church plants for networks and without a parish had begun in 1994[38] and, by 2005, there were some 40 more.[39] Thus the old cross boundary issue has become a non boundary consideration. They posed the question 'must church in Anglicanism be only parochial'? Chaplaincy could have told us this was not so. Sunday also turned out not to be the only day for being a church. We also noticed church being created for segments of the population. Youth was the earliest and most frequent example. Since then we have seen examples for the Arts community, cases in the workplace and within enduring sub-cultures such as Goths, Hip-Hop, Skateboarders and Surfers. This development raised both fresh fury and interest

---

[33] G. Lings and S. Murray, *Church Planting: Past Present and Future* (Grove Evangelism no.61, Cambridge: Grove Books, 2003), p. 7.

[34] See P. Harris (ed.) *Breaking New Ground*, p. 49.

[35] For an overlapping yet different list, see R. Hopkins, *Planting New Churches*, pp. 15–16.

[36] The Nine O' Clock Service in Sheffield, Visions in York, the Late service in Glasgow and Third Sunday service in Bristol would be best known.

[37] See *News from Anglican Church Planting Initiatives* Issue 7 (Sheffield: ACPI, autumn 2000), p. 3. The number of Base Ecclesial Communities in the Church of England was tiny but was a congruent trend.

[38] G. Lings, *New Ground in Church Planting*, pp. 8–10. This tells the story of one of the first of this kind.

[39] We have data for 9 Network churches from 1992–98 and 34 for 1999–2005. However, the figures for all 1999–2005 examples are unpublished and provisional.

in the so-called Homogenous Unit Principle.[40] Often what seems to be ignored in the critique is that churches in such cultures do contain a heterogeneous diversity of gender, personality types and range of ages. Also much traditional Anglicanism is significantly culturally specific too, well suited to middle England in terms of cultural tastes and the age range of attendees. These and other variants such as café church, church arising from community engagement and midweek church were becoming known and were eventually described in the fourth chapter of the 2004 report *Mission-shaped Church*. We began to give a few headlines, drawn from theological reflection and strategic considerations, about why such diversity might be applauded.[41]

A further complexity was the range of generic terms for this variety. By the time *Mission-shaped Church* was penned at least three different candidates were around, some with tribal loyalties and sensitivities. For example, in the British Isles, for a time 'emerging church' was code for communities that hitherto had been labelled Alternative Worship, rendering that problematic as a generic term.[42] Partly for this reason the report tried, in coining the new term 'fresh expression of church', to be inclusive of this variety while critiquing the helpfulness of some other terms.[43]

Another element in this transitional period was the creation in 1997 by the *Church Army* of its research unit, the Sheffield Centre. Set up to investigate trends in culture, practice in evangelism and creation of church plants, it has disseminated its findings through speaking, consultations and, since 1999, telling extended stories through its quarterly publication *Encounters on the Edge*.

Its work has usually been qualitative more than quantitative, trusting the power of story for the re-imagination of church and of narrative rather than systematics to be more appropriate for the culture of post-modernity. All this became part of the evidence submitted to the *Mission-shaped Church* group.

As the 21st century began to unfold there was also a rise in the sheer number of examples. Sheffield Centre currently has records for around 387 fresh expressions begun in the period 1999–2005.[44] Thus a few of us asked in 2001 for a second report to be written. The Church of England agreed and once again a group formed

---

[40]   Critique and dismissal can be found in J. Hull, *Mission-shaped Church: A Response* (London: SCM, 2005) and A. Davison and A. Milbank, *For the Parish: A Critique of Fresh Expressions* (London: SCM, 2010).

[41]   G. Lings and S. Murray, *Church Planting,* pp. 23–24. Further work was offered in Archbishop's Council, *Mission-shaped Church* (London: Church House, 2004), pp. 20–21, 35–6.

[42]   However this term, 'emerging church', has different connotations in the USA. For examination of its use on both sides of the Atlantic see E. Gibbs and R. Bolger, *Emerging Churches* (London: SPCK, 2006).

[43]   Archbishop's Council, *Mission-shaped Church*, pp. 33–4.

[44]   Such figures are provisional.

with a Bishop as the chair. I was part of the process and we worked from 2002–04 to produce *Mission-shaped Church*.

The Impact and Main Messages from *Mission-shaped Church*

The Archbishop of Canterbury, Rowan Williams, wrote a short but important introduction, describing the English church as being 'at a real watershed.' This language refers to a change of understanding. He continued '... there are many ways in which the reality of church can exist ... we are going to have to live with variety.' The chairman, Bishop Graham Cray, spelt out how significant that change was. He looked back to *Breaking New Ground*'s view of planting as a 'supplement' and commented 'the most significant recommendation of the report is that this is no longer adequate.' He went on to say that parochial thinking and practice *alone* is 'no longer able fully to deliver its underlying missionary purpose.' This change signals a both/and mentality, not one of either/or. This 'mixed economy' of parishes and fresh expressions is the framework, whatever critics or the fearful may claim.[45]

The 1994 word 'supplement' now had to be changed to 'complement'.[46] The difference is profound. To supplement is to provide a minor addition to something major. To complement is about two different realities needing each other for mutual benefit. It is another case of change in mission practice leading to change in ecclesial belief. The Church continues on a journey away from uniformity into principled unity in diversity. It is a journey that values both tradition and innovation. By this, what was fringe activity has become a central practice. Twelve different kinds of fresh expression and how they engaged with different cultures in British society were described. This diversification has continued to grow and, at present, we know of nearly 20 different kinds.

The report also made working with social networks more important as they had become more significant in British society. It also identified the culture of consumerism as the major challenge faced by the Church.[47] The incarnation was seen as the theological basis upon which this culture had to be entered and then challenged by the counter-cultural claims of Christ.

Across the diversity and part of this deeper unity, five values ran through the report. They are seen as five marks of missionary churches – to run beside the Anglican Consultative Council's five marks of mission. The report saw any missionary church as: Trinitarian, relational, incarnational, disciple-making and transformational. Furthermore, following the lead of Archbishop Rowan Williams, it held that the Church is formed Christologically. In his words 'church is what happens when people encounter the risen Jesus'. It also affirmed the long

---

[45]   Archbishop's Council, *Mission-shaped Church*, pp. vii, xi.

[46]   Ibid., p. 146.

[47]   Ibid., p. xii–xiii.

held view of one of our earliest church planting experts, Revd Bob Hopkins, who connected church to *Missio Dei* and kingdom thinking. Back in 1991 he wrote that Church planting is 'part of the mission of God to express God's kingdom in every geographic and cultural context.'[48]

Mission-shaped Church suggested that Church has a DNA. It is significantly known through four dimensions, perhaps better described as relationships, with God, within its own community, with the world and with the wider church. These relationships can be related to the creedal words: Holy, One, Apostolic and Catholic – the last in its universal sense.[49] Yet at the same time being church is derived from Christological roots and the accompanying indwelling of the Spirit. The dimensions are not in themselves fully diagnostic.

Breaking New Ground in 1994 emphasized safety and gradual development. But its questions about how to do this were, by 2004, being overtaken by a deeper digging into what Church is and what it is for. As I have shown, the second report went far further. It also showed that there was much that could change and yet what was emerging was still church. Hence the term – fresh expressions of Church – was coined. Here is a list of what might change, for mission reasons.

- Church need not stay inside parish boundaries.
- Church need not only be congregational.
- Church need not be on Sunday.
- Church can happen outside dedicated buildings.
- Church need not be led by clergy.
- Church can be for segments of the population.
- Church is about more than public worship and attending it. Growing quality of community and serving others in mission are of equal priority.

Changes since *Mission-shaped Church*

The report has travelled extraordinarily well, across both denominational and national boundaries. It is now read in many commonwealth countries and has been translated into both German and Japanese. This may be because it tries to deal in principles and stories. Deliberately it did not adopt a 'how to' methodology, precisely because it advocated the DNA of Gospel and Church being contextualized, taking discernment in context. In these ways it was generic rather than denominational.

Thus it has delighted some but also alarmed others. Davison and Milbank argue that it has changed Church of England ecclesiology[50] but they seem

---

[48]   Ibid., p. 29.

[49]   Ibid., pp. 96–9.

[50]   A. Davison and A. Milbank, *For the Parish: A Critique of Fresh Expressions*, p. viii and many other pages.

curiously blind to the historical changes within Anglicanism and beyond the Anglican Church.[51] The report is both radical, in the sense of seeking roots, and developmental in asserting the legitimacy of principled change. It draws attention to what is already happening more than it asks the Church of England to start what is not yet happening. Hence it urges evolution not revolution. Thus it has also made recommendations, of which some have become reality.[52] Church law has been changed. In the past incumbents could block the start of further churches in their parishes. The new legislation, a Bishop's Mission Order, gives a Bishop the right to allow the creation of fresh expressions of Church which cross parish boundaries, where local context and diocesan strategy show they are needed.

Paul Bayes, the national adviser in evangelism, was given the job of acting as a focus person across the dioceses to try and keep track of the development of planting fresh expressions of Church and to encourage dioceses to keep records and form strategy. A process was started to identify and train people with the calling and gifts to pioneer new Christian communities, now called Ordained Pioneer Ministers. We are still learning how best to train without domesticating, how best to deploy without frustrating and how to nurture a life-long calling to this kind of ministry. Millions of pounds have been set aside by the Church Commissioners for beginning work in our large areas of new housing. Dioceses have put in bids for this money and a system set up to learn lessons from the process.

We have seen the arrival of a major new fresh expression called *Messy Church*. It has a focus on the values of building family life, releasing creativity, modelling hospitality and providing celebration. Its website directory[53] cites over 500 cases and in several denominations.[54]

We simply do not know the overall total number of fresh expressions of Church started since the report but estimates of over 1,000 do not appear fanciful.[55] There are signs that certain kinds are prolific. Several dioceses have records of up to 100 alleged examples, although I am sure not all of these are fresh expressions in the terms described in *Mission-shaped Church*.

In addition the Archbishop created the Fresh Expressions team in 2004. It was led for the first four years by Steve Croft as the Archbishop's missioner. He and his team have visited every diocese and made presentations. He and others have been able to walk the corridors of power and been active players in the legal and

---

[51] See, for example P. Avis, *The Anglican Understanding of the Church* (London: SPCK, 2000).

[52] Archbishop's Council, *Mission-shaped Church*, pp. 145ff.

[53] www.messychurch.org.uk/ accessed 15 January 2012.

[54] For an account of a diagnostic case see G. Lings, Messy Church – Ideal for all Ages? *Encounters on the Edge* no. 46 (Sheffield: Church Army, 2010).

[55] On average each diocese had about 20 examples. The revised and pruned Sheffield Centre database holds 777 specific records for the overall period 1992–2008. Some of those years contain 100 records each, thus an overall figure by 2011 of 1,000+ is posited.

ministerial changes. The team from the start included Methodists and the United Reformed Church has come alongside since.

This case of ecumenical partnership is in contrast to generally weak links with other groupings. Personal connections, but little structural engagement, exist with Baptists and with the previously styled 'House Churches', begun in the 1970s. Much the same is true with the vigorous but rather different Black Majority Churches. Within fresh expressions we have little hard evidence beyond an anecdotal preponderance of growth from de-churched returners and those existing Christians who relocate and choose a church. There are notable examples of winning the non-churched but these are probably in the minority. Anglicans also have fewer examples of mega-churches and, perhaps, a less favourable disposition toward them as well as to revivalist models. In conjunction with this our national distribution pattern is different, including serving sparsely populated areas because of the parish system.

Until now our Anglican learning has been very largely from within, although with a considerable theological debt from overseas mission. Any talk of which denomination is leading the others in all this raises a danger of competitiveness, not to say hubris. The widespread influence of *Mission-shaped Church* should not be seen in such a light. The slow-moving Church of England story, when compared to that of the Black Churches, has one unique contribution in the wider debate about growth and decline. It should confound any critic trying to maintain that a sustained story of growth, by intentional and creative starting of further Christian communities, is only seen among the newer denominations, white or black, and those serving specific ethnic immigrant groups.

The ecumenical Fresh Expressions team has created a national year long course called *Mission-shaped Ministry* and several thousand people have attended it. A web based resource *Share the Guide*, edited by Michael Moynagh, has put thinking about the discipline on the web. In partnership with Church Army two posts have been created: one to administer and update the website and the other to form learning networks among pioneering practitioners. Their communications team has made four successive DVDs containing local stories which put flesh on the bones of theory and evoke possibilities. Steve Croft also edited a number of academic books exploring different aspects of how fresh expressions of Church relate to Scripture and to Church doctrine and of how their life may develop.[56] Since 2008, when Steve Croft became Bishop of Sheffield, the team has been led by Bishop Graham Cray. This two way connection with bishops shows how central the movement has become.

Current Dangers and Frailties

In observing various church initiatives over 40 years it seems there is a corrupting influence which arises when an idea or process becomes popular. Some are merely

---

[56]   S. Croft (ed.), *The Future of the Parish System* and *Mission-shaped Questions* (London: Church House, 2008).

re-badging existing activities as 'fresh expressions': the 'annual Christmas tree lighting service' is an entry on a recent database that entertains me most and convinces me least. Or there is the danger of changes in motivation or that the DNA is distorted and the results fruitless.[57]

A quite different set of dangers, and certainly frailties, consists of unrealistic expectations surrounding those in the leadership of many fresh expressions. They are not a panacea; they cannot be done on the cheap.[58]

There is an even wider developmental issue. Fresh expressions of Church are brought to birth in order to grow communities of Christian disciples among the majority of the population who do not find the inherited way authentic or helpful. Such young churches have never been old or fully mature. So much is new and there is so much to learn.[59] But here is the rub, they cannot simply copy the inherited church, although they will be wise to learn from her.

Another danger is that the big battalions in the Church are only partially engaged in the fresh expressions agenda. The vast majority of larger English churches are still operating in the Church Growth paradigm. I remember examining the different sets of strategies spread across 20 years and all of them were short on creating diversity, advocating dispersal and giving away resources. In addition, as finances get tighter in the wider church, there is more pressure to support the existing fare-paying parishes in preference to the, usually subsidized, fresh expressions. This is no easy matter. It demeans the issue by applying unappealing economic categories, yet it may concentrate the mind. The question is how the superstore of the church divides its investment between the long established, but maybe declining, brands and the intriguing but uncertain patterns of new ones.

Spring Moves to Summer

I end with a seasonal and horticultural analogy. Perhaps 2004–09 was a springtime in the Church with lots of new growth (though Davison and Milbank may retort that it was mainly weeds). There is little doubt that the Church of England now knows it can start further congregations and smaller groupings. The more pressing issue is whether we know how to sustain them.

A summer time has further challenges: what has been planted now needs watering. This is akin to the questions of resources – time, people and money. Will fresh expressions be watered or left to fend for themselves? There remain questions around how best we train leaders, lay and ordained, and how they keep going for the longer term. Disciples too need to be nurtured but not spoon fed.

---

[57] G. Lings, *Messy Church*, p. 3.

[58] G. Lings, *Do Network Churches Work?* Encounters on the edge No. 41 (Sheffield: Church Army, 2009).

[59] G. Lings, Evaluating Fresh Expressions of Church, *Anvil*, 27, 1, 2011.

There is a task of weeding. I do think we need to work harder at recognizing that not all that grows is a fresh expression of Church. Some things are pale imitations, or even plastic copies, of the real deal and need exposing. Some things may not even be Christian. Some are honourable mission initiatives from an existing church. But their aims, to assimilate newcomers into existing church, and the lack of intention to begin further churches are clear indications that they are not fresh expressions.

Summer brings heat. How will the planted churches cope when the sun shines relentlessly? How will they fare when what was new becomes familiar and they face the internal issues of discipline and the complexities of pastoral care.[60] How will they build structures that are stable enough to last and flexible enough to grow? We have come a long way in 30 years and at a noticeably faster pace in the last six, but I judge that there is far further to go.

---

[60] S. Savage, 'On the analyst's couch', in S. Croft (ed.), *Future of the Parish System*, pp. 16–32.

Chapter 11

From the Margins to the Mainstream: New Churches in York

David Goodhew

There is striking evidence of church growth in and around London.[1] This chapter looks at the situation well away from the capital. Amongst mainline churches, such as the Anglican Church, there is a noticeable divide between London, where there is substantial church growth, and much of the rest of England, where there is mainly small-scale and large-scale decline. This is especially true of the North of England, where the Anglican Church has seen very substantial decline in recent decades.[2] Moreover, Church growth has in significant measure correlated with ethnic diversity. What does this mean for communities which are less cosmopolitan than the major urban centres?

This chapter examines the recent history of a medium-sized town in the north of England, the city of York; a city which contains a mix of affluence and poverty, a city not noted for ethnic diversity. The research shows that 27 new churches have started up in York during the last 30 years. Whilst some of these remain small, a number have grown markedly and are now larger than many of the churches of longer established denominations. These churches illustrate new church growth, which is a widespread phenomenon in contemporary Britain, extending well beyond London and the South East.[3] A study of a single town offers the potential to map the way church growth is changing the face of British Christianity as a whole. York suggests that churches once on the margins are moving into the 'mainline'. This chapter has two sections: the first section surveys the number of new churches in York founded since 1980 and the chronology of their development; the second section explores the nature of these churches in terms of theology, ecclesiology, missiology and sociology.

---

[1]   See, for instance, Chapter 2, J. Wolffe and R. Jackson, 'Anglican Resurgence' and Chapter 7, H. Osgood, 'Rise of the Black Churches'.

[2]   B. Jackson, *Hope for the Church* (London: Church House Publishing, 2002), pp. 37–40: B. Jackson, '*Hope for the North*?', presented at Church:North conference, Cranmer Hall, Durham, 26 February 2011.

[3]   At least 5,000 new churches have been founded in Britain between 1980 and 2010. See Chapter 1, D. Goodhew, 'Church Growth in Britain', pp. 7–8.

York's New Churches, 1980 to the Present

Nomenclature can be confusing when studying recent church history with references to house churches (which rarely, if ever, meet in houses), restorationist churches, neo-Pentecostal churches, charismatic churches and so on. This chapter refers to 'new churches', by which it simply means congregations which have been founded since 1980.[4] Amongst them it has included four church plants which came from older congregations but which are in essence new.

York is a good place to study this development. It is a substantial community with a broad social mix, neither wholly affluent nor wholly poor. Its recent religious history is comparatively well recorded. Through the work of Robin Gill, its patterns of mainline church attendance are better researched than those of any other city in Britain, whilst Rob Warner's work offers suggestive pointers regarding some non-mainline churches.[5] Gill's work shows that mainline churches in York broadly followed national trends in recent decades. Despite pockets of growth, most mainline churches are in long-term decline.[6] Even the Roman Catholics, who had kept growing after Anglican and Free Churches began to shrink, have declined markedly in recent years, although immigration may yet bolster their numbers.[7]

Tables 11.1 and 11.2 show the size of 27 new churches founded in York since 1980, illustrating their variety and vitality, especially in comparison with many mainline churches.

---

[4]   New churches tend to fly beneath the radar of contemporary academic discourse but background to their growth can be found in: S. Hunt, M. Hamilton and T. Walter (eds), *Charismatic Christianity: Sociological Perspectives* (Basingstoke: Macmillan, 1997); W. Kay, *Pentecostals in Britain* (Carlisle: Paternoster, 2000); L. Thompson, 'New Churches in Britain and Ireland' (PhD, Queen's University, Belfast, 2000); W. Kay, *Apostolic Networks in Britain: New Ways of Being Church* (Milton Keynes: Paternoster, 2007).

[5]   Some of the churches discussed in this chapter are surveyed in: R. Warner, 'York's Evangelicals and Charismatics: An Emergent Free Market in Voluntarist Religious Activities', in S. Kim and P. Kollontai (eds), *Community Identity: Dynamics of Religion in Context* (London: T&T Clarke, 2007).

[6]   R. Gill, *The Empty Church Revisited* (Aldershot: Ashgate, 2003), p. 199. Whilst Gill's work is invaluable for mainline churches in York, it provides little information about new churches.

[7]   M. Hornsby-Smith, 'English Catholics at the New Millennium' in M. Hornsby-Smith, (ed.), *Catholics in England, 1950–2000: Historical and Sociological Perspectives* (London: Geoffrey Chapman, 1999), p. 300.

Table 11.1   New Churches in York

	Adult Attendance (Sunday)	Under-18s. Attendance (Sunday)	Year Founded
The Ark	40	6	2003
Calvary Chapel	200/100*	65	1997
Chinese Church	45	5	2003
Clifton Moor LEP	40	18	1990
Christ the Light	40	20	2007
Crossroads C.F.	30	30	2003
Elim	150	26	2004
G2 (Anglican)	160/90*	25	2005
Gateway C.F.	150	35	1981
Global	120	80	2005
Groves Pentecostal	30	-	2003
Hope Centre Church	15	8	2011**
Living Word Church	50	15	1987
Korean Church	25	5	2004
New Hope Ministry (Portuguese)	20	5	2008
Orthodox (Antioch)	20	3	2004
Orthodox (Greek)	15	3	1980s
Orthodox (Ecumenical Patriarchate)	10	-	1995
Orthodox (Ethiopian	-	-	2011
The Rock	250†	30	1993
Trinity Church	45/27*	6	2009
York City Church (NFI)	110	20	1999
YCC	200	55	1993
YEC	120	25	1982
Vine Apostolic	26	5	1999
Vineyard	63	24	2008
Visions/Transcendence Mass	18/90‡	5	1991

Notes: Data for this table were initially gathered in 2007 and revised in 2011 from interviews with church leaders, web pages, participant observation and secondary literature. Abbreviations are as follows: LEP, 'Local Ecumenical Project; CF, 'Christian Fellowship'; NFI, 'New Frontiers', a network of charismatic churches based in Brighton, YCC, 'York Community Church'; YEC, 'York Evangelical Church';* UniversityTermtime/Out of University Termtime; ** A branch of the Nigerian-based Redeemed Christian Church of God; †Warner, 'York's Evangelicals and Charismatics', p.190l. ‡The first figure is for Visions' weekly attendance; the second figure is for the monthly 'Transcendence Mass'. The 'Transcendence Mass' has shrunk slightly since 2007, partly because it has been started in two additional venues – in Leeds and Beverley.

Table 11.2: Adult Sunday Attendance at Mainline Churches in York, 1948–2001

	1948	**1989**	**2001**
Anglican	3,384	2,989	2,248
Free Church	3,763	2,335	2,013[*]
Roman Catholic	3,073	3,160	2,540

Source: R. Gill, *Empty Church Revisited*, p. 199.

Note: * The 'Free Church' category includes a handful of the new congregations, without which Free Church decline would be more pronounced.

Four of the new churches have come from within the established denominations. These churches and a number of other mainline churches have shown significant signs of vitality in the past decade – with evidence that decline has bottomed out for some of them and evidence of significant growth in a small number of mainline churches.[8] The epitome of establishment, York Minster, has itself seen significant congregational growth in recent decades.[9]

However, this does not match the remaining new congregations founded in York across the last three decades. The chronology of their development is striking. A steady stream were founded in the 1980s and 1990s but their growth has markedly quickened in the last decade. More than half have been founded since 2000. The churches founded in the last decade have a noticeably more international flavour – including Chinese, Korean and Nigerian churches. Whilst some new churches have struggled rather than grown, most are consolidating their place on the religious landscape of the city and a number are substantial entities. New churches now represent a very substantial stream of church life in a town hundreds of miles away from London which does not have large ethnic minority communities. In size the new churches constitute a 'new non-conformity', outstripping the old nonconformity represented by the Methodist, Baptist and United Reformed churches. Their particular strength amongst children and young adults suggests that they may well catch up with the Anglican church during the next decade.

The Nature of the New Churches

Theology

The majority of such churches can be described as 'evangelical-charismatic' in theology, worship style and organization. This said, one further development is that four of the new congregations are Orthodox. Almost all new churches have

---

[8] York Deanery Attendance Figures, 2006.

[9] Interview with Canon Glyn Webster, 4 July 2010.

an orthodox view of Bible and doctrine, expressed by emphasis on the literal truth of such doctrines as the bodily resurrection, the uniqueness of Christ and the requirement of faith in Christ as the sole basis for a believer's salvation. In concrete terms this usually entails prominence for preaching in worship – it is rare for such churches to allocate less than 30 minutes for a sermon – and Bible study as central to mid-week home groups. Pastor Hyun Jin Jang of York's Korean Church commented 'Koreans expect a good sermon. The whole week is about preparing one sermon.'[10]

Only one new church could be described as utilizing a less conservative theology, 'Visions', which is connected to the Anglican parish of St Michael-le-Belfrey. Visions began in 1991 as part of what was then known as 'alternative worship'. It has mixed multimedia technology with a concern to be church for those who struggle with mainline Christianity, particularly those who are part of club culture and the artistic world. Whilst preaching is important to this new church, it is given less space and offered with a less conservative theology than is the case for other new churches in York. Yet Visions, as well as being one of the oldest of the new churches in York, is also one of the smaller new churches; its monthly 'Transcendence Mass' in York Minster attracts 80–90 people, while around 20 people attend its weekly worship.[11]

The label 'evangelical-charismatic' is a broad term and it is important to recognize the variations between new churches. Such congregations stress the authority of the Bible but do so in different ways. Some have been started by existing denominations (Anglican, Elim Pentecostal, Assemblies of God) which colour their individual approach. Some are part of newer evangelical-charismatic networks (Calvary Chapel, a highly conservative California-based church; New Frontiers, Abundant Life, and Ministries Without Borders [also known as Covenant Ministries]) – which mostly sprang from the British charismatic movement of the 1970s. York Evangelical Church is independent, with Baptist and Brethren roots, but adheres to the Calvinist Westminster Confession. York Community Church is independent but has Brethren roots and an ex-Baptist pastor. Gateway Christian Fellowship came as a breakaway from a charismatic Anglican church in the early 1980s but now has connections with New Frontiers. Some have a strong ethnic base – as is the case with the Ethiopian, Portuguese, Korean and Chinese churches. The result is a movement which is organizationally diffuse, with a theological 'family likeness' – but which retains significant theological variation. Some happily see themselves as 'charismatic' (City Church, Gateway); some explicitly do not (York Evangelical Church).[12]

---

[10]   Interview with Hyun Jin Jang, York 10 June 2007; Global, Main Worship, 24 June 2007.

[11]   Communication from Sue Wallace, 19 September 2008.

[12]   Interview with C. Runciman (York Evangelical Church), 23 May 2007; Interview with S. Hurd (City Church), 6 June 2007; Interview with J. Wilson (Gateway Church), 7 June 2007.

Orthodox congregations are a different world again. Some have strong ethnic roots – as is the case for the Ethiopian and, to a lesser degree, the Greek congregations. The Antiochene Orthodox congregation is ethnically diverse and uses English in worship. The Orthodox community includes a small congregation centred on a monastery based in the garage of a terraced house.[13] While less numerous than many other new churches, the vigorous Orthodox presence in York indicates the way this strand of Christianity has spread across Britain in recent decades.[14]

Other theological trends can be seen in the use of the Alpha Course by around half of new churches, allowing them access to an internationally known stream of spirituality which mixes evangelicalism, Pentecostalism and a light dusting of Anglicanism. Alpha acts as an informal theological yardstick – implying conservative theology alongside a blurring of divides between evangelicals and a vague approval of the charismatic.[15]

The above analysis shows the new churches to be decidedly Protestant in orientation, but this does not make them unsacramental. York Community Church, which arose as a split from a Brethren congregation, retains the Brethren stress on communion. 'The Ark' – a split from 'The Rock' (the local Assemblies of God church) has communion every other week, stressing 'The bread and the grape juice are symbols, but obedience makes them a point at which God can minister blessing to us.'[16] The 'Living Waters' church has communion once a fortnight but the elements are present at every service and their minister sees them as an important symbol – an unconscious echo of a more Catholic reverence for the elements of communion.[17] At the opposite extreme, Global is so focussed on outreach that it does not include communion in its main acts of worship. 'It doesn't mean anything to people' said the main leader, fearing those coming to worship would find it 'odd, religious'.[18] Baptism is mostly seen in terms of believer's baptism. A distinctive twist to this in York has been the practice of the new Archbishop of York, John Sentamu, of baptizing adults by immersion on Easter Day in conjunction not just with local Anglican churches but with the non-Anglican new churches.[19] This distinctive form of ecumenism raises the question of whether such new churches are being 'Anglicanized', or whether the Archbishop is being 'Pentecostalized'?

One facet of new church theology which influences a handful of churches is what is sometimes called the 'prosperity gospel'. This is evident mainly in

---

[13]   www.exarchate.org.uk/st-annes-house-and-chapel-york, accessed 1 June 2011.

[14]   K. Ware, 'The Orthodox Church in the British Isles', in C. Chaillot (ed.), *A Short History of the Orthodox Church in Western Europe in the Twentieth Century* (Paris: Inter-Orthodox Dialogue, 2006).

[15]   N. Gumbel, *Questions of Life* (London: Kingsway, 2001).

[16]   www.the-ark.net, accessed 15 May 2009.

[17]   Interview with D. Lavery 31 May 2007.

[18]   Interview with D. Shore, 18 June 2007.

[19]   See, www.onevoiceyork.org.uk, accessed 1 July 2011.

Global – an independent congregation which has strong links with Paul Scanlon's 'Abundant Life Church' in Bradford. Global's main leader, Dave Shore, has been influenced by the teachings of the American Pentecostalist Kenneth Copeland, who sees poverty as a curse to be overcome by faith.[20] Whilst Global prefers to talk in terms of 'God's Favour' rather than explicitly speaking of 'the prosperity gospel', there is a distinct stress that believers should seek to grow in wealth and that faith will be rewarded by riches.[21]

Missiology

Most new churches place a high priority on mission. Mission is seen primarily as about encouraging non-Christians to become Christians – hence the importance of courses such as Alpha and other courses which nurture faith.[22] This approach is clearly bearing fruit. A number have seen significant growth over the last two decades – and not simply 'transfer' growth from other churches.[23]

Schism has played a major part in the genesis of a number of the new congregations. Gateway Church started in the early 1980s as a break-away from David Watson's Anglican congregation at St Michael-le-Belfrey, a large evangelical-charismatic congregation in York, but Gateway has itself seen two groups leave it in recent years to form 'Global' and 'Crossroads', with the latter body having also recently split, leaving 'Crossroads' and 'Hope Centre Church'. On a smaller scale, there is clearly a good deal of 'traffic' of individuals between churches. Unpicking the root causes of such divisions is difficult, especially since many are quite recent. To the outside observer, such divisions seem to have been fuelled by disagreements about leadership style and/or doctrine which then mesh with personal differences. Since most of the new churches have only loose oversight from any other body there is little to prevent division hardening into a formal split. It would be a mistake to assume that schism is a wholly negative phenomenon. A number of churches which have split have gone on to grow and exercise valuable ministries.

---

[20] A. Anderson, *An Introduction to Pentecostalism* (Cambridge: CUP, 2004), pp. 220–21.

[21] Interview with D. Shore, 18 June 2007; visit to Global, 24 June 2007.

[22] Those who have or continue to use Alpha are: The Ark, the Chinese Church, Clifton Moor LEP, Crossroads, Elim, G2, Gateway, Global, Living Waters, York City Church, York Community Church. York Evangelical Church utilizes 'Christianity Explored'. Calvary Chapel uses denominational material.

[23] Those which have seen significant growth include: Calvary Chapel, Elim, Gateway, Global, The Rock, York City Church, York Community Church and York Evangelical Church and various congregations connected with St Michael-le-Belfrey (G2 and the Chinese Church) Vineyard, Trinity Church; see also www.yorkcommunitychurch.org, accessed 15 May 2009; interview with D. Shore 18 June 2007.

It would also be a great mistake to view new churches as merely the result of 'transfer growth', as merely the shuffling of a fixed number of committed believers into a new configuration. There is significant evidence of conversions from those outside faith and of recommitment amongst those whose faith had previously been dormant.[24] In a rapidly expanding city, new churches have had particular success in attracting those new to York, especially students and members of ethnic minorities.[25] Growth amongst the city's long-established white working class has proved harder to achieve, but some churches, such as The Ark and Global, are beginning to connect with this section of society.[26] It is impossible to account for the expansion of the new churches by merely attributing it to the decline of other churches.

Whilst evangelism is primary, new churches are deeply aware that Christian discipleship involves action as well as proclamation. Gateway and Ark have consciously sited themselves in the poorer areas of the city and their programmes involve a variety of social action projects, from debt advice to drama clubs to fundraising for cancer treatment. York City Church has sponsored a new agency which seeks to counsel those facing an unplanned pregnancy. Global puts particular emphasis on work with young people: 'See those chavs', commented Global's ebullient leader Dave Shore, 'no-one else will touch them, but we'll work with them.'[27]

There is a wide variety of attitudes to the wider culture. Conservative theology can feed into a pessimism about the world in general. Thus, the American-backed 'Calvary Chapel' contains a number of members who choose to home-school their children, wary of the influence of the state education system. The new churches tend to be conservative with regard to contentious ethical issues, with the exception of the Anglican 'Visions' congregation. Yet conservative social attitudes did not prevent, for instance, the pastor of Global conducting a funeral for a lesbian woman connected with his fellowship. Equally, there is a willingness to engage with the state in surprising ways: Global offers youth services which have been widely taken up by the city council, generating corresponding funding from the local state.[28]

More generally, culture is enthusiastically embraced where it is seen as a means to connect with non-church members. Thus new churches are consistently better at utilizing electronic media than many mainline churches.[29] Most new churches

---

[24]   Interviews with S. Redman, (the Ark) 4 May 2007; J. McNaughton (YCC) 27 June 2007; D. Shore, 18 June 2007; G. Hutchinson, (Elim) 3 June 2007.

[25]   Interviews with M. Salmon (Calvary Chapel), 20 May 2007; G. Hutchinson, 3 June 2007; S. Redman, 4 May 2007; J. McNaughton, 27 June 2007.

[26]   Interviews with S. Redman, 4 May 2007; D. Shore, 18 June 2007.

[27]   Interview with D. Shore, 18 June 2007.

[28]   Ibid.

[29]   This can be illustrated by examination of the websites of, for instance: The Ark, Elim York and Global – and comparison of them with those of mainline denominations in York.

worship in secular buildings. Partly they do so out of necessity, but partly out of recognition than many people feel more at ease entering a secular building than a church. 'I'm not Oliver Cromwell', said one of the elders of YEC, commenting on how he loved the architecture of York Minster. But he went on to stress that his church deliberately chose to site itself in a community building (a local school) rather than seek its own premises, since it felt it would be more accessible to non-churchgoers that way. New church music is mostly offered in a post-1960s idiom, utilizing overhead projectors or PowerPoint – rather than organs and hymnbooks.[30]

Politically, new churches tend to take an apolitical stance. York's new churches steer clear of aligning themselves with any specific party, programme or politician. The ecumenical body most popular with the new churches, One Voice York, has held meetings with city councillors, but on a carefully non-partisan basis. One new church, York City Church, has set up 'Reflect', an agency seeking to encourage women facing an unexpected pregnancy to think through the decision and consider the various options. What is striking is how their conservative views on abortion are combined with a low public profile – the accent is on gentle reflection not placard-waving. York's new churches are very different to America's Christian right and tread warily into the public arena.

Ecclesiology

New churches possess a range of ecclesiologies but tend to be strongly voluntarist. Their very existence is an implicit or explicit critique of establishment. One pastor regarded his local Anglican church as 'a grey crematorium' which showed, in his eyes, little interest in the surrounding population.[31] Another new church, Calvary Chapel, has its roots in America and sees itself as rekindling faith in a Europe which has largely abandoned Christianity, with the corollary that most other churches are assumed to be defective to a greater or lesser degree. Its York pastor wrote in 2006, England is the country that had once evangelised the world … Now the country is spiritually dark. Some call it a post-Christian nation; Muslim mosques and the occult abound.[32]

A number of new church leaders spoke of difficult experiences which they had had with mainline denominations where the Christian faith (as they saw it) had been watered down.[33] New church ecclesiology can, in significant measure,

---

[30]   Interview with C. Runciman, 23 May 2007; www.rockchurch.org.uk., accessed 1 July 2011.

[31]   Interview with 'A', 3 June 2007.

[32]   *Calvary Chapel Magazine*, 29, Fall 2006.

[33]   Interviews with M. Salmon, 1 June 2007; J. Wilson, 7 June 2007; C. Runciman, 23 May 2007.

be seen as a reaction to what leaders and members perceive as the liberalism and laxity of mainline churches.[34]

Part of this self-definition involves church government. The new churches vary between those who are strongly linked to a wider network – such as Calvary Chapel and New Frontiers – and those who jealously guard their independence – such as Crossroads Christian Fellowship, YEC and YCC. A further divide is between a more Episcopalian and a more Presbyterian model of church leadership; those who are centred around a key leader – as is the case with Global and Calvary Chapel – and those who stress some kind of eldership – YEC and YCC. Thus York Community Church's high regard for the eldership and congregation and wariness of clerical dominance is expressed in the way its website notes that 'The church employs a full-time pastor, a full-time youth worker and an office administrator.'[35]

This voluntarism does not necessarily mean hostility to ecumenism; some new churches stand apart from other local churches but many are prepared to be involved in ecumenism. Yet such involvement tends to be on their own terms. York's new churches have tended to avoid traditional ecumenical structures and have created their own, called 'One Voice York'. Initially a leaders' prayer meeting, it has branched out into holding periodic ecumenical times of worship and prayer, evangelistic, youth and pastoral events. It has a distinctly evangelical-charismatic ethos but includes members of all the denominations – including Anglicans, Roman Catholics and free churchpeople. There is irony in its adoption of the name 'One Voice' – given that it offers an alternative voice to that of the existing ecumenical structure, Churches Together in York. One leader commented to the author in private that its stress on intercession was a means of sorting out what he saw as the theological 'sheep' from the 'goats', since, he believed, liberal Christians would have little time for such a practice.[36] Nonetheless, there is overlap and cooperation between the two – with One Voice on occasion organizing an ecumenical Good Friday open air act of worship on behalf of the existing ecumenical body, Churches Together in York.[37] York's new churches, for all their stress on independence, suggest that a new form of ecumenism may be growing up alongside older forms such as the 'Churches Together' groups. These new forms of ecumenism are shaped around prayer and mission, underpinned by a more conservative theology.

As has been shown, church disunity has played a key part in the rise of new churches in York, many of which arose as splits from other churches. What is clear is their implicit or explicit independent, voluntaristic view of church planting. There is an enthusiastic readiness to start new congregations with little or no concern for what is currently happening in an area. At best, a new church may

---

[34]   W. Kay, *Apostolic Networks in Britain: New Ways of Being Church* (Milton Keynes: Paternoster, 2007), pp. 252, 285.

[35]   www.yorkcommunitychurch.org accessed 15 May 2009.

[36]   Interview with 'B', 3 June 2007.

[37]   See: www.onevoiceyork.org.uk, accessed 22 July 2011.

write to local leaders, explaining its plans to start a new congregation but, in such communications, there is an assumption of the right to do so.[38] One church leader commented that, since 90% of the population had no obvious interest in the Christian faith, he did not see the need to be overly careful about where he started up a new congregation.[39] York's new churches embody a kind of ecclesiastical entrepreneurialism which is both innovative and uncompromising.

William Kay's *Apostolic Networks in Britain* tries to find a new sociological typology for the new churches, seeing them as moving beyond the division between sects and churches and as embodying the network society, creating a structure which does not fit the categories devised by past sociologists. Kay's thesis helps identify the vitality and organizational innovation of a number of new churches.[40] However, whilst a number of new churches claim not to be traditional denominations, York's experience suggests that there are, in effect, a number of new denominations arising in the UK, the most cohesive of which are the New Frontiers, Vineyard and the Calvary Chapel churches.[41]

Sociology

York is a medium-sized northern city, managing the transition from older declining industries (such as railways and confectionery) to an economy based more on tourism and the knowledge sector (in just over 40 years it has acquired two universities). It is fast growing (the city council claim it is the fourth fastest growing city in the country) and, having been predominantly white, it is now becoming more ethnically diverse – although it remains less ethnically diverse than most British cities. York contains pockets of considerable affluence and of considerable deprivation – all in all an average sort of community.[42]

York is far less ethnically mixed than London or many other parts of Britain but it is, nonetheless, being touched by globalization. Calvary Chapel is a plant from a California-based parent denomination. The advent of Chinese, Portuguese and Korean churches, of Hope Centre (a branch of the Redeemed Christian Church of God, led by Nigerian Pentecostals) and the four Orthodox congregations in York demonstrate the role of immigration in church growth. Those churches closest to the university tend to be more multi-ethnic than the wider population. The largest congregation in the city – St Michael-le-Belfrey – has included a Kenyan as one of its leaders in recent years, whilst the Anglican Church in the North is led by a Ugandan. Such churches implicitly (and

---

[38]   Letter from Destiny Church, York to church leaders, 1 May 2007.

[39]   Interview with S. Redman, 4 May 2007.

[40]   Kay, *Apostolic Networks in Britain*, pp. 273–92.

[41]   For more on these networks see: Kay, *Apostolic Networks in Britain*.

[42]   R. Macefield and D. Caulfield, *The City of York: Future Population and Housing Growth* (City of York, 2007).

on occasion explicitly) undermine attempts to connect Christianity with a white British identity.

Another key social shift affecting faith is the burgeoning student population of the city. A map of new churches shows a marked concentration around the two universities and a number of new churches (notably Calvary, YEC, City Church, YCC, G2) draw many members from the students and staff of York and York St John Universities. Here are many issues. Student Christianity is arguably one of the most important aspects of religious history in modern Britain. To a degree it is one of the few success stories for contemporary British Christianity, mostly within the paradigm of evangelical and charismatic Christianity.[43] Thus it is to be expected that where there is a large concentration of students there will be fertile ground for new churches – and York supports this insight. What is striking is that there appears to be a shift within student Christianity. Whereas, a generation ago, the main churches attended by students were evangelical-charismatic churches within the mainline churches, especially Anglican and Baptist churches, now there is a much greater variety of churches attended. They remain mainly conservative in theology, but far more are now outside the mainline denominations.[44]

New churches tend to be conservative on matters of gender. In many, the leading of worship, preaching and the overall government of churches are mainly or solely the preserve of men. As has been shown in other conservative churches, however, this does not mean that women are uninfluential. Indeed, leadership is often rooted in a pastor and his wife – with the latter a key figure in her own right.[45] Furthermore, not all new churches are conservative on gender issues. Those from an Anglican stable tend to be much more positive about women as leaders and preachers. The Chinese Church was effectively started by a woman member of a large Anglican congregation.[46] The Brethren influenced York Community Church split from its parent Brethren chapel because it believed the latter was failing to permit the gifts of women to be exercised. It now permits women to preach and lead communion – but not to be elders.[47]

Conclusion

York shows astonishing evidence of church growth, with an average of one congregation a year founded across 30 years. Whilst church growth in contemporary

---

[43]   D. Goodhew, 'The Rise of CICCU', *Journal of Ecclesiastical History*, 54.1 (2003).

[44]   In York, the main student churches are: St Michael-le-Belfrey, G2 (all Anglican), Heslington Church (Anglican/Methodist); York Evangelical Church, Calvary Chapel, York City Church, York Community Church and Elim. A similar pattern can be seen developing in other cities such as Durham and Cambridge.

[45]   Calvary Chapel and Global are examples of couple-based ministry.

[46]   Interview with D. Wooldridge, 27 June 2007.

[47]   Interview with J. McNaughton, 27 June 2007.

Britain is being led by London, it is happening in a significant scale outside of London and outside of the South of England. The resulting churches show signs of stability and the capacity to grow – they are very far from a 'flash in the pan'. The rate of foundation of new churches has markedly increased in the last decade. The result is a profound and permanent change in the city's religious ecology. These new churches are overwhelmingly orthodox in belief, but culturally highly flexible. They show a tendency to split, but this has often increased their reach, even whilst it has caused discord. York remains a largely white city, with small immigrant communities, yet even here immigration has had a marked effect on the formation of new churches, especially in the last decade. Whilst not immune from change and decay, many of the new churches are in better shape than many of the mainline congregations in the city – although a number of the mainline churches are growing too.

Alongside developments amongst black churches, the experience of York offers a degree of support for Rational Choice Theory (RCT), discussed in the introduction, which argues that a pluralist culture and a religious 'free market' enable churches to grow, rather than hamper growth.[48] The new churches embrace pluralism with vigour. They are ecclesiastical entrepreneurs, energetically offering salvation to all. They assume a kind of spiritual marketplace in which people can be persuaded to consider faith, but where they can never assume that the population retains a sense of religious obligation. York suggests that a more pluralist wider society is no bar to church growth and may be facilitating it. Contrary to RCT, there may be contexts in which both established and voluntarist churches grow. On a different level, the new churches of York offer support to Dean Kelley's thesis, insofar as they show that, in Britain as well as in America, conservative churches are growing.[49]

York could be seen as something of an ecclesiastical 'hot spot'. New churches have been noticeably more numerous and vigorous there than in poorer, less ethnically mixed or less socially mobile areas such as Hull or Middlesbrough.[50] Yet the new churches of York are far from an isolated phenomenon. A number of York's new churches have been instrumental in planting congregations in nearby towns[51] and there is considerable evidence of new church vitality across the UK.[52] At least 5,000 new churches have started in England alone between

---

[48] See Chapter 1, D. Goodhew, 'Church Growth in Britain', pp. 14–17.

[49] See: D. Kelley, *Why Conservative Churches are Growing: a Study in Sociology of Religion* (Macon: Mercer University Press, 1996).

[50] See, for instance, P. Forster, (ed.), *Contemporary Mainstream Religion: Studies from Humberside and Lincolnshire* (Aldershot: Avebury, 1995).

[51] Calvary Chapel has planted in Bridlington and Harrogate; New Frontiers International (the parent body for York City Church) have planted in Hull and Teesside (Interviews with M. Salmon, 1 June 2007; S. Hurd, 6 June 2007).

[52] A. Greeley, *Religion in Europe at the End of the Second Millennium: a Sociological Profile* (New Brunswick, New Jersey, 2003), pp. xi, 73–4; Kay, *Pentecostals in Britain*;

1979 and 2010.[53] York's new churches come in part from mainline denominations but mostly they come from denominations founded within the last 100 years or which are only very loosely affiliated to any other churches at all. York shows that a significant sea-change is taking place within British Christianity. That which might once have been seen as on the margins is becoming mainstream. The rise of the new churches represents one of the most significant developments in the Christian Church over the past 50 years.

Thompson, 'New Churches in Britain and Ireland', p. 221; Chapter 7, H. Osgood, 'Rise of Black Churches' and Chapter 13, K. Roxburgh, 'Growth amidst Decline'.

[53]   Chapter 1, D. Goodhew, 'Church Growth', pp. 7–8.

Chapter 12

The Diversification of English Christianity: The Example of Birmingham

Colin Marsh

Birmingham has seen profound change across recent decades in its economic and social fabric – but also in its Christian community. Just as the town as a whole has had to adapt to the decline of the manufacturing industries which were once its mainstay and to the dramatic growth of ethnic diversity, so its churches have faced similarly sizeable changes. Alongside the decline of many mainline churches, there has been a dramatic diversification of Birmingham's churches, to the extent that, in this major British city, churches which were tiny or completely absent from Birmingham 50 years ago may shortly form the bulk of the Christian community. Change need not always mean decay.

With a population of over 1 million, Birmingham has become one of the most culturally and ethnically diverse cities in Britain, with 32% of its citizens from Black and Minority Ethnic (BME) groups.[1] The sustained migration of peoples from across the world indicates that the city will continue to diversify in the years ahead. Fifty years ago, the Christian community was dominated by the 'mainline' churches – Anglican, Catholic, Methodist, Baptist, United Reformed Church, Society of Friends and Salvation Army. As in many other parts of Britain, the twentieth century saw marked decline amongst many of such churches.[2]

Yet the growth of non-mainline churches in recent decades means that Birmingham's Christianity has diversified and mainline decline may be less important than before. A survey undertaken by Birmingham Churches Together in 2007 showed that they represented only 60% of the 700 Christian places of worship in Birmingham and neighbouring Solihull.[3] The remaining 40% represent a wide range of traditions, including 'Black Majority' Pentecostal Churches (for example, Church of God of Prophecy, New Testament Church of God and Wesleyan Holiness Church); new evangelical/charismatic churches (for example, Vineyard, Newfrontiers and Oasis) and over 50 other traditions with origins from across the

---

[1]   Office for National Statistics, http://www.neighbourhood.statistics.gov.uk/dissemination/, accessed 17 July 2011.

[2]   S. Parker, *Faith on the Home Front: Aspects of Church Life and Popular Religion in Birmingham, 1939–45* (Oxford: Peter Lang, 2005), pp. 47–54, 213–19; I. Jones *'The Mainstream Churches in Birmingham, c. 1945–1998'* (PhD, Birmingham, 2000).

[3]   http://www.birminghamchurches.org.uk/find-a-church/, accessed 17 July 2011.

globe, including Evangelical, Pentecostal, Apostolic and Orthodox Churches from Latin America, Africa and Asia.[4] In the same way that Birmingham is moving towards becoming a majority minority city, so too the Christian community will continue to diversify and present day minorities may well form the majority of the Christian community in the next decade.[5]

The absence of accurate statistics for church attendance for each place of worship means that close examination of the implications of diversity is not possible.[6] In any case, crude comparison of Sunday attendance figures can obscure as much as it reveals.[7] However, further insight can be gained by examination of individual churches, outside the 'mainstream' traditions, which have experienced exceptional growth during the period 1980 to 2010.[8] These churches are making an impact across the life of the city through their contribution to community orientated programmes and engagement in the public space. The examples are presented through the lens of founding leaders or leaders who have presided over a period of growth. They are naturally positive and do not emphasize the more negative aspects of the inner workings of their congregational life. However, they provide insight into the relationship between strategies leading to growth and the groups of people who are attracted to join.[9]

---

[4]   The term 'Black Led' is used in preference to 'Black Majority' as this is the term most frequently used in the context of Birmingham. J. Aldred, *Respect: understanding Caribbean British Christianity* (Peterborough: Epworth, 2005), p. 109. M. Sturge, *Look what the Lord has Done! An exploration of Black Christian Faith in Britain*, (Bletchley: Scripture Union, 2005), pp. 29–35. An 1892 religious census estimated that, in Birmingham, 13% of Christian attendees were from smaller, independent fellowships, quoted in I. Jones, 'More desperate than any other diocese in England?: Christianity in Modern Birmingham' in *Islam and Christianity in School Religious Education*, N. Holm (ed.), (Religionsvetenskapliga skrifter, 52, Abo, 2000), p. 155.

[5]   L. Simpson, preface to *Population forecasts for Birmingham*, Cathie Marsh Centre for Census and Survey Research, University of Manchester, CCSR Working Paper 2007-12. This report indicates that, based on current trends, the white population of Birmingham will become less than 50% no earlier than 2024.

[6]   There is no accurate record of attendance figures for the 40% of places of worship that are outside the 'mainstream' churches.

[7]   I. Jones, 'More desperate than any other diocese in England?: Christianity in Modern Birmingham', p. 143.

[8]   J. Wilkinson, *Church in Black and White* (Edinburgh: St Andrew Press, 1993), p. 6. Wilkinson uses 'mainstream' to denote historic, white-led, established denominations and contrasts it with 'Black Led'. Wilkinson acknowledges that 'no terminology is available which is entirely accurate and non-judgemental'. See also J. Aldred, *Respect: Understanding Caribbean British Christianity* (Peterborough: Epworth, 2005), pp. 85–91.

[9]   The interviews were in the form of guided conversations: H. Rubin and I. Rubin, *Qualitative Interviewing: the art of hearing data* (London: Sage, 1995), Chapter 6.

Church of God of Prophecy: Aberdeen Street, Bishops McCalla and Richards[10]

As Jamaican Christians arrived in the West Midlands during the 1950s they gathered in homes for fellowship, friendship and mutual support. Although from different Christian backgrounds and traditions, they found a common bond as West Indians living in the UK and were joined by friends from other parts of the Caribbean.[11] In Birmingham the early leadership and style of worship came from Jamaicans who belonged to the Church of God of Prophecy. Their tradition of Pentecostal worship resonated with Caribbean culture and those from other traditions welcomed the strong sense of connection and belonging offered through the fellowship.

An early meeting place was a home in Ennwood Court Road, Birmingham where they met for prayer and Bible study. They offered mutual support as together they negotiated their transition to a new culture. After securing a school room to rent in Grove Lane, Handsworth, 10 Christians began meeting for Sunday worship in September 1957. As their number grew they faced complaints from neighbours who were unhappy with the noise of their exuberant worship. An afternoon Sunday School, enabled stronger contact with families. Throughout this period they maintained connection with the national overseer for the Church of God of Prophecy, Herbert England, a white Englishman living in Bedford.[12]

Within five years their services had grown to 200 people, attracting people by inviting friends and acquaintances to join their regular prayer meetings. A strong emphasis on evangelism brought new converts into the fellowship. They faced an uphill struggle to find larger appropriate accommodation to rent. Consequently they began exploring other options and were informed of a former Methodist mission building for sale in Peel Street, Winson Green. It was not in good shape, nor did they have sufficient funds to purchase it and they struggled to negotiate with the banks for loans. In the end, one of their members offered a loan after receiving financial compensation from an injury at work. When they moved into Peel Street during 1963 there were no chairs or furniture and it was in great need of repair and decoration. With about 160 members they made it their home.

Their numbers were growing elsewhere in the West Midlands and the larger congregations were asked to send people to support fledgling small new churches. In 1963 T.A. McCalla was sent to pastor a church in Wolverhampton and another small group left to form a Church in Quinton. When T.A. McCalla returned to Peel Street as pastor in 1970 the fellowship had outgrown the building. Its Sunday School had become one of the largest across the whole worldwide

---

[10]   Interview with Bishop Basil Richards on 1 June 2011 and Bishop McCalla on 8 July 2011. The national body of the Church of God of Prophecy is a member of Churches Together in England.

[11]   For a review of the Christian traditions in Jamaica, J. Aldred, *Respect: Understanding Caribbean British Christianity* (Peterborough: Epworth, 2005), p. 59.

[12]   See also J. Aldred (2005), p. 93.

Church of God of Prophecy, with over 200 children meeting in an afternoon. They began to make financial preparations to purchase a building or property. They were upfront with people in the community about their aspirations and organized door-to-door collections, utilized wholesalers to purchase bulk goods to save money, and invited new members to take fundraising on board.

Initially they looked at redundant church buildings on the property market, but these were old with high maintenance needs. Instead, after prolonged discussions with Birmingham City Council, they bought land in 1974 at a nearby site in Aberdeen Street. A new building was opened two years later as the first purpose-built church for the Church of God of Prophecy in England, using £300,000 raised entirely through the endeavours of its members. Its seating capacity of 600 allowed it to be used to bring together churches from across the Midlands for occasional shared services. It was a period of spiritual revival with occasions when 20 to 30 people were baptized during a single service. By the time that Bishop McCalla left to work in Nigeria in 1991, the membership of Aberdeen Street had grown to about 375.

In subsequent years, the membership fluctuated through two-way movement of new people arriving and existing members moving away or transferring to other fellowships. In 2005, when Bishop Basil Richards was appointed pastor of Aberdeen Street, its membership was about 350, with a regular Sunday attendance of 250 to 300. Rather than focusing exclusively on the wider Caribbean Christian community, now spread more widely across the Midlands, they began to reach out within the local neighbourhood of Winson Green. This emphasis has resulted in renewed growth and attendance has reached between 350 and 400 worshippers, with new members drawn from different ages but mainly teenagers through to people in their 30s or 40s. The majority are from the Caribbean community who are reconnecting with Christian faith, frequently after attending a service for the baptism of a family member or through curiosity after hearing about the Church through word of mouth.

Presently they are actively raising their profile within the surrounding streets. They are doing this through prayer walks, using a nearby park for the occasional open-air service and engaging with a nearby prison and hospital. Encouraging their leaders to participate in this work is not new; rather, the priority given to it is greater than previously. More recently they have acquired a former doctor's surgery to use as an additional facility for youth work and conferences and this is used by outside community groups serving people in the area. This year they welcomed into their membership a fledgling British-Asian congregation of 80 people and are exploring a closer partnership with this group of recent converts from Sikh and Hindu backgrounds. As a result of these priorities they have created the perception that Aberdeen Street is a Church for Winson Green, not solely for the commuting Caribbean community.

Church of God of Prophecy: Mansfield Road, Bishop Alfred Reid.[13]

From the initial meeting in Grove Lane, Handsworth at the end of the 1950s a small number left in 1959 to establish a Sunday fellowship at a junior school in Perry Barr and later in Westminster Road. Under the leadership of Pastor E.L. Plummer and Cynthia Brown they continued meeting in homes for weekday gatherings. Their ambition was to purchase their own building but at this stage they were unable to procure a bank loan. It was into this fellowship that Bishop Alfred Reid joined after arriving in Birmingham from Jamaica in 1961. Despite the many obstacles faced during this period, including the frequent overt racism of the host nation, they set about saving for a building to accommodate their Sunday meetings.[14] Money was given sacrificially as members managed the competing demands of establishing a new life in the UK and supporting families in the Caribbean.

Through their generous corporate giving, within a decade they purchased outright a former Methodist church building in Mansfield Road, Aston in 1972. Under the leadership of Bishop S.A. Mcken they continued to grow by welcoming new arrivals from across the islands of the West Indies. Using the informal networks of the Caribbean community, they called at the homes of newcomers to offer a warm welcome, prayer and an invitation to join their fellowship. They soon established a Sunday School for the children of young families and, following a pattern adopted within their Caribbean culture, they purchased minibuses to take children to and from Mansfield Road. This work enabled Church members to build friendship with parents who were invited also to participate in their developing spiritual life.

As Mansfield Road grew, small groups of members left to establish new fellowships elsewhere in the city, including Acocks Green during the 1970s and West Bromwich and Nechells in the 1980s. Integral to the nurturing process of new fellowships and the strengthening of those already established were 'revival outreach' services held on a regular basis in different locations across the West Midlands. Frequently organized around the needs of young people, the outreach was supported by nearby churches to encourage the new fellowships. Further growth came during the 1990s for Mansfield Road as young children from the Sunday School became adult members and new members came to faith, joining through baptism and sharing of testimony. This was an active period of visiting in the community to invite people to church services and social activities. Under Bishop Reid's leadership in the 1990s, Mansfield Road grew from 50 to 200 members.

Since reaching a peak of 200 members at the turn of the millennium, increased social mobility within the Caribbean community has led to some members moving

---

[13]   Interview with Bishop Alfred Reid, 20 June 2011.

[14]   See also, M. Barton, *Rejection, Resistance and Resurrection: Speaking Out on Racism in the Church* (London: DLT, 2005).

away. During this period the cultural connection with young people has weakened. Today there is an increasing focus on supporting women whose partners or family members are facing prison sentences and also on engaging with the needs of a younger generation who feel more strongly alienated from wider society than their parents did as children. However, this challenge is now being passed on from the previous generation of leaders represented by Alfred Reid to new leaders such as Derek Dunkley, who grew up as part of Mansfield Road and is now pastor of the Living Well fellowship in Highgate, Birmingham. Furthermore, the worldwide fellowship of Christians belonging to the Church of God of Prophecy has brought another generation of migrants to the city, with a new Ethiopian fellowship of about 80 members recently moving out from Mansfield Road to open their own church building.

Mount Zion Community Church: Pastor Calvin Young[15]

Mount Zion Community Church originated as Mount Zion Pentecostal Church in 1954 and was pioneered by Mr and Mrs Hadley, who moved out from Hockley Pentecostal Church to establish it as an Assemblies of God Church. As a predominantly white led church, the fellowship relocated to Thomas Street in 1984, was renamed the Aston Christian Centre and its leadership handed to Bill and Ruth Hopley.[16] In the years that followed black people began to attend, reflecting the changing demographics of the area. Under Mr Hopley's ministry it made a transition from a mixed congregation to a predominantly black church as white people moved away through migration or left for other places of worship. During these years, the size of the congregation fluctuated, with high and low periods, but declined after the Hopleys left in the early 1990s.

Calvin Young belongs to a group of black pastors who were the first appointed to leadership positions in the Assemblies of God in England. He arrived in the UK from Jamaica in 1973 and came to faith in Bristol, where he was encouraged to move into full time Christian ministry. Asked in 1994 to become the pastor of the Aston Christian Centre, Calvin and his wife Pauline found a congregation of between 40 to 60 members with only one or two white people in attendance. There was a strong weariness and considerable uncertainty about the future. However, it was also evident that, within the foundation of the church, there was a healthy level of faith. Calvin grew in the belief that the fellowship was being called by God to be an influence across the city. Early on, he realized that the normal focus of ministry around Sunday morning worship was not going to work and there was a need to develop relationships between the Aston Christian Centre and people living in the surrounding neighbourhood. It was apparent also that the church had not begun to address issues relating to young people being excluded from

---

[15]   Interview with Pastor Calvin Young, 29 June 2011.

[16]   Bill and Ruth Hopley were the daughter and son in law of Mr Hadley.

school or to tackle the impact of fatherless children on either the church or the wider community. The realization of these needs led to the setting up of a youth empowerment project. Its aim was to mentor young people through music and offer education and schooling for the excluded. As a result the Aston Christian Centre became home for a project supporting expelled young people.

To develop the support for this work within the Christian community, the Sunday evening meeting of 15 people took the step of engaging with the annual Handsworth Carnival in September 1994 by setting up a stage with a worship concert of contemporary music, testimony and drama. It was a significant step for Aston Christian Centre and helped raise the profile of Black Christians, demonstrating their potential to participate in the wider community life of the city. This approach resulted in a number of new converts to Christian faith, thus providing momentum and encouragement. Responding to the influx of new members and to encourage existing members to get to know each other, they started 'link' groups during the week. They trained leaders to enable the groups to be places where newcomers could belong. During the period that followed other new people came to faith, offering themselves for adult baptism and publically declaring themselves as Christians.

As a church they were seeking to be contemporary and were willing to explore issues that, at that time, churches in the area were not talking about, in particular unemployment and fatherlessness. As they listened to black young people, they created opportunities to explore these issues from Bible passages relating to the presence of black people. The aim was to express their faith in ways relevant to the local social context of Aston. Another innovation was the development of a ministry in local public houses. They were assisted by a leader in London who brought with him a group of Jamaicans. By advance arrangement with landlords, they used music and story to share the Christian message. Up to that point, Black Led Churches in the city did not have a strong community presence. This new work created media attention and provided growth to the church. In subsequent years, the church has helped to facilitate others to be involved in their community, for example through Street Pastors.

Soon they were holding two services on a Sunday in St Thomas Street. This proved unsatisfactory and at the end of the 1990s Sunday services moved to King Edward School and then to Parkland Banqueting Suite before settling at Aston University for a number of years, growing from 200 to between 300 and 350. There was a strong sense of being a church for people who did not attend church. However, the high costs of renting from the University led them, in 2005, to return to St Thomas Street, using their old building again. This resulted in a slight decline of numbers but they began increasing after relocation in 2007 to a nearby building with a large auditorium, additional meeting rooms and office space.

Renamed as the Mount Zion Community Church, since moving their numbers have doubled from about 200 to 400 on a Sunday morning. For Calvin, the hallmark of the Church is to combine the Christian Gospel with a care for the community in a way that relates to the needs of people. This was highlighted in the aftermath of a high profile shooting of two sisters leaving a New Year party in 2003. Mount Zion was integral to the churches' response and the subsequent focus on issues of guns and gangs within local communities.

Riverside: Nick Cuthbert[17]

Nick Cuthbert, the founder of Riverside, came to Birmingham to work at St Philip's Anglican Cathedral in the early 1970s. In the early days of his ministry, living in an area to the South of the city he and others initiated 'Moseley Alive' as a monthly meeting for Christians from any church or fellowship. It pointed to the emergence of something new during a period when many Christians were becoming disgruntled with traditional patterns of church and a new house church movement was developing across England.

In the early 1980s Nick and his wife Lois started meeting for fellowship in a home with three other couples who were at that time churchless. At the same time a children's club was started in Sunday mornings at a house in Kings Heath by two or three people who belonged to a small house group that was breaking up. The two groups joined together and soon 15 or 16 people were meeting and deepening friendship. Through their corporate ministry a number of new people came to faith, whilst other Christians in the area heard of their fellowship and linked in with their gatherings. By the beginning of 1985 the Sunday house meetings were frequently packed to the doors. They explored the possibility of becoming a congregation within a local Church of England parish. When this suggestion did not work out they began, in July 1985, to use Swanshurst Girls School in Kings Heath, calling themselves Moseley and Kings Heath Fellowship. From the outset they were concerned to avoid creating a reputation of encouraging people to leave their denominations and were committed to sending people back if they came from other locally established congregations. By now they had grown to about 40 people who lived in the area and either were not attending a local church or were new to an active Christian life. From this core group, the fellowship continued growing, including Christians who commuted distances for Sunday worship, but lived in the area. About a quarter of new members were people coming to faith for the first time.

In 1986, inspired by the pattern of Icthus fellowship in South West London, they decided to start a second congregation when they reached about 150 members. They agreed it was more creative to split than to manage a transition to a larger sized church. Within two years about 25 people left to meet at Park Hill School, Moseley. The new group was full of enthusiasm and eager to grow. To maintain fellowship between the two groups they began an evening meeting at Swanshurst School which became attractive to students. They quickly reached an attendance of

---

[17]   Interview with Nick Cuthbert, 15 March 2011.

100 people, occasionally nearer to 250 at its peak. Other Sunday morning services were initiated in Kings Heath South, Ladywood and Selly Oak.

By 1989 they were holding services in five different locations across the South of the city and a sixth was planned in Balsall Heath; each group had its own leader and plenty of life. Their numbers increased as people came to faith through an outreach strategy that included drama events, 'Make Way' marches[18] and events in homes. Others joined through searching for a church after moving to Birmingham. However, the strategy was leading to tiredness – a sense of not necessarily doing anything very well – and they encountered numerous difficulties in the hire of buildings. Consequently they decided to regroup again as a single fellowship. In searching for an appropriate place to convene they were introduced to Queensbridge School, which was seeking to raise £100,000 to develop its status by establishing a Performing Arts School. As the school struggled to reach the sum required the church donated a significant proportion of the money. This also enabled them to work with the school to equip the hall for their use. The gesture helped to reinforce their reputation within the area as an outward looking and caring Christian community. In moving to the school they adopted the name of 'Riverside' to symbolize a flow out from the church into the world. In 1994 they started two Sunday services and developed a monthly service for people to bring guests. Their emphasis moved away from students to focussing on developing friendships with non-churchgoers, welcoming people moving into the area and offering Alpha courses. From a membership, including students, of about 300 during the mid-90s, they have maintained growth and today Riverside has about 550 adults with an additional 150 to 200 children.

From the outset in the 1980s they have fostered a culture of members reaching out in friendship to people who do not belong to church. For Nick, small mid-week groups combined with the principle of service and volunteering are integral to sustaining the life of the church and enabling people to belong. Today the number of people moving into the area and joining Riverside is balanced by those leaving the city. There is also a degree of movement between churches and a loss to other new churches being formed. The result is a high turnover and about half the church membership changes in each three year period. A survey in 2006 showed that, on average, approximately a quarter attend services almost every week, a quarter once a month, and a half attend once every two or three weeks. This trend is a reflection of a changing culture and the extent to which people are away visiting relatives, on holiday or pursuing other activities. Today a high percentage live within two miles of Queensbridge School and most live in Kings Heath and Moseley with the result that many walk to services.

---

[18] 'Make Way' is the title of a Graham Kendrick song from which the title of the march was taken.

Solihull Renewal Centre: Bishop David Carr[19]

The Solihull Renewal Centre grew out of a friendship between two couples, David and Molly Carr and Geoff and Althea Greenaway, who began meeting for fellowship in August 1972. Over the next four years their group expanded to about 50 people meeting in a brand new library theatre in the centre of Solihull. After holding an outreach mission in October 1976 they doubled in number and began co-sharing with St Ninian's United Reformed Church to develop evening worship, weekday activities and a youth service alongside the morning service in the theatre. From the outset new members were encouraged to join mid-week house fellowship groups to discuss the Sunday sermon and grow in their faith. As new members continued joining, by the early 1980s there were over 250 members with 120 attending in the morning service at the theatre and 220 for evening worship at St Ninian's. In addition to new converts to faith, many coming into the fellowship were Christians without church affiliation. Any seeking to transfer from other churches were asked to provide a reference before being accepted for membership. Through their corporate giving they purchased, in 1984, a former primary school building for services. Within two years this space also became too small. However, they retained the building for midweek and youth activities and hired a larger space at Lyndon School, Solihull for Sunday services. They soon outgrew its 400 seating capacity and transferred to the 900 capacity Solihull Civic Hall for Sunday services.

Throughout this period David Carr continued working as a Director of the Professional Footballers Association. Driving 40,000 miles a year across England he combined this work with being senior pastor for the Renewal Centre and superintendent of 32 Elim Pentecostal Churches. However, this changed in dramatic fashion in 1997 following a heart attack. Brought up short, he re-evaluated his priorities and relinquished outside roles to concentrate time and effort as senior pastor in Solihull. The following year a factory came onto the market in Lode Lane, Solihull. Although they did not submit the highest offer for the property, their bid of £720,000 was accepted and the local authority permitted a change of use within an industrial area. With a seating capacity of 1,000 in a space at the heart of the building complex, they have continue growing and today over 2,000 people attend at least one of their two Sunday morning services or a midweek service.

For David, the bedrock of this growth has been a pattern of making people welcome, sharing compassion and befriending people. Members are encouraged to 'love the word of God and love people' and apply Christian principles in their everyday life in a way that is relevant without being overly religious. The preaching seeks to expound a Gospel message that is understandable to a wide audience. The Centre has grown in its understanding of being church over the years and Matthew 25:35–36 was especially significant in bringing to the fore

---

[19]   Interview with Bishop David Carr, 1 July 2011.

the importance of Christian action towards those in need as part of the Christian Gospel:

> for I was hungry and you gave me something to eat, I was thirsty and you gave me something to drink, I was a stranger and you invited me in, I needed clothes and you clothed me, I was sick and you looked after me, I was in prison and you came to visit me.[20]

The Centre endeavours to put this into practice through a wide range of activities, including bereavement counselling and a debt advice service. They support a family centre in partnership with the health and police authorities and work with 26 local schools and 16 other churches to maintain an extensive food programme for destitute and marginalized households.

From the outset, small mid-week home meetings were central to enabling members to grow in Christian faith. Today, in addition to homes, some groups are held in cafés and other public places. During the 1990s priority was given to mentoring new leaders who, in turn, would mentor others. In 2001 a leadership course was started for anyone in the church to help nurture a new generation of leadership. For David Carr, another important element of the church's growth has been the role of voluntary youth workers who enable children to enjoy Sunday services. This has encouraged parents to attend with their children. Over the past 10 years, the congregation has diversified as Christians from minority ethnic backgrounds have become members. From a small percentage in the 1990s, today 40% of newcomers represent black and minority ethnic communities, including second and third generation black British. Conversely, there are occasions when members leave the fellowship to contribute to the life of other churches and the Centre has begun to support new churches elsewhere in the Midlands, for example a Sunday afternoon service in Chelmsley Wood, an area to the north of the Solihull Borough.

The Renewal Centre began its life in the 1970s as part of the Elim Pentecostal family of churches. David speaks of a period when he was considering greater responsibility within the Elim Churches, at which time he experienced through prayer a strong sense that God was leading him to review the place of the Centre within the Pentecostal family. Reaching back into his Methodist roots through baptism as a child, he describes what he understands as God's leading him to connect with the Free Methodist Church in the USA. At that time, the Free Methodists were actively praying for new pastors to bring spiritual renewal to their Church.[21] In 2002, the Centre affiliated with the Free Methodist Church and David Carr was appointed in 2008 as a national overseer for the UK.

---

[20]   New International Version.

[21]   The Free Methodist Church has a presence in 80 countries across the globe, including the UK and Europe.

Conclusion

These four case studies provide valuable insights into the dynamics of Church growth in England during a period of decline in Church attendance in many mainline churches. The initial groups who provided the growth for the Church of God of Prophecy were predominantly from the Caribbean and from a Christian background and, more recently, were either adults from Christian families returning to Church or African migrants, such as the Ethiopian fellowship. Alongside a steady flow of new converts from the black community, Mount Zion Community Church has appealed to a second generation of African-Caribbean people, many of whom are adults returning to Church, having attended as children. The growth of Riverside and Solihull Renewal Centre has benefitted from non-Church going Christians who were disillusioned with other local churches and Christians transferring membership after moving to the area. Nevertheless, they continue to make headway in drawing people from outside the Christian faith into their fellowships.

Steve Bruce comments that only sustained and widespread religious growth would undermine the secularization thesis.[22] It is unclear yet whether this is happening in Birmingham with regard to Christianity (although once other religions are factored in, there may be a case for saying so). What is clear is that the decline of mainline denominations is being offset, if not balanced, by the growth of other churches. The primary cause for the presence of new traditions in Birmingham is the arrival in the city of Christians from across the world seeking to establish culturally relevant worship or the result of groups breaking away from existing churches, rather than the consequence of a wave of new conversions to Christianity. Yet, however their members are drawn in, these new churches represent a large and potentially dominant aspect of Birmingham's Christian community.

The increasing priority on community engagement through social action to connect preaching with practical application has significantly increased their impact in the public arena, including with local authorities. They partnered the Anglican Diocese to form a Birmingham Mission Network for Church Leaders in 2005 and are represented at meetings of the city's senior church leaders, organized by Birmingham Churches Together. They are major contributors to events with a city-wide focus, including an annual Carols in the City and a recent Redeeming the Communities event.[23]

---

[22]   S. Bruce, *God is Dead: Secularisation in the West* (Oxford: Blackwell, 2002), p. 173.

[23]   Consultation with this group of Churches was integral to a review of Birmingham Churches Together in 2006. At present they are contributing to the drafting of a new constitution for Birmingham Churches Together so that its membership can more accurately reflect the broad diversity of the city's Christian community. See www.redeemingourcommunities.org.uk, accessed 20 July 2007, for information on an event held

During the interviews, two concerns were expressed that related to sustaining growth: the questions of leadership succession and maintaining the outward-looking focus. On the question of leadership succession the example of Aberdeen Street is informative, as recent leadership has renewed growth and established a connection with a group of British Asian Christians from Sikh and Hindu backgrounds. At Riverside, Nick Cuthbert recently stood down as leader and it is too early to assess whether the fellowship is continuing to grow. However, they have demonstrated the ability to grow beyond the 150 threshold which they considered problematic in the early stages. In order to retain the outward-looking focus that provided their original growth, the interviewees were concerned about maintaining a healthy church life that avoided complacency, but provided practical ways that members could connect with people outside Church.

---

in November 2010 at Birmingham's National Indoor Arena organized in partnership with the West Midlands police and Birmingham City Council. See also http://carolsinthecity.org. uk/, accessed 20 July 2007. This event includes street stalls offering free parcel wrapping to passers by.

PART IV
Scotland, Wales
and Northern Ireland

Chapter 13

Growth Amidst Decline: Edinburgh's Churches and Scottish Culture

Kenneth Roxburgh

The twentieth century has not been kind to Christianity in Scotland. A country which had been marked by significant levels of Church and Sunday school attendance has, since the 1960s, experienced a steep decline in the number of members in churches of every denomination. The challenge of engaging contemporary culture in Scotland with the Christian message is not new, but one which the Church has attempted to accomplish throughout its history with varying degrees of success and failure.

The decline had its roots in the earlier days of the twentieth century and many factors have been involved in this phenomenon. Much of the debate surrounding the secularization thesis advocated by Steve Bruce[1] and the views of Callum Brown,[2] focuses around the question of when religion began to be displaced from the centre of the cultural life of countries such as Scotland. Although there is much more to this question than an analysis of Church membership statistics, it is clear that this is one of the major indicators of how seriously people are taking their faith as Christians. As fewer and fewer people appear to be worshipping on a regular basis in the churches of Scotland, then it seems clear that there is either a 'loss of faith or a loss of interest' in Christianity.[3] The percentage of people attending church in European countries in general, and Scotland in particular, has fallen and in no case has this decline been reversed except in some specific congregations, which this chapter will address.

This decline has not been due to any lack of enthusiasm among Scottish Churches in seeking to engage in evangelism and mission. The period following the Second World War witnessed an emphasis on evangelism throughout the United Kingdom, including Scotland. Tom Allen, leader of the Tell Scotland movement in the 1950s wrote that 'at no time during the last fifty years has the subject of evangelism been more widely discussed than it is today.'[4] By the end of

---

[1]   See S. Bruce, *Secularization: In Defense of an Unfashionable Theory* (Oxford: OUP, 2011).

[2]   C. Brown, *The Death of Christian Britain: Understanding Secularization 1800-2000* (London: Routledge, 2001).

[3]   S. Bruce, *Secularization*, p. 3.

[4]   T. Allen, 'Evanston and Tell Scotland: The Mission to those Outside' in *Life and Work* (August 1954), p. 195.

the war however the conclusion was reached that 'Scotland ... is caught in a cycle of very low spirituality, and that religious fervour, which had been on the wane for half a century, has reached its nadir.[5]

One of the responses of the Church in Scotland to this perceived decline was the invitation to Billy Graham to conduct a six-week mission centered in Glasgow,[6] including numerous radio links to various locations throughout Scotland. His visit created great interest in religion although he generally attracted a majority of people who already had some connection with the Christian Church and he himself admitted that he attracted very few, comparatively speaking, who had been totally outside the Christian sphere of influence. In Scotland the total number of 'decisions' came to 53,542. The most reliable guide to the initial impact of the crusade on church life comes from John Highet's survey of church attendance in Glasgow in 1954–6.[7]

The results showed that the three-Sunday average rose from 56,503 in 1954 to 67,078 in 1955 and fell in 1956 to 62,224. Highet's conclusion remains valid that

> the crusade stirred some existing but dormant members into attendance for a week or two, and that after this first flush of revived enthusiasm they relapsed into paper membership ... while some new, post-Crusade attendees fell away during the months that followed, some before becoming members of a Church and some after joining.[8]

In 1945 some 42% of Scots had a connection to a Christian Church. As a result of the various evangelistic enterprises this figure rose to 46% in 1956 and then began its steady, inexorable decline.[9] Every denomination in Scotland has experienced severe decline in membership and attendance since the 1960s. The main denomination, the Church of Scotland has seen it membership drop from 1,301,280 in 1960 to 470,640 in 2010 and a similar decline is clear evident in other denominations as well.

In recent research David Voas and others have demonstrated that religious decline in contemporary Scotland has been continuous and has affected religious affiliation and congregational attendance, as well as religious beliefs.[10] Citing the research of Voas, Penny L. Marler speaks of how the

---

[5]   *Free Church Monthly Record*, December 1945, pp. 188–9.

[6]   See K. Roxburgh, 'The Mission of the Protestant Church in Scotland, 1940-1960', in the *Welsh Journal of Religious History*, 3 (2008), pp. 100–122.

[7]   J. Highet, in J. Cunniston and J. Gilfillan (eds), *Third Statistical Account: Glasgow* (Glasgow: Collins, 1958), pp. 956–7.

[8]   Ibid., pp. 730–32.

[9]   See C. Brown, *Religion and Society in Scotland since 1707* (Edinburgh: Edinburgh University Press, 1997), p. 158.

[10]   D. Voas, 'Religious Decline in Scotland' in *Journal for the Scientific Study of Religion* 45.1 (2006), pp. 107–118; D. Voas and A. Crockett, 'Religion in Britain: Neither

proportion of people raised in Scotland in a context of no religion increased from about 5% in 1905 to nearly half the population by 2000 ... largely at the expense of those raised in the Church of Scotland who dropped from over seventy per cent to less than 30% over the same period.[11]

Several writers have raised the question of whether Scotland has become truly secular and if many people are not turning away from religion per se, but from institutionalized Christianity. Heelas and Woodhead speak of a turn from 'theistic' religion to a more internalized 'spirituality' and identify these people as mainly female, well educated and middle class.[12] John Drane argues that 'alleged secular' people are far more religious than for many generations – 'it's almost avant-garde to be engaged in the spiritual search' – although he rightly concludes that 'it is unlikely to have a place for whatever the Church has to offer.'[13] For Crockett and Voas, 'both believing and belonging have declined in equal measure.'[14]

Two of the most accurate assessments of membership, as well as of adherence, in Scottish Christianity come from the three Church censuses which were conducted in 1984,[15] 1994,[16] and 2002.[17] In 1984 some 75% of congregations took part and in 1994 this rose to 81%, although the number of congregations responding in 2002 was only 52%. In 1984, the census demonstrated that Church attendance was declining quicker in the Roman Catholic Church than in the Church of Scotland,[18] although 17% of the adult population still attended a worship service each week.[19] Between the three censuses, however, attendance in 1994 had fallen by 19% on 1984 and a further 18% decline took place between 1994 and 2002.[20] Over a period of 18 years between 1984 and 2002, the number of people in Church dropped by 33%. The three censuses showed that, although some growth had taken place

---

Believing nor Belonging' in *Sociology*, 39.1 (2005), pp. 11–28.

[11]   P. Marler, 'Religious Change in the West: Watch the Women' in K. Aune, (ed.), *Women and Religion in the West: Challenging Secularisation* (Ashgate: Aldershot, 2009), p. 35.

[12]   P. Heelas and L. Woodhead, *The Spiritual Revolution: Why Religion is Giving way to Spirituality* (Oxford: Blackwell, 2005), pp. 7, 94. For a critique of this argument see S. Bruce, *Secularization: In Defense of an Unfashionable Theory*, pp. 79–99.

[13]   J. Drane, *Evangelism for a New Age* (London: Marshall Pickering, 1994), pp. 183ff.

[14]   A. Crockett and D. Voas, 'Generations of Decline: Religious Change in 20th century Britain' in *Journal for the Scientific Study of Religion*, 45.4 (2006), p. 582.

[15]   P. Brierley and F. MacDonald, *Prospects for Scotland: Report of the 1984 Census of the Churches* (Edinburgh: National Bible Society of Scotland, April 1985).

[16]   P. Brierley, *Prospects for Scotland 2000: Trends and Tables from the 1984 Scottish Church Census* (Edinburgh: National Bible Society of Scotland, 1985).

[17]   P. Brierley, *Turning the Tide: Report of the 2002 Scottish Church Census* (London: Christian Research, 2003).

[18]   P. Brierley, *Prospects*, April 1985, p. 5.

[19]   Ibid., p. 5.

[20]   P. Brierley, *Turning the Tide*, p. 15.

between 1984 and 1994 among newer house church/charismatic congregations, this had dissipated by 2002.[21] In each category of age, gender, etc. recorded by the 2002 census, the rate of decline increased from previous measurements.[22] The only growth that was identified by the census was within mainstream evangelical congregations between 1994 and 2002.[23]

Voas argues that the change in affiliation within Scottish Christianity is not explained by denominational switching (only 5%), or by conversion from another or no religion (fewer than 10%), but is rather accounted for by people quitting Church altogether.[24] Crockett and Voas conclude that 'religious decline in 20th century Britain was overwhelmingly generational in nature; decade by decade, year by year, each birth cohort was less religious than the one before.'[25]

Edinburgh – Case Studies of Growth in the Midst of Decline

Edinburgh is a useful case study when examining the decline of affiliation with the Church in contemporary society. Michael Fry suggests that 'Edinburgh … is a mirror of Scotland.'[26] Religion in the city has experienced steep decline although, as we will see, incidents of real growth within several congregations have taken place. The city of Edinburgh, with about 100 congregations, had a total attendance of 40,670 people during the 2002 census, a decline of 19% from the 1994 figures.[27] Edinburgh is no longer 'bible-black, pickled in boredom by centuries of sermons, swaddled in the shabby gentility of the Kirk,'[28] but growth in the midst of decline is occurring.

Church of Scotland – Morningside United Church

The congregation of Morningside United Church is a union of the United Reformed Church (formerly Congregational) and the Church of Scotland.[29] They intentionally seek to be inclusive, open to dialogue and not to draw boundaries. As a result, they are an eclectic mix of people from almost every Christian background and many nations, a liberal and inclusive congregation. Their current minister, John Smith was ordained into the Ministry of the Congregational Union of Scotland and entered into the United Reformed Church. He began his current ministry in Morningside in 1998 and was Moderator of the Presbytery of Edinburgh 2007–08.

---

[21] Ibid., pp. 19–20.

[22] Ibid., p. 55.

[23] Ibid., p. 151.

[24] D. Voas, 'Religious Decline in Scotland', p. 117.

[25] A. Crockett and D. Voas, 'Generations of Decline', p. 581.

[26] M. Fry, *Edinburgh: A History of the City* (Edinburgh: Macmillan, 2009), p. 388.

[27] P. Brierley, *Turning the Tide*, p. 37.

[28] T. Nairn, 'Festival of the Dead' in *New Statesman* (10 November 1967).

[29] Interview with the minister, Revd John Smith on 15 June 2011.

The congregation, like many others in Edinburgh, has declined in membership but has been one of only two which experienced any growth in membership over the last decade.[30] When he arrived in Morningside the congregation was virtually independent with membership in two denominations. The congregation which does not receive funding from either denomination, however, is paid for locally, although it contributes money to its sister denominations. This has allowed the congregation to develop its ministry and mission in ways that are financially sustainable. John discovered that the parish had 13 care homes for the elderly but no local authority schools within the parish. The resident population of just over 5,000 shows a higher than average representation of the student group (16–24 years) – 21% compared to 14% for the city – and a lower than average representation of all other age groups except for the very elderly (85+ years). They decided to make ministry towards the elderly a main focus of their mission and began to employ full-time pastoral staff in this area, often utilizing Americans who were studying at New College. Indeed, in the 1970s, about 20% of the Kirk session was American. Although Government legislation reduced the number of care homes from 13 to four, their emphasis on care for the elderly has continued to bear fruit in the congregation's ministry and mission within the local area. This has occurred at a time when the Presbytery of Edinburgh is seeking to reduce the number of full-time ministers in the city from 98% to 78.2% over a 10 year period from 2012 to 2022.

They have also worked very closely with the Episcopal Church directly across the main road and share a youth worker and associate pastor with that congregation. They have formed a strong connection with candidates for the ministry of the Church of Scotland who have worked alongside the Church in developing their own formation in ministry and, at the same time, contributing to the ministry of the Church. This has continued the strong intellectual component of the congregation. The congregation has also supported the *Radical Welcome* initiative of the United Church of Christ in the USA and England, as well as the Zero Intolerance program of the United Reformed Church. These 'mission' opportunities reinforce the overall goal of the congregation in seeking to welcome people of all perspectives, including those who are gay or lesbian in their sexual orientation. The congregation is currently supportive of allowing gay ministers to be ordained and inducted into the ministry of the Church of Scotland.

Like many other churches in Edinburgh, United Morningside is seeking to fulfill the mission of God in the life of the city and its local community, offering a place of meeting for enquiring minds. As with other growing churches, it has clearly identified its areas of mission and is seeking to minister the good news of Jesus Christ through both ordained and other paid-staff, as well as utilizing

---

[30]   Holy Trinity in Wester Hailes, an urban priority area on the outskirts of the city, has grown over the last few years from 172 in 2002 to 206 in 2008 under the ministry of Revd Kenny Borthwick.

lay members in making it clear that the good news of Jesus Christ is one of unconditional welcome to all people.

Scottish Episcopal Church – St. Paul's and St George's

There are 57 Episcopal churches in Edinburgh and the outlying areas, reporting 8,529 communicants in 2001 although those who take communion are not necessarily Church members. This number rose to 8,922 in 2002, an increase of 393 people. The churches boasting the highest rise in attendance include Balerno Episcopal Church on the outskirts of the city and St. Paul's and St. George's in the city centre. This slight growth has continued within these two congregations which are identified with the evangelical tradition.

St. Paul's and St. George's Church (known colloquially as 'Ps and Gs') is a Church located on York Place in the east end of Edinburgh's New Town. In 1932 the congregation of St. Paul's merged with that of St. George's Church, also located on York Place. In 1985, following a period of decline, the Episcopal Church in Corstorphine was invited to take responsibility for the congregation and the Bishop installed Roger Simpson as the new rector. A large number of members of St Thomas's moved to a building that had become almost empty, with only 25 people attending. During the following 10 years the Church experienced significant growth and the congregation recently undertook a £6,900,000 refurbishment project – £6,200,000 given by members of the congregation – and normal giving has risen by 50%. World mission giving is also up each year and comes in much more quickly.[31] The congregation holds three services each Sunday with attendances of 75 at 9 am, 450 at 11 am and 220 at 7 pm. The current rector, Dave Richards, estimates that growth has been as a result of both conversion (50%) and transfer (50%).

Conversions have often taken place as a result of the Alpha courses which are held twice a year. One further activity which has attracted people to the Church is a marriage preparation course which had 30 couples attending in 2010, about 22 of which were unchurched. The large number of young families has led to growth in their mother and toddlers groups, up from 80 to 220, meeting in three groups rather than one. Richards believes that the four major characteristics of the Church which have led to growth have been the use of Alpha courses on a regular basis, a focused youth and children's ministries with full-time workers, contemporary worship and an informal and welcoming community. The Church is predominantly middle class, with many young professionals and students making up the 800 people who are members of the congregation. In 2004 Richards spoke of the congregation as one which seeks 'to be friendly and open and to make Church relevant and interesting to people in the 21st century. We try to make the atmosphere welcoming

---

[31]   Much of the information came from a discussion of the author with Revd Richards on 9 January 2011.

and we have a strong evangelical element that helps to keep spreading interest in what we do.'[32]

Roman Catholic Church – the Polish Immigrants[33]

Between 1984 and 2002 the Roman Catholic communion throughout Scotland experienced a decline, from 345,950 attending mass in 1984 to 175,029 in 2010.[34] This is also reflected in the city of Edinburgh where the Catholic population fell from 125,000 in 1980 to 111,540 in 2008. Recent figures of those attending mass also declined from 37,396 in 2001 to 29,791 in 2009. There are indications that over the period of decline amongst Roman Catholics, influences have included a lessening of attachment to mass attendance on a weekly basis. Parish loyalty has also changed and most Catholics in Scotland would attend mass in congregations which held services at times which were more convenient to their family schedules.

This decline in mass attendance would have been even more serious if it was not for the presence of Roman Catholic immigrants from Europe, especially Poland. In 2006, the Catholic Church in Scotland said its dwindling congregation had been bolstered by as many as 50,000 Polish immigrants. Church officials reported an influx of thousands of new worshippers since Poland and other East European states joined the EU in 2004.

About 20,000 Poles now live in Edinburgh, and many of them are boosting Church membership in the capital. Every Sunday there are two Polish masses at St Mary's in Edinburgh, each drawing about 1,000 people, and the celebration of the Eucharist is presided over by two Polish priests. In 2000, St. Mary's Cathedral had 1,203 people in attendance at Mass whereas in 2010 this had risen to over 2,000.[35] The influx of Poles has also led, as a result of marriages to Scottish spouses, to a rise in the number of people seeking confirmation within St. Mary's Cathedral. Furthermore, on 3 June there were 35 children confirmed and 16 of these were Polish. In addition to the weekly Polish Mass, there is a daily celebration each evening of the week, when approximately 30 people attend the service.

The visit of Pope Benedict to Edinburgh in 2010 demonstrated that, although the official Roman Population has declined over the previous 30 years, the interest in religion has not dissipated entirely. From 8 am on the morning of his visit, Princes Street began to fill with people from all over Scotland who were anxious to catch a glimpse of the Pope and, when he left Edinburgh, the streets of the city from the home of Cardinal Keith O'Brien to the city bypass were lined with people bidding him farewell. In total, Edinburgh police estimated that some 100,000 people turned

---

[32]   *Scotsman Newspaper*, 23 February 2004.

[33]   Interview with Father Michael Regan on 17 June 2011.

[34]   P. Brierley, *Turning the Tide*, p. 16.

[35]   C. Marshall, 'Polish incomers swell Good Friday congregations in city', *Scotsman Newspaper* (22 March 2008).

out to see the Pope. Scotland's First Minister, Alex Salmond's comment to the BBC appears to have been fulfilled, that 'sceptics … may well be confounded today.'[36]

Baptists – Morningside Baptist Church

In Edinburgh the majority of the 14 Baptist congregations experienced decline between 1990 and 2010.[37] The largest congregation, Charlotte Baptist, fell from 786 members in 1990 to 579 members in 2010. The only exception to this trend is Morningside Baptist Church which had 342 members in 1990, declining to 213 in 1997 but rising in recent years to a figure of 458 in December 2010.

The Church experienced a division over leadership in 1993 and when Andrew Rollinson arrived from Newcastle in 1995 the membership figure had declined by more than 100, from 327 in 1992 to 221. His ministry was marked by a period of reconciliation and consolidation but also involved the use of Alpha courses as a means of mission.[38] Rollinson commented that the Church became 'alpha addicts' with three courses running each year. By the conclusion of his ministry in 2003, almost a third of the congregation spoke of the impact of Alpha on their lives. As a result the membership of the Church rose to 238 over an eight-year period.

In 2005 the congregation appointed Karl Martin as their new pastor. Martin came from a Baptist congregation in Leeds and deliberately designated himself as senior pastor, even though he was the only full-time member of staff. This has enabled him to appoint staff members who also are full-time to facilitate growth in specific areas, such as working with children, youth and students. There were only 5 students attending the Church in 2003 but by 2010 the number had increased to over 200. Martin changed the leadership of the Church from deacons to elders, who give direction and vision to the Church, and the staff are given the responsibility of implementing this vision. In 2009 the elders closed down 35 home groups that were primarily focused on fellowship and pastoral care and began to establish Missional Expression groups throughout the city. There are now 23 of these groups with 50% of the congregation currently involved. Martin speaks of the Church as moving from being very Baptist to 'not particularly Baptist' in its identity, from moderately evangelical to overtly evangelistic, charismatic and contemporary in its worship and intentionally missional.[39]

The Missional Expression groups 'are the vehicle by which we as a Church live out the vision that God has given us – to introduce our friends, colleagues and neighbours to Jesus Christ and encourage them to be fully devoted followers of

---

[36]   See http://www.catholicherald.co.uk/news/2010/09/16/papal-visit-2010-live-blog/ accessed 22 June 2011.

[37]   Figures from *Scottish Baptist Year Books*.

[38]   Information on this period of ministry comes from an interview with A. Rollinson on 17 June 2011.

[39]   Interview with K. Martin, 16 June 2011.

Him.'[40] Some of the groups continue to use the Alpha course in a variety of different small group settings. Yet, unlike many conservative evangelical congregations, it also has groups focusing on social issues such as poverty, personal debt, ecological issues, the arts and theatre, physical healing and working with those involved in the sex industry in Edinburgh. The diversity of ways in which the congregation views mission and evangelism has enabled the Church to make contact with many people with little or no previous connection with the Church.

The growth of the congregation has been exceptional. Between 2006 and 2010, the congregation saw 92 people baptized, 107 people who transferred from other congregations and 106 people professing faith for the first time. From 2006 to May 2011, due to expanding numbers, MBC held Sunday services in both the Holy Corner Church and the Braid Centre, Morningside. In June 2011 the Church purchased Methodist Central Hall in Tollcross to accommodate increasing numbers. During University term times, 40 to 60 people attend the early contemplative service at 9.30 with 450 attending the family worship at 10.30 and a further 250 meeting in the evening. Martin's vision of Church growth is based on the mega-Church model and he recognizes that the growth he has seen in the congregation is due both to conversion and transfer growth from other churches. Morningside Baptist Church is also becoming better known in the Edinburgh evangelical community and draws many Christians who move to Edinburgh from other areas of the country. He attributes the growth to the strong leadership given by the elders of the congregation as well as to the key staff appointments which he has made over the last six years.[41]

New Churches – Destiny

Destiny Churches began life in Glasgow through the leadership of Andrew Owen who worked with the Restoration House Church movement in Bradford in the 1980s. They are evangelical and charismatic and have been established throughout Scotland, Germany, India, Ireland and Kenya. The Church in Edinburgh began in 1998 and now welcomes hundreds of people from different age groups, cultures and backgrounds to their Sunday gatherings in two locations in the city. The congregation in Edinburgh is led by Peter Anderson, along with several elders, as well as by 14 members of staff. Peter Anderson is the lead pastor who started the Church in his flat in Haymarket in 1998 with about five people, while working for an architect's firm in the city.[42]

The Church grew slowly over the first five years of its existence until it reached about 60 people in 2003. During this initial period of growth they moved into a

---

[40]   *MBC Bulletin*, 5 June 2011.

[41]   Interview with K. Martin, 16 June 2011.

[42]   Interview with P. Anderson, 21 June 2011. See also *The Journal*, Issue 8, (24 April 2008), and www.destinyedinburgh.com, accessed 20 July 2011.

local school in Tollcross. At the beginning of 2004 they purchased an old cinema in Leith. During 2004 weekly Church attendance grew through the 100 mark and in 2005 was over 200. They purchased a second property in Gorgie. Up to 50% of their congregation live in Leith and Gorgie. The population of Gorgie in 2008 was heavily weighted to the student and young adult age group (i.e. 16 to 44 years) representing 74% of the total population compared to a city average of 47%.[43] They draw about 100 students to their weekly gatherings which number between 600 and 750 during University term time. The congregation mainly consists of people in the 20 to 40 age group. They currently have three services in two locations, with the same sermon being preached in each location and little or no overlap of people attending more than one service.

The Church deliberately attempts to grow as the result of conversion growth. Anderson claimed that between five and 15 decisions are made each Sunday and for example, in the first six months of 2011 about 50 people were baptized into the life of the congregation. Between 2003 and 2011 the congregation has seen 500 people make first time decisions to become Christians. Their hope is to see this attendance growth continue until it reaches 1% of the city's population (5,000 people) by 2027.[44]

The particular areas of ministry include working with the unemployed, singles and people with drug and alcohol addictions. The Church employs a psychotherapist and counsellor as well as a worker who leads social action initiatives within the Church. Their stated mission is to be a contemporary and significant Church, to introduce as many people as possible to Jesus in Edinburgh, regularly communicating this timeless gospel in contemporary, creative, relevant and engaging ways in the city.

They run three mothers and toddlers groups, as well as one for mums and babies with special needs. They offer a free counseling service as well as free English classes for the growing Polish community. They also have a food store and four teams of volunteers give out food parcels to the homeless, working with the Bethany trust, a long established city centre ministry. They advertise a social ministry called 'Destiny Angels' who will respond to calls for practical help in refurbishing homes, cutting grass and other practical ministry within the community. There are about 30 to 40 people who act in this capacity. Their reputation of care has been recognized in the local area and social work agencies in Edinburgh often refer people to the Church for help.

Their early beginning in an Edinburgh flat means that they run dozens of 'home groups' where people can meet, pray and study the Bible together. This ethos means that they give attention to community, encouraging social networks among the membership, welcoming people from different age groups, backgrounds and cultures, with a special emphasis on those from deprived socio-economic backgrounds. The Church has people attending their services from about 50 different countries. They

---

[43] I am grateful to Fiona Tweedie for these figures. Leith is also heavily weighted towards young adult workers (25–44 years) age groups that account for 42% of the residents, compared with a city average of 33%.

[44] Interview with P. Anderson, 21 June 2011.

are currently exploring the possibility of purchasing property in two further locations within the city in order to facilitate growth, although they will probably increase the number of Sunday services to six in their two current locations in the interim.

Anderson attributes their growth to strong leadership, both locally and in connection with the lead, apostolic pastor in Glasgow, Pastor Owen, to whom Anderson is accountable for local developments. He also speaks about proclaiming a clear and simple evangelistic gospel message at each service, inviting people at the conclusion of each sermon to become Christians. They also have a strong consolidation programme which includes an initial 10 week membership course, as well as integrating new members into their house groups for fellowship and nurturing.

Conclusion

A study of Scottish Christianity, especially that of the city of Edinburgh, at first sight appears to confirm the dominant narrative of inexorable decline within the Christian Church. Yet, as we have seen, several churches have grown and have exhibited real spiritual vitality in recent years. The growth in Edinburgh has not just been among the new churches but can also be detected in mainline Protestant and Roman Catholic faith communities. The largest expressions of growth are, however, to be found among those congregations which are within the evangelical and charismatic Churches.

The growth in Edinburgh is to be found in or near to the city centre and is clearly linked to a focused mission and vision of the social and geographical needs of the particular communities of the area. Each congregation has identified the social setting of its 'parish' and has determined to appoint staff, mainly paid and full-time to engage with particular needs. Each congregation has a clear sense of its mission and has sought in its own unique way to share the good news of God's love in appropriate contextual forms. The growth has occurred within congregations that have been free to appoint specific leaders and staff, whether these be Polish priests, youth workers or counsellors to address the needs identified by the congregational leadership, as well as empowering lay people to use their gifts in the service of others.

In a city which is a mirror image of Scotland, the needs of different areas are very diverse. Congregations which in recent years have struggled with decline and a lack of growth can learn, not by duplicating what others are doing but by prayerfully discerning the challenges of their own communities and seeking to be the presence of Christ with and for the citizens of their own communities.

Chapter 14

Economic Factors in Church Growth and Decline in South and South West Wales

Paul Chambers

In a recent article Steve Bruce suggested that Wales is becoming increasingly 'indistinguishable from metropolitan Britain in its secularity' and 'more like everywhere else'.[1] The picture that Bruce paints is clear: Welsh mainstream religion is declining and will continue to wane. Implicit in this portrayal is the assumption that Wales is increasingly conforming to the secularization paradigm. Wales has never sat easily within this paradigm given that modernization and industrialization were the motors that led to an incremental growth in indigenous religious institutions. Religious decline in the twentieth century has been a by-product of Wales-specific cultural and economic factors, with links to the secularization paradigm being tenuous at best. While general indifference to organized religion in Wales should not be discounted, religious belief (however attenuated) as it is expressed in the 2001 Census remains buoyant, with only 18.5% stating that they have no religion and 72% describing themselves as 'Christian'.[2] Attendance at services of worship remains low at 8–9% of the general population, although this figure actually represents a slight increase on previous years.[3] Given Bruce's attention to statistical detail, I am surprised to see him assert again that the trajectory of decline is neither 'arrested or slowed'.[4] This is in marked contrast to recent surveys which suggest that current attendance might even be considered fairly stable when compared to the 1995 Welsh Churches Survey.[5]

Secularization, as understood by Bruce, is the by-product of the unintended consequences of the process of modernization. Religion loses its presence in everyday life and its sense of mission, and ultimately its being becomes hard to sustain. Religion, in as much as it has a future, is in a highly privatized, hard

---

[1] S. Bruce 'Religion in Rural Wales: Four Restudies', *Contemporary Wales* 23 (2010), pp. 219–39.

[2] D. Dunkerley, 'Wales's Changing Population: A Demographic Overview', *Contemporary Wales*, 19 (2007), pp. 116–25.

[3] J. Evans, *Faith in Wales: Counting For Communities* (Cardiff: Gweini, 2008), pp. 20–23; J. Ashworth and I. Farthing, *Churchgoing in the UK; A Research Report from Tearfund on Church Attendance in the UK* (Teddington: Tear Fund, 2007), pp. 5–18.

[4] S. Bruce, *Religion in Rural Wales*, p. 219.

[5] J. Evans, *Faith in Wales*, p. 7; J. Ashworth, *Churchgoing in the UK*, pp. 5–22.

sectarian or cultic form.[6] This is very much a generalized macro-level theory and, while it contains a certain plausibility, the reality on the ground can be quite different. As I have argued elsewhere, religion and religious praxis are accomplished in local settings according to local conditions.[7] These can and do differ. For example, one of the unintended consequences of recent global migration has been an explosion of multicultural religion in the larger British cities, locales that were previously assumed to be highly secularized environments.[8] Religion in Europe has consequently come under the media and public policy spotlights and been the subject of rights legislation.[9] This legislation seeks to protect the rights of faith groups' belief and practice, while parallel rights legislation seeks to protect citizens from the prejudices of faith groups, notably within the sphere of human sexuality. Rather than retreating into the private sphere along the lines that the orthodox secularization thesis suggests, dialogue *about* religion increasingly encompasses the field of community cohesion, the nature of identity and conflict – notably the struggle for power to influence public opinion between different worldviews and between groups that have secular and faith orientations.[10] This raises interesting questions about the secularization paradigm in the light of changing circumstances. Ultimately one has to question its continued efficacy as an explanation of religious change in modern pluralist societies.

Perhaps a more fruitful theoretical avenue lies within the work of Pierre Bourdieu and his concepts of 'fields' of action and the generation of 'symbolic capitals'.[11] Fields can be overlapping and cross-cutting and are understood in their relation to values. Clearly, the overarching dominant cultural and social 'field' relevant to this discussion is secular and liberal in nature and function, reflecting significant changes in society and culture. Various symbolic capitals have different values in the sense of how they relate to fields and to current policy discourses surrounding the positive and negative values of religion. Thus, some types of religious and social capital are seen as more or less useful than others. In this

---

[6]   S. Bruce, *God is Dead: Secularization in the West* (Oxford: Blackwell, 2002), pp. 1–43.

[7]   P. Chambers, *Religion, Secularization and Social Change* (Cardiff: University of Wales Press, 2005), pp. 75–167.

[8]   G. Smith, 'Religion as a source of social capital in the Regeneration and Globalisation of East London' *Rising East*, 4.3 (2001), pp. 128–57.

[9]   H. Davis, *Human Rights Law: Directions* (2nd ed.; Oxford: Oxford University Press, 2009), pp. 358–73.

[10]   D. Herbert, *Religion and Civil Society: Rethinking Public Religion in the Contemporary World* (Aldershot: Ashgate, 2003), pp. 119–54; O. Riis, 'Modes of Religious Pluralism Under Conditions of Globalization' in M. Koenig and P. de Guchteneire (eds), *Democracy and Human Rights in Multicultural Societies* (Aldershot: Ashgate, 2007), pp. 251–66; A. Billings, *God and Community Cohesion: Help or Hindrance?* (London: SPCK, 2009), pp. 95–124.

[11]   P. Bourdieu, *The Logic of Practice* (Cambridge: Polity Press, 1990).

way government can co-opt faith groups into projects of community cohesion or regeneration because faith groups are deemed to have 'appropriate capital', while in other contexts and discourses religious values might be seen to be out of kilter with a largely secular and liberal field, with faith groups deploying 'inappropriate' capital. Symbolic capital can also be seen to have 'bridging' or 'bonding' aspects with the former facilitating connections with other groups – which is very important in, for example the context of mission – while the latter tends to promote group cohesion while also being potentially insulating. The point to be stressed here is that the whole gamut of fields, values and capitals is dynamic and subject both to change and to unintended consequences. Compared to this fluid approach, the secularization thesis appears increasingly ossified. In the almost two decades that I have been studying religion in Wales I have consistently approached religious institutions through the medium of local congregational studies, focusing as much on areas of local religious growth as on decline. While not discounting the wider effects of societal trends on religious institutions, I would argue that congregational growth and decline is best explained through local socio-environmental factors. Religion is something largely accomplished at the local level and in the local field and this is the perspective from which analysis should proceed. A limited focus on religious decline blinds us to the many interesting developments in the contemporary religious field, not least to successful strategies for engagement with local populations and, ultimately, growth among congregations committed to this approach.

In my previous studies of church growth and decline in South West Wales, engagement with or disengagement from local communities was largely dependent on the nature of social networks.[12] Declining congregations tended to have weak or non-existent links to their local communities or these links mainly encompassed the elderly population. Without robust links, recruitment becomes unlikely and long-term sustainability questionable. Congregations age and atrophy while becoming increasingly insular. Where significant congregational growth is achieved it tends to be through the presence of robust, outward-looking networks. Mission is also dependent on actions, the careful auditing of needs among local populations, the setting of appropriate goals and a level of internal congregational resource capable of realizing these goals. Despite the overall decline of institutionalized religion in Wales there is increasing evidence of a leaner, fitter Church that is more attuned to emerging local community needs.[13] This chapter will explore recent trends in South Wales, arguing the case for the continued salience of the Church in Welsh society and its likely role in the future. While the case study is Wales, much of what I have to say is mirrored in developments in similar regions of Britain, notably those areas that have experienced significant de-industrialization.

---

[12] P. Chambers, *Religion, Secularization and Social Change*, pp. 199–229.

[13] P. Chambers, 'Out of Taste, Out of Time: The Future of Nonconformist Religion in Wales in the Twenty First Century', *Contemporary Wales*, 21 (2008), pp. 86–100.

Economic Factors and Social and Religious Change in South and South West Wales: The Last Three Decades

Rather than waning in the face of modernization religion in Wales waxed with a growing economy. Religion expanded into the newly industrialized regions and consolidated itself as a major component in Welsh identity, reaching a high point during the 1904–05 Welsh Religious Revival. Subsequent progressive industrial and economic decline in the twentieth century was mirrored by religious decline.[14] The year 1980 saw Britain move into economic recession and in Wales that year saw the laying off of almost 6,000 workers (half the workforce) at the British Steel Corporation plant in Port Talbot.[15] Not only did this rip the economic heart out of the town, it significantly disrupted traditional social networks and identities, ultimately undermining customary notions of community and the local institutions (including churches and chapels) that were predicated upon solidarity-based industrial communities. While local congregations played their part in helping their communities to come to terms with these changes, many skilled workers migrated far afield in search of employment and the character of communities such as the huge Sandfields Estate changed as the Local Authority took the opportunity to re-house and concentrate many 'problem families' in the area. What had been a bastion of working class respectability became known locally as 'Little Beirut'.[16] As recession grew, the very narrow base of the Welsh economy began to contract and come under increasing pressure. Many mines were becoming increasingly unworkable with miners being deployed to increasingly distant but still viable pits, a process that kept them in work but undermined the strong local social solidarities developed in their 'home' pits. The steel industry continued to contract as it sought to adapt to competition from foreign competitors. Many workers increasingly sought employment in manufacturing (such as it was) and the service sector, leading to much greater differentiation in terms of social identity and undermining the formerly homogenous nature of local communities.[17] Local institutions such as Miners Institutes and the chapels become much less salient to the locales in which they were situated. D. Ben Rees' study of Nonconformity in the Aberdare Valley clearly links the decline of the local mining industry (and more broadly industrial change) with the progressive loss of social salience of the chapels in those settings. More specifically, he also points to congregations becoming insular

---

[14]   P. Chambers, 'The Changing Face of Religion in Wales', *The Expository Times*, 122.6 (2011), pp. 271–79.

[15]   C. Harris, *Redundancy and Recession*, (Oxford: Blackwell, 1987).

[16]   P. Chambers and S. Gorard, R. Fevre, G. Rees and J. Furlong, *Changes in Training Opportunities in South Wales 1945–1998: The Views of Key Informants* (Cardiff: School of Education, Cardiff University, 1998), pp. 12–15.

[17]   G. Day, *Making Sense of Wales: A Sociological Perspective* (Cardiff: University of Wales Press, 2010), pp. 116–40.

and ossified, offering little relevance both to potential newcomers and to the younger generations.[18]

During the 1980s, all the traditional Nonconformist denominations were haemorrhaging members, attendance was spiralling downwards and new recruits to the ministry were drying up.[19] Conversely, the profile of Pentecostalism was growing both through transfer and conversion.[20] For churches based upon the parish system, matters were somewhat better and arguably this was because many church halls still constituted hubs for local voluntary associations. Indeed both the Anglican and Roman Catholic Churches were experiencing some limited growth in the large and medium urban conurbations of Wales but, tellingly, not in the industrial valleys. The miners' Strike of 1984 represented what was to be the last hurrah for traditional local community solidarity and it was often church or chapel premises that provided focal points for the miners' support groups in what proved to be a difficult year. Indeed, the Christian community in South and South West Wales did much to try and mediate between the strikers and employers. While ultimately unsuccessful in this project this was nevertheless a clear demonstration that the churches could, under the right conditions, reach out into their communities and intercede with the powerful on behalf of those communities.[21] The end of the strike saw the decimation of mining with all coal production in the iconic Rhondda Valley ceasing within the span of a few months. Pit closures both negatively affected the social fabric of communities and stored up problems that were to play themselves out in the 1990s – a decade that also brought significant challenges to the religious community.

By 1990 there were five remaining working mines in South and South West Wales and steel production had largely ceased throughout Wales. The nature of working-class life was changing and participation in pub, club and chapel life was now becoming a marker of social and cultural differentiation rather than of commonality.[22] Social identities were changing and becoming more individualistic, raising challenges for religious institutions predicated on 'community'. This was reflected in the increasing isolation of many congregations from their surrounding populations. While this comprises the broad picture there are exceptions to the rule, with Charles *et al* noting that, in some traditional communities in Swansea, while personal religiosity had ebbed significantly, local religious organizations continued to facilitate and provide 'a framework for many people's personal

---

[18] D. Ben Rees, *Chapels in the Valley: A Study in the Sociology of Welsh Nonconformity* (Upton: Fynon Press, 1975), pp. 147–214.

[19] P. Chambers, 'Out of Taste'.

[20] D. Densil Morgan, *The Span of the Cross: Christian Religion and Society in Wales 1914–2000* (Cardiff: University of Wales Press, 1999), pp. 265–6; P. Chambers, *Religion, Secularization and Social Change*, pp. 56–63.

[21] D. Densil Morgan, *Span of the Cross,* pp. 269–71.

[22] G. Day, *Making Sense of Wales*, pp. 131–2.

networks and as a form of social capital'.[23] The more general experience in Swansea, however, was of a socially and geographically mobile population which occasionally visited their 'home' church or chapel for baptisms, weddings and funerals. As elsewhere in Wales, the biggest area of religious decline was among the Welsh medium denominations. This is reflected in data from the baseline 1960 survey and its 2002 restudy. Whereas in 1960 30% of 'Welsh' respondents were affiliated to a Welsh nonconformist denomination, in 2002 only 6% of respondents cited some sense of identification or attachment to religious organizations.[24] Elsewhere the lowest levels of personal religious affiliation (to both Welsh and English medium faith groups) were in the de-industrialized counties of Rhondda Cynon Taff and Blaenau Gwent.[25] This arguably reflects the progressive internal fracturing of these socially excluded communities.[26]

In conversations that I have had with Christian faith group leaders in South Wales it is clear that they now see these areas as mission fields. The collapse of local church and chapel affiliation has less to do with a turning away of local populations from religion *per se* and more with the preoccupation of these people with trying to cope with poverty, crime (particularly the vice-like grip that heroin, alcohol and other drugs have gained on these communities) and general social exclusion. Clearly, economic factors are still at work and, if religious institutions are symbolic mirrors of society, the parlous state of many churches and chapels reflects the condition of the local communities in which they are situated. Along with local people, churches and chapels have struggled to make sense of these changes and to adapt to a world where all the certainties that underpinned customary community life have been blown away by the effects of deindustrialization. Arguably, it is now when the very foundations of the welfare state are being brought into question and where frontline services are being rapidly eroded in a bonfire of public service finance cuts that local organizations, whether religious or secular, are progressively more needed. The key question here is: are Christian congregations able to step up to the mark?

For the majority of nonconformist congregations the answer is no. Wales has too many small congregations housed in too many buildings. These congregations neither have the human and financial resources to make an impact on their local communities, nor are they in the long term sustainable. The historic churches struggle with material and human resources but are able, through the use of church halls and school buildings, to maintain meaningful links with their local communities. Many (but by no means all) evangelical congregations are perhaps the best placed of all in terms of resources (human and financial) and sustainability.

---

[23]   N. Charles, C. Aull Davies, C. Harris, *Families in Transition: Social Change, Family Formation and Kin Relationships* (Bristol: Policy Press, 2008), pp. 198–9.

[24]   N. Charles, *Families*, p. 38.

[25]   D. Dunkerley, 'Wales' Changing Population', pp. 123–4.

[26]   Bevan Foundation *Poverty and Social Exclusion in Wales* (Cardiff: Bevan Foundation, 2010).

Even if they have the means, however, they do not always demonstrate the will. The evangelical culture within Wales for most of the twentieth century leant towards insularity and separation. Matters changed with the establishment of the Evangelical Alliance Wales and particularly its support for political devolution in Wales in 1997, the appointment of a political officer in 1998 and the establishment of the Gweini (literally, 'to serve') network of socially involved congregations in 1999.[27]

Gweini, The Council of the Christian Voluntary Sector in Wales, is now a relatively mature organization with growing levels of experience in many fields of social action and social entrepreneurship. It is also committed to making this experience available to the wider Christian community and to encouraging congregations to work towards becoming a transforming influence within their local communities. In essence this looks very much like a return to the 'nonconformist' conscience whereby effective 'social work' becomes a channel for the spiritual revival of communities.[28] This was echoed in the theme of the 2010 Gweini National Autumn Conference, *The Church and the "Big Society"*. Speakers and delegates repeatedly emphasized that this concept was nothing new for them and that they had been 'doing Big Society' for a decade prior to Cameron's co-option of the term. The mainstream denominations and Churches have also recognized the need to engage meaningfully with local communities and training for clergy and laity has been ongoing throughout the past decade.[29]

Faith in Wales – Faith in Communities

Arguably, the current long-term economic crisis (and the recent change of government) offer opportunities to faith groups to pursue this vision as civil society is being called upon to plug the gaps opened by the progressive contraction of the Welfare State at both national and local levels. Taking David Cameron at his word, the idea of 'Big Society' also seeks to expand civil society as an end in itself. As I shall demonstrate from recent research, there is increasing evidence in Wales (and in the UK generally) that faith groups are progressively getting involved in community development and regeneration and that they can still make a very significant contribution to community wellbeing.[30] Working within socially

---

[27]   P. Chambers and A. Thompson, 'Public Religion and Political Change in Wales' *Sociology*, 39.1 (2005), pp. 29–46.

[28]   For a helpful overview of related issues, see G. Bowpitt, 'Working with Creative Creatures: Towards a Christian Paradigm for Social Work Theory, With Some Practical Implications' *British Journal of Social Work*, 30 (2000), pp. 349–64.

[29]   P. Chambers and A. Thompson, 'Public Religion', pp. 43–5.

[30]   G. Smith with G. Kulothungan, *Newham Twenty Years On: A Research Report for Communities in Transition and CULF* (London: Communities in Transition and CULF, 2006), pp. 32–50.

excluded communities can be daunting and overwhelming, as Bowpitt notes in his study of ministry in Urban Priority Areas, but it can also be rewarding both in terms of the personal development of congregations and in terms of mission and raised congregational profiles.[31] While active involvement in communities is not a guarantee of church growth it nevertheless can establish and nurture those social networks that are a necessary, if not sufficient, condition for church growth. Moreover, from the perspective of local communities, their expectations of faith groups seem to lie rather more with what groups do than with what they preach.

For example, in a recent survey commissioned by the Presbyterian Church of Wales in 2009, containing data from 1,009 interviews with adults resident in Wales, the most recognized denomination was the Salvation Army (87%). I think it is fairly safe to say that this high recognition rate relates mainly to the social work activities that the Salvation Army is known for or possibly their fairly high visibility when fundraising. It is unlikely to be due to the conservative theology or the fairly puritanical lifestyle of its members. The point being made here is that, quite often, non-churchgoers have a set of expectations based around 'good works' rather than theological niceties and around social capital rather than spiritual capital. This is reflected again in the fact that 70% (rising to 80% of people aged 55+) of respondents saw a continuing role for churches and chapels in their local communities. In terms of potential Christian involvement in communities, comments from non-members surveyed included a desire to see churches orientated more along community centre and advice shop lines, more focus on the community rather than 'religion', support for the children of lone parents and the provision of these services with no religious strings attached. These sentiments were most strikingly summed up by the respondent who said 'Just try and step away from all that Bible stuff, chapter this and that. Take what they've learned and apply it to people's real lives.' In this same survey, some PCW members argued that, despite the parlous general situation of the church, some congregations were engaging with local communities and that, where possible, this was the way forward. These engagements included strong links with local schools, children's clubs and the homeless and support for charities and debt advice, as well as making buildings available to local community groups.[32]

Within this same report, the Roman Catholic Church receives almost as high a recognition score as the Salvation Army with the Church in Wales coming in fourth. Arguably, this high visibility is linked to the number of primary and secondary schools that both churches operate in Wales. Around 55,000 pupils attend 168 Anglican schools and 99 Catholic schools that are fully integrated into the Welsh

---

[31]   G. Bowpitt, *The Clergy in the Local Community* (Nottingham: York House Publications, 1999), pp. 134–45.

[32]   A. Blunt and O. Bowyer, *Presbyterian Church of Wales: Key Research Findings* (Cardiff: Beaufort Research, 2009).

educational system (Welsh Assembly Government, 2009).[33] Both churches set great store by the schools, which are seen as an investment in the future. So much so that the former Catholic Archbishop of Wales, Peter Smith, in an interview with the author (Cardiff, 1 July 2008) indicated that he would be prepared to close most, if not all, of his churches in order to safeguard Catholic education. As he pointed out, Mass can just as easily be said in a school hall as in a church. Anglican commitment to their places of education also remains strong. Parish churches still remain important social hubs in communities, most notably in rural areas where the parish church and church hall are virtually synonymous with 'community'.[34] Drilling down into one diocese, Swansea and Brecon, a dedicated rural advisor has established regular contacts with farmers at eight markets and works closely with small communities in decline or in danger of decline. With rural pubs and shops shutting and the closures of rural schools, the parish church is quite often the only local institution left. Faith in Families, a new initiative, runs eight family and child orientated projects in some of the most deprived areas of Swansea. These include Family Centres and 'Flying Start' projects. They are now developing a new Family Centre in Brecon. In a pattern that is becoming increasingly common these projects are part funded by Welsh Assembly Government, Local Government, Children in Need and Gwalia Trust, with the shortfalls being made up by the Mothers Union, the Diocese and local parishes.[35]

A relatively recent report carried out jointly by Gweini and The Wales Council for Voluntary Action seeks, for the first time in Wales, to quantify the contribution made by Christian faith communities to Welsh civil society.[36] Based on a national survey of all existing faith communities (and with a 50% response rate), it identifies what churches are doing, the numbers of mobilized volunteers and the spaces made available to civil society groups, as well as the general picture in terms of the contribution of faith groups to Welsh society. Thirty-five areas of service were recognized, the most numerous being 'traditional' areas of activity such as hospital visiting, children's work, social activities including lunch clubs and coffee bars, marriage preparation and bereavement. There has been a concerted move to engage with emerging needs including employment training, alcohol and drugs awareness and personal debt and this trend looks likely to increase with many indications of interest from congregations.

Two thirds of those faith congregations surveyed reported at least one form of community service with most being involved in an average of five activities. These services are delivered by over 42,000 volunteers and the total numbers of hours put into these activities is estimated at approximately 80,000 per week,

---

[33] Welsh Assembly Government, *Schools in Wales: General Statistics 2009* (Cardiff: WAG Statistical Publication Unit, 2010).

[34] C. Harris and R. Startup, *The Church in Wales: The Sociology of a Traditional Institution* (Cardiff: University of Wales Press, 1999).

[35] *Swansea and Brecon Directory* (Cardiff: Church in Wales Publications, 2010).

[36] J. Evans, *Faith in Wales*.

equivalent to 2,000 full-time workers. The 1,400 paid staff are also employed by faith groups, putting in 23,000 hours weekly, equivalent to 575 full-time workers. Another important dimension of community involvement is the provision of premises for local community use, arguably enhancing civil society in Wales. Some 18,000 faith groups rent rooms to other groups, often at a nominal charge, and 11,000 offer free accommodations. In total this amounts to 35,000 room hours per week. There is also a growing trend among congregations to replace outmoded places of worship with 'new build' community centres and there are now 600 of these in Wales. Faith groups also maintain 1,600 listed buildings with 200 categorized as Grade 1, welcoming 2.5 million tourists a year while being heavily involved in supporting the Welsh language – around 800 congregations provide Welsh language classes or activities for Welsh speakers. All in all, the Wales Council for Voluntary Action estimates that the economic value of all these activities is conservatively equivalent to £102 million per year. Much of this is self-financed by faith groups but there is also a growing trend towards partnership with government, charities and the National Lottery and 500 faith groups are participating in government sponsored regeneration activities or local Community Strategies. The Welsh Assembly Government (WAG) has been, from its inception, willing to work with faith communities and more so with the recent successful referendum for greater devolved law-making powers. This arguably opens up the potential for greater faith group recognition in the fields of social action and entrepreneurship. Without wanting to step outside the Welsh remit of this chapter, none of this is going on in a vacuum and similar trends appear to be present in England and Scotland, particularly within the *Faithworks* movement. [37]

Doing the Stuff

Much more research needs to be carried out on the linkages between faith groups, social entrepreneurship and community regeneration and cohesion. One such recent study by Rhys Price deploys four case studies in order to explore these themes at the level of local communities.[38] All four congregations are evangelical churches committed to social action within their surrounding communities by means of generating bridging social capital. Three are based in urban areas and one in a former mining village. All are ministering in areas of varying social deprivation and are orientated towards meeting locally articulated needs.

'Centre A' was established in 1999 and is a purpose-built community centre prominently located in the shopping complex at the heart of a local authority estate built in the late 1980s. The community has a significantly higher number

---

[37]   www.faithworks.info, accessed 20 July 2011.

[38]   R. Price, *How Can Organisations with a Significant Christian Ethos use the Social Enterprise Model in Delivering Significant Community Benefits?* (MSc, University of Glamorgan Community Regeneration Unit, 2010).

of ethnic minority residents than is usual in Wales. Originally a church plant with a clear vision of local service, it immediately set about surveying the residents of this estate and three surrounding estates with a view to establishing what services were needed. A Community Interest Company was established and this provides a nursery, coffee shop, conference and seminar hire facilities. The centre is open 12 hours a day, seven days a week and constitutes a hub for local social activity, including adult education which involves training and health advice (a qualified nurse works two and a half a week and also does home visiting). The centre services a number of contracts for the local authority (including *First Opportunity*, a scheme for disadvantaged children) and has aligned itself with Welsh Assembly Government regeneration policy priorities. The centre is self-financing and is breaking even. It employs a number of local people as well as deploying many unpaid volunteers and providing work experience opportunities for young people. Approximately 200 to 300 clients a week visit the coffee shop and many of the services are accessed through local word of mouth. The centre (after some soul searching) also provides a prayer room for local Muslims, reflecting its ethos of responding to what local people want. After 12 years the centre has a prominent role within the local community and has built up high levels of trust and many collaborative connections with other local organizations.

'Centre B' is situated in a former mining village which scores fairly high on the Wales Index of Multiple Deprivation in terms of unemployment, chronic illness and lack of educational qualifications. The congregation originated in the wake of the 1904 religious revival and the first church building was erected in 1933. This building was demolished in 2005 to make way for a purpose-built, community-relevant centre, including fitness facilities, training rooms and conference facilities (it was partly funded by Welsh Assembly Government and various charities who matched the initial £120,000 raised by the congregation). This was in response to a strong vision of re-positioning the church as a potential hub of community transformation by taking the gospel to the community in practical ways. By 2006 the congregation had trebled and the centre is extensively used by local residents. There is a strong emphasis on sport and children's activities and the centre is often utilized by the local authority, the local health trust and other organizations. Fifty volunteers are currently engaged in running a food and furniture bank. They also run a nationally recognized youth mentoring project, which works in tandem with the local youth offending team and which originated from within the congregation. The centre is a partner with the local authority in engaging with young people in education, employment and training. All their education courses are fully subscribed. While initially deeply dependent on grants (and this remains so with some activities), the centre is moving to becoming financially self-sustaining in many areas of activity. This church has been used by WAG as a model example for community regeneration. The church leadership is committed to collapsing the distinction between sacred and secular activities and represents a successful record of development from a traditional church to a multi-purpose community hub.

'Centre C' was built in the mid-1970s as a combined church and sports centre (at the same time as the housing estate it is based in was built) and was converted into a multi-purpose community centre in the mid-80s. Its ethos is to serve equally both the spiritual and material needs of local people. It is situated in an area of mixed housing with some areas of marked social deprivation. These deprived areas have high levels of crime and various forms of anti-social behaviour, low incomes and an education, skills and training deficit. Two wards feature in the top 10% of the Welsh Multiple Deprivation Index. The purpose-built centre is situated in a housing estate that is part of a Neighbourhood Improvement Programme and offers sporting facilities and an arts and advice centre. The congregation identifies strongly with the local community and is a mission-focused church. Other activities include work with the homeless, the elderly and debt advice. The Centre is very actively involved in work with young people, including parents and toddlers groups, schools visits, youth clubs and work with young people at risk, as well as providing building space for voluntary groups. The Centre has two full-time youth workers and members of the congregation are trustees in schools and the Centre works closely with the local authority's Community Education Officer.

Active involvement with volunteers from the local community is exemplified in community work parties that seek to improve the local environment and, significantly, volunteers are recruited through word of mouth, suggesting a high level of penetration into the local un-churched community. Financing for these activities is mainly generated internally through sustainable sacrificial giving, although this is augmented by grant monies for specific partnership initiatives and activities. Relations and co-operation with local government are good and the Centre receives substantial funding from the Legal Services Commission for its Advice Centre work, which is carried out in its main office and a number of out-centres. This work is not insignificant and in one year (2006–07) helped 1,118 clients access over £1 million additional benefits and to write off or re-negotiate nearly £4 million of debt. Underpinning all these activities are careful research into local conditions and needs, a commitment to a theology of personal spiritual growth and a commitment to the vulnerable and to good relations within the local community. It has adapted from a 'church' to being an organization that has become a significant provider of local services for the benefit of the local community. In terms of its status as 'church' it benefits from high levels of local trust, reflecting its presence since the inception of the surrounding estate.

'Centre D' is a purpose-built community centre located in an urban setting on a large local authority housing estate with significant levels of deprivation, including a level of male unemployment 38% above the city norm. Managed by a seven-person trust established in 1999, this is a private limited company with charitable status whose aims are to encourage and develop a local sense of community through practical care and support and to promotion personal self-development, primarily through a Community Education Centre. The centre is largely self-financing through room hire and related grants. Services are, once again, taken up largely through local word of mouth, suggesting a significant degree of local penetration into the surrounding community. Unlike the cases highlighted above, this faith group exhibits more open tensions between members committed to the social vision of community development and those who would seek to prioritize conventional evangelism. This spills over into occasionally difficult relations with the local authority, although not with WAG. The centre constitutes a highly visible hub for the local community. Local people are supportive of both its activities and the fact that it has now been a presence in the local community for over a decade. This case is perhaps more representative of where many churches are in relation to their local communities and in terms of internal tensions over their overall mission vision.

Future Trends

These churches, and many thousands more like them in England, Wales and Scotland are off the radar for most academics, like Bruce, who are concerned with focussing on statistical measures of religious belief and church membership. This needs to be redressed, not least because the trends rehearsed above appear to represent a significant sea change and a potential new direction for faith communities through which they can reconnect with their local communities in mutually meaningful ways. Within the evangelical sphere this represents a significant theological shift, although in many conversations with faith group leaders they see this trend as a re-appropriation of nineteenth century evangelical custom and practice. What is more novel, and this also positions them alongside their mainstream counterparts, is the growing partnership with both government and other local voluntary groups.

Proponents of the secularization thesis would probably want to argue that this is a form of 'internal secularization' but from the perspective of faith groups this is seen in more pragmatic terms. Increasingly, WAG may be seeking to co-opt faith groups into community projects but it is apparent that many of these groups retain a clear sense of religious mission. For the foreseeable future and given the current threatened rolling back of the public sector, opportunities for faith-related community work are likely to wax rather than wane. Increasingly, the will is there and, through matched spending particularly, so are the means. Rather than the progressive marginalization of religion we are arguably witnessing increasing cases of a return to public significance at the local level and the opening up of opportunities to reconnect with local un-churched and de-churched populations through the establishment of bridging networks.

This certainly opens up the prospect of church growth for congregations willing and able to re-invent themselves for twenty-first century conditions. While the political situation in England is more fluid in terms of commitment to the idea of 'Big Society', government in Wales has consistently sought to engage with and make use of the particular talents and levels of commitment that faith groups can bring to the community regeneration table and has been prepared to back this with funding. This has been made easier by the fact that faith communities are well integrated into the quasi-governmental Wales Council for Voluntary Action.

The jury remains out on how and in what ways the Westminster government might facilitate faith-based community involvement in community cohesion and regeneration. These trends in Wales are not happening in a vacuum and there are similar developments in England and Scotland.[39] With a nod to Bruce, one also has to recognize that mainland Britain is a far less religious and far more secular society, (although, arguably, this may be less the effect of declining or changing religious beliefs and more the consequence of a general decline in voluntary associations, secular and religious as noted by Day).[40] In Wales, the resulting problem for the churches is that there are far too many congregations and places of worship relative to the general population. These are in the main ageing congregations whose lack of sustainability is clear to any engaged observer. An emerging, leaner and fitter Church with far more local impact, however, is not a bad trade off and, at the very least, means a continued visible and viable social role for Christianity into this century.

A Conclusion of Sorts

This chapter began with a critique of Steve Bruce's theoretical position. I have a number of reservations about Bruce's take on the secularization paradigm. Firstly, it focuses almost entirely on statistical measures of contemporary religious decline and ignores or denies areas of religious growth on the ground. Secondly, it is increasingly out of kilter with the modern world and that includes, at the very least, the recent experience of Britain's major urban conurbations. Thirdly, it focuses primarily on the nature of religious belief, ignoring or not understanding that religious practice encompasses far more than belief and is as much about belonging and the mundane affairs of this world. Fourthly, it is essentialist in character, seeking to impose theory on a social and cultural world that is far more diverse and dynamic than developmental theories of modernity will allow. Fifthly, it refuses to admit that, historically, faith groups have demonstrated a great capacity to adapt to social, cultural and economic change. Within the Welsh context, religion has largely adapted to primary economic change and the social and cultural developments that have accompanied these changes. While one might stretch the secularization thesis to encompass all aspects of modernity, including economic change, it then becomes a theory so broad in its reach that it has little or no concrete efficacy. Certainly the Welsh experience has historically shown little congruence with the orthodox secularization paradigm and continues not to do so.

It seems to me that the turn to Bourdieu within the sociology of religion can prove helpful with respect to many of these problems. In jettisoning the idea of

---

[39]   www.faithworks.info, accessed 20 July 2011.

[40]   G. Day, *Making Sense*.

secularization as a process in favour of the recognition of fields of action and the generation of symbolic capitals, we regain the potential to marry theory with data in ways that do not distort the reality on the ground. Clearly the dominant field in UK society is secular but this does not preclude faith groups from having the right types of capital (or the wrong types) to operate within this field. Certainly, at this moment in time, some faith groups are increasingly able to generate types of social capital that resonate both with their local fields and with the Welsh political and governmental field. Particularly important here is the notion of bridging capital that allows for the building of fairly robust social networks, joining congregations with their surrounding local population and opening up the possibility of church growth. At the same time it is clear that many of the failing congregations of Wales have an overabundance of bonding capital that actively inhibits them from any meaningful wider local engagement. The challenge for faith groups in Wales is to negotiate the transition from holding vast amounts of bonding capital to repositioning themselves in relation to their local social environments and creating bridging capital. I do not want to imply that this transition is easy but, as the Welsh research data rehearsed in this chapter demonstrates, it can and is happening.

Chapter 15

Northern Irish Protestantism: Evangelical Vitality and Adaptation

Claire Mitchell

Rumours of Northern Ireland's secularization have been greatly exaggerated. Whilst recent social and political changes in the region have been transformational, religion in Northern Ireland is interesting for its persistence as much as for its change. This is particularly the case for evangelical, or born-again, Protestantism in Northern Ireland, which has demonstrated a remarkable capacity for adaptation. As the peace process has taken root, evangelical Protestantism has begun to move away from its traditional political roles and is less likely to make headline news. Instead, it is finding cultural relevance in other arenas, for example in debates around sexual morality for conservative, or social justice for liberal, evangelicals.

The fact that religion continues to thrive in Northern Ireland may be surprising to commentators who assume that secularization is the natural order of things, except for where religion props up deeper ethnic divisions.[1] The logical conclusion of this argument is that, once conflict wanes, religion will follow suit. This, however, is manifestly not the case. Levels of church attendance in Northern Ireland continue to be high, belief in God, heaven and hell remain strong and attitudes to morality are more conservative than in any other part of the UK. Based on indicators like these, Fahey, Hayes and Sinnott argue that Northern Ireland still ranks amongst the most religious societies in Europe and indeed the world.[2]

Of course different religious subgroups within Northern Ireland are changing in different directions. A group of people who identify as having 'no religion' has emerged over the last 20 years and is slowly growing. Catholicism has undergone significant individualization alongside some decline in traditional practices. But Protestantism in Northern Ireland is holding more of its traditional shape. Levels of churchgoing, always around the 40–50% mark, have not changed radically

---

[1] J. McGarry, and B. O'Leary, *Explaining Northern Ireland* (Oxford: Blackwell, 1995); S. Bruce, *God is Dead: Secularisation in the West* (Oxford: Wiley Blackwell, 2002).

[2] T. Fahey, B. Hayes and R. Sinnott, *Conflict and Consensus: A Study of Values and Attitudes in the Republic of Ireland* (Netherlands: Brill Academic Publishers, 2005).

since the 1960s.[3] And whilst mainline Protestantism is undergoing some decline, evangelical, or born-again, Protestantism has actually experienced some growth.[4]

This chapter focuses on evangelical Protestantism in Northern Ireland, arguing that it presents a formidable challenge to the assumptions of secularization theory. Evangelicals are those Protestants who believe that one must be converted or 'born-again', that the Bible is the inspired word of God, that the crucifixion was necessary to save the world and that faith must be exercised through social action and evangelism.[5] Sometimes evangelicalism is characterized as conservative Protestantism[6] but it also contains people with more liberal dispositions who share a commitment to these basic tenets. It is an active subgroup within Protestantism that is growing around the world[7] and represents roughly one third of Northern Ireland's Protestants.[8] This chapter shows how evangelicals have found ways to adapt their faith in the face of rapid social and political change and to remain numerically strong and culturally relevant. It underlines the diversity of ways in which evangelicals have responded to change – from those who have become more conservative, even apocalyptic in their beliefs, to those who have taken their faith in a more post-modern direction.

A 'Subcultural' Theory of Cultural Adaptation

Berger argued in 1967 that modernity brings individuals into contact with other perspectives and erodes religious certainties. A generation ago, sociologists predicted that this would inevitably lead to secularization and the decline of religious identities.[9] But this has turned out not to be the case. Instead, increasing attention is now being paid to the ways in which religion is appropriated,

---

[3] C. Mitchell, *Religion, Identity and Politics in Northern Ireland: Boundaries of Belonging and Belief* (Aldershot: Ashgate, 2005).

[4] J. Brewer, 'Continuity and change in contemporary Ulster Protestantism,' *The Sociological Review*, 52.2 (2004), pp. 265–83.

[5] D. Bebbington, *Evangelicalism in Modern Britain: A History from the 1730s to the 1980s* (London: Unwin Hyman, 1989).

[6] R. Johnston, 'Evangelicalism', in A. Hastings, A. Mason and H. Pyper (eds), *The Oxford Companion to Christian Thought* (Oxford: Oxford University Press, 2000), pp. 117–220.

[7] P. Berger, ed., *The Desecularization of the World: Resurgent Religion and World Politics* (Grand Rapids: Eerdmans, 1999).

[8] C. Mitchell and G. Ganiel, *Evangelical Journeys: Choice and Change in a Northern Ireland Religious Subculture* (Dublin: UCD Press, 2011).

[9] S. Bruce, *God is Dead: Secularization in the West* (Oxford: Wiley-Blackwell, 2002); C. Brown, *The Death of Christian Britain: Understanding Secularisation 1800-2000* (London: Routledge, 2001).

transformed, resisted, revised and used to make sense of the complexities of late modern societies.[10]

One of the seminal studies in this area is Christian Smith's book on American evangelicalism.[11] Smith calls evangelicalism a 'subcultural identity' that 'thrives on distinction, engagement, tension, conflict and threat' from and with wider society.[12] Drawing from social identity theory,[13] Smith argues that the human desire for belonging is satisfied by orientation to social groups, that groups seek to maintain boundaries between themselves and other social groups and that groups often define themselves against relevant out-groups. Smith maintains that religious groups have always adapted to their cultural surroundings. In contemporary societies pluralism strengthens religion as it clearly delineates out-groups, as well as meaning that religion now satisfies a need to belong in an increasingly unsettling late modern world.

As Smith develops these ideas in the context of American evangelicalism, we begin to see how religious movements creatively adapt to cultural and political changes over time. Where the evangelical enemy may once have been Communism, now secular modernity and Islam have taken centre stage. Whereas television and cinema were once anathema for evangelicals, now most have accepted their role in modern society and in fact use these media for their own ends. Indeed, the literature is full of examples of how personal religion is shaped by wider social and political change.[14] The questions posed in this chapter then, are how far evangelicals in Northern Ireland have adapted to change and what this might tell us about secularization in late modern societies.

A Brief Profile of Religious Change in Northern Ireland

Before exploring evangelicalism in depth, it is worth taking a moment to locate it within the wider context of religious change in Northern Ireland. One trend

---

[10]   N. Ammerman, 'Religious identities and religious institutions', in M. Dillon (ed.), *The Handbook of The Sociology of Religion* (Cambridge: Cambridge University Press, 2003), pp. 207–24.

[11]   C. Smith, *American Evangelicalism: Embattled and Thriving* (Chicago: University of Chicago Press, 1998).

[12]   Ibid., p. 89.

[13]   H. Tajfel and J. Turner, 'An integrative theory of intergroup conflict', in W. Austin and S. Worchel (eds), *The Social Psychology of Intergroup Relations* (Monterey, CA: Brooks-Cole, 1979), pp. 33–47.

[14]   For example, M. Dillon and P. Wink, *In The Course of a Lifetime: Tracing Religious Belief, Practice and Change* (Berkeley: University of California Press, 2007); E. King, *The Image as an Agent in the Social Construction of Identity: Shifting Images and Evolving Religious Identifications in Contemporary Northern Ireland* (PhD, Queen's University Belfast, 2007).

that has emerged is religious de-identification. Overall 12% of respondents to the Northern Ireland Life and Times Survey in 2009 said that they have no religion.[15] This is significantly higher than the 364 people who identified themselves as atheists, freethinkers or humanists in the 1961 census.[16] However, it is interesting to note two things about those with 'no religion'. First, that although their growth has been steady, it is also slow, and the non-religious remain a minority within Northern Ireland. And, second, that this group may not be as secular as we might think, with 33% of those with 'no religion' saying they believe in God,[17] 39% believing that the Bible is the word of God,[18] and 10% even praying on a daily basis.[19]

Of the two major faiths in Northern Ireland, Catholicism is following the trajectory of the secularization thesis most closely. In 1968, 95% of Catholics reported that they attended mass every week, compared to 53% in 2009.[20] Across Ireland, Catholics' religious beliefs are becoming increasingly individualized as people sift through aspects of traditional doctrine, accepting some tenets and rejecting others.[21] Moreover, the moral authority of the Church has been seriously damaged in the wake of the sexual abuse scandals of the 1990s and 2000s.[22] Catholicism continues, however, to form a significant part of identity in Northern Ireland and still plays a large role in organizing social life.[23] But for some it has become a communal identity that does not need to be accompanied by religious beliefs or practices. In this sense, we can argue that, although Catholicism is far from being a dimly burning flame in Northern Ireland, secularization has steadily chipped away at its dominance over the last 30 years.

---

[15]   *Northern Ireland Life and Times Survey 2009* (NILTS). Data available at: http://www.ark.ac.uk/nilt/, accessed 20 July 2011.

[16]   R. Rose, *Governing Without Consensus* (London: Faber and Faber, 1971).

[17]   *Northern Ireland Life and Times Survey 2008* (NILTS) . Data available at http://www.ark.ac.uk/nilt/, accessed 19 January 2012.

[18]   *Northern Ireland Life and Times Survey 2004* (NILTS). Data available at http://www.ark.ac.uk/nilt/, accessed 19 January 2012.

[19]   *Northern Ireland Life and Times Survey 2008* (NILTS). Data available at http://www.ark.ac.uk/nilt/, accessed 19 January 2012. See also C. Mitchell, 'Is Northern Ireland abnormal? An extension of the sociological debate on religion in modern Britain', *Sociology*, 38.2 (2004), pp. 237–54.

[20]   T. Fahey, B. Hayes and R. Sinnott, *Conflict and Consensus*; (NILTS 2009), data available at http://www.ark.ac.uk/nilt/, accessed 19 January 2012.

[21]   T. Inglis, 'Individualisation and Secularisation in Catholic Ireland' in *Contemporary Ireland: A Sociological Map* (Dublin: University College Dublin Press, 2007); T. Inglis, *Moral Monopoly: The Rise and Fall of the Catholic Church in Modern Ireland* (2nd ed., Dublin: University College Dublin Press, 2007); E. King, *Material Religion and Popular Culture* (London: Routledge, 2009).

[22]   T. Inglis, 'Catholic Identity in Contemporary Ireland: Belief and Belonging to Tradition', *Journal of Contemporary Religion*, 22.2 (2007), pp. 205–20.

[23]   C. Mitchell, *Religion and Politics in Northern Ireland.*

In contrast, levels of church attendance amongst Protestants are not dramatically lower than they were 40 years ago. In 1968, 46% of Protestants attended church weekly.[24] In 2009, 34% attended at least weekly and a further 11% attended two or three times a month.[25] So it is probably fair to say that 45% of Protestants are currently regular church attenders.

Analysing the Northern Ireland Social Attitudes Survey in 1991 and the Northern Ireland Life and Times Survey in 1998, Brewer concludes that the 1990s saw reduced levels of religious commitment, a liberalization of Christian beliefs, declining levels of regular observance and participation and an ageing membership amongst mainstream Protestants.[26] Brewer underlines that the loss of interest in mainstream Protestantism is particularly pronounced amongst young people.

But this is only part of the story. Brewer observes the growth of people identifying as 'other Christian', instead of Protestant, in recent years[27] and points out that smaller Protestant denominations, such as Pentecostal, charismatic and new churches, are growing.[28] Some of these are American offshoots, such as the Vineyard churches, whilst others are locally conceived, such as the Whitewell Metropolitan Tabernacle, an inner-city mega-church which attracts thousands of worshippers each week.[29] Reflecting global trends, Pentecostalism tends to be most popular amongst Northern Ireland's working classes whilst the charismatic churches have more – but not exclusively – middle class members.[30] Some of the members of these churches are new converts, whilst others are former mainline Protestants who have either moved to a more conservative evangelical position, or who have been attracted to 'the livelier and more youthful Christian traditions, which are evangelical but more Sprit-led than doctrinal'.[31]

Analysis of more recent Northern Ireland Life and Times Survey data also points to a degree of growth within evangelical Protestantism. Religious beliefs actually intensified for Protestants between 1998 and 2008. As many as 75% of Protestants said they believed in heaven in 1998, rising to 80% in 2008; 64% of Protestants said they believed in hell in 1998, rising to 69% in 2008. Most strikingly of all, whereas 46% of Protestants believed in miracles in 1998, this had risen to 57% in 2008. In addition to beliefs, more Protestants said they took

---

[24]   R. Rose, *Governing Without Consensus*, p. 264.

[25]   Northern Ireland Life and Times Survey (NILTS) 2009. Data available at http://www.ark.ac.uk/nilt/, accessed 19 January 2012.

[26]   J. Brewer, 'Continuity and change'.

[27]   J. Brewer, 'Are there any Christians in Northern Ireland?', in A. Gray, K. Lloyd, P. Devine, G. Robinson and D. Heenan (eds), *Social Attitudes in Northern Ireland: The Eighth Report* (London: Pluto, 2003).

[28]   J. Brewer, 'Continuity and change'.

[29]   L. Murphy, *Believing in Belfast: Charismatic Christianity After the Troubles* (Carolina: Carolina Academic Press, 2010).

[30]   D. Martin, *Pentecostalism: The World Their Parish* (Oxford: Blackwell, 2002).

[31]   J. Brewer, 'Continuity and change', p. 271.

part in church activities outside of church attendance in 2008 – 28%, compared with 21% in 1998. Looking at all of these measures together, we might argue that there has been an increase in religiosity in Protestantism. And, given the emphasis on conservative beliefs, this looks very much like a growth in the evangelical, charismatic and/or born-again grouping within Protestantism.

The remainder of this chapter is set within the context of these numbers, but presents a qualitative analysis of the ways that evangelicalism in Northern Ireland is changing. It shows how evangelicals have managed to remain culturally relevant as violent conflict has waned. What follows is informed by qualitative interviews conducted with evangelical Protestants in Northern Ireland over the last 10 years. Most of the data is from Mitchell and Ganiel's *Evangelical Journeys* which analyses interviews with 95 evangelicals and ex-evangelicals in Northern Ireland.[32] This research was interested in why people change their religious beliefs over time and shows how conservative and liberal evangelicals have changed in different directions in recent years, adding not only to the diversity, but to the vibrancy of the wider tradition.

Cultural Adaptation

Fifty years ago, evangelical teachings about life-style in Northern Ireland, as in America, were extremely strict. At the beginning of the twenty-first century, however, this has changed significantly. For example, Sabbatarianism, once a defining feature of Northern Irish evangelicalism, has now been softened.[33] Brewer points out that even the most conservative of evangelicals, the Free Presbyterians, have experienced some liberalization in their behaviour and attitudes.[34] Whilst they may ban line dancing at social functions, other attitudes such as beliefs about women in the church have liberalised to some extent.[35]

There are plenty of examples of these kinds of cultural adaptations in the interviews Ganiel and I conducted for Evangelical Journeys. Jan, a Free Presbyterian teacher in his 30s, for example, says he has retained 'the basics' of faith, but has liberalized his views on whether women should wear trousers and whether Christians can consume alcohol. Fifty-year-old civil servant Alexander continues to identify as a 'traditional evangelical', but he now allows his children not only to work in a cinema but to work on Sundays as well. In fact, many evangelicals say they hold fast to the important moral issues, such as an opposition

---

[32]   C. Mitchell and G. Ganiel, *Evangelical Journeys*.

[33]   N. Southern, 'Ian Paisley and evangelical Democratic Unionists: an analysis of the role of evangelical Protestantism within the Democratic Unionist Party', *Irish Political Studies*, 20.2 (2005), pp. 127–45.

[34]   J. Brewer, 'Continuity and change'.

[35]   See F. Porter, *Changing Women, Changing Worlds: Evangelical Women in Church, Community and Politics* (Belfast: Blackstaff Press, 2002).

to homosexuality, abortion and divorce. But they have compromised on peripheral cultural issues.

Daniel, a Baptist minister in his 50s, says that his way of being a conservative evangelical is 'very radically different' from that of his parents. He says:

> Everything about it is probably different. I remember the first Sunday I wore a blue shirt to church, oh wow, they made me take it off. Our model was you dressed a certain way to go to church, and that was always a white shirt under a suit and that would have been taken as part of what mattered. Now the Church I go to has no dress code, people could come as they come and that's up to them … Alcohol, cinema going … They are just not issues any more.

In these ways, evangelicals in Northern Ireland have managed to update their faith in relation to the changing world around them, so that they can be culturally relevant. In other words, evangelicals are able, slowly and over time, to adapt the social and moral issues that define them so that they can 'fit in' to an extent with the rest of society whilst retaining a distinctive religious view of the world.

Evangelical Strengthening in Response to Unionist Political Loss

Evangelicalism has always had an important connection to the politics of conflict in Northern Ireland. In fact, some commentators argued that conservative evangelicalism was only strong in Northern Ireland because it played political roles, providing ideological support for violence, passionate clergy who articulated unionist ideas and a rationale for anti-Catholic beliefs.[36] The assumption was that once conflict waned, evangelicalism would follow suit. Since the 1990s the political situation in Northern Ireland has changed dramatically. Violent conflict has decreased and even the strongest forms of unionism and loyalism are engaged in a political relationship their republican former enemies.

But just because the DUP have accepted the reality of working with Sinn Féin, it does not follow that all or most of their supporters (including both conservative evangelicals and secular non-evangelicals) approve of political change. In fact many Protestants feel that, whilst they have lost out from change, they have no option but to accept it. They have had to accept, for example, that the days of unionist dominance are over.[37] Police reform, restrictions on Orange Order parading and the release of political prisoners – all stemming from the 1998 Good Friday

---

[36]   S. Bruce, *The Edge of the Union: The Ulster Loyalist Political Vision* (Oxford and New York: Oxford University Press, 1994).

[37]   J. McGarry and B. O'Leary, *The Northern Ireland Conflict: Consociational Engagements* (Oxford: Oxford University Press, 2005).

Agreement – have been traumatic for many Protestants.[38] Some feel that a united Ireland is 'a done deal' and that nationalists have won the political argument.[39]

So what have conservative evangelicals made of this new political order? Has their faith been made redundant by the decline in violent conflict? So far, anyway, it seems that this is not the case. In fact, political change has made some evangelicals' faith even stronger. And it is *precisely because* they feel they have lost the political argument that some conservative evangelicals have come to experience a deeper faith. This argument is made in full in Mitchell and Ganiel's *Evangelical Journeys*, where a significant number of conservative evangelicals describe a deepening of their faith in the years since the 1998 Agreement. Amongst this group there was a withdrawal from politics and a renewed focus instead on saving souls, evangelism and conversion.

Some have come to view the Good Friday Agreement as a 'sign of the end times,' a signal of the second coming of Christ.[40] Billy, an Elim Pentecostal council worker in his 50s, for example, says that 'providential circumstances are being created in Northern Ireland to bring about evangelical testimony.' Helen, a public servant in her 40s and a once ardent supporter of the DUP who considered politics as a career, says she is now disillusioned with politics and asks 'why bother?' For her, the presence of 'murderers' in the Northern Ireland Assembly ties in with predictions in Revelation that in the last days evil men will rule the earth. She says:

> That's why politics – it is nothing. It certainly doesn't fire me up any more. I have absolutely no desire for it at all. The only desire now is to warn people, that Armageddon is definitely coming, that the apocalypse is not far off … the fact is that Christ is coming back, he's going to come back and sort out this mess.

Amongst this group of conservative evangelicals, global political developments also point towards the immediacy of the end times. Helen lists earthquakes, famines and floods as pointing to Armageddon whilst Billy lists political developments in Afghanistan, India, Pakistan and Israel. A shopkeeper in his 50s, Jeremy, agrees that the recent extreme weather is a marker of the end times and talks about the encroachment of the Anti-Christ.

Many conservative evangelicals in Northern Ireland, then, have been adapting to political change in exactly the way that Christian Smith described. They are revising and updating their faith to take account of wider political changes.

---

[38]   P. Shirlow and I. Shuttleworth, '"Who is going to toss the burgers?" Social class and the reconstruction of the Northern Irish economy', *Capital and Class*, 69 (1999), pp. 27–46; S. McKay, *Northern Protestants: An Unsettled People* (Belfast: Blackstaff, 2000).

[39]   C. Mitchell and J. Todd, 'Between the devil and the deep blue sea: nationality, power and symbolic trade-offs among evangelical Protestants in contemporary Northern Ireland', *Nations and Nationalism*, 13.4 (2007), pp. 637–55; C. Mitchell, *Religion and Politics in Northern Ireland*.

[40]   See also C. Mitchell and J. Todd, 'Between the devil and the deep blue sea'.

Indeed, Northern Ireland has changed so drastically from some conservative evangelicals' point of view that they have given up hope of achieving their aims politically. But rather than losing their faith, many individuals' evangelicalism has actually helped them adapt to this situation and, in some instances, has pulled their religious beliefs in an ever more apocalyptic direction. There is also evidence that ethno-national identities have become less important for this group as religious identity has taken precedence.[41] This is a fascinating example of how engagement with the modern political world can actually strengthen people's faith and poses a significant challenge to secularization theory.

New Public Roles: Conservative Evangelicals' Morality Agenda

If a focus on the 'end times' points to some Northern Irish evangelicals' serenity in accepting the things that they cannot change, a renewed focus on moral issues in political life highlights a courage to change the things that they can. As it became increasingly clear over the course of the 2000s that religiously informed unionism and loyalism in Northern Ireland were unpopular, an interesting trend began to emerge in which evangelicals began to explore how the new political structures could be used to promote some of their other religious goals – for example, opposition to homosexuality. This is interesting because it highlights how religion can stay *publically* relevant in modern societies, rather than simply being confined to the private sphere.

Analysis of the 1991 Northern Irish Social Attitudes Survey and the 1998 Northern Ireland Life and Times Survey highlighted evangelicals' growing emphasis on moral issues in public life during the 1990s.[42] For example, the DUP began to use equality legislation to argue that evangelicals ought to be allowed to set up faith schools with public funding.[43] They began to see that alliances could be made with Catholics in the SDLP and Sinn Féin to oppose abortion legislation.[44] Aghast at the legalization of civil partnerships in 2004, evangelical unionist politicians and advocacy groups began to see how the devolved administration at Stormont could be used to stave off secular legislation from the UK.[45]

---

[41]   C. Mitchell and J. Todd, 'Between the devil and the deep blue sea'.

[42]   C. Mitchell and J. Tilley, 'The Moral Minority: evangelical Protestants in Northern Ireland and their political behaviour', *Political Studies*, 52.4 (2004), pp. 585–602.

[43]   G. Ganiel, 'Explaining new forms of evangelical activism in Northern Ireland: Comparative perspectives from the USA and Canada', *Journal of Church and State*, 50 (2008), pp. 475–93.

[44]   In fact in a 2007 debate in the Northern Ireland Assembly, all four main political parties in Northern Ireland opposed the extension of the 1967 UK Abortion Act to Northern Ireland.

[45]   G. Ganiel, 'Ulster says maybe: The restructuring of evangelical politics in Northern Ireland', *Irish Political Studies*, 21.2 (2006), pp. 137–55; G. Ganiel, *Evangelicalism and*

What we can draw from this renewed emphasis on conservative morality is that evangelicalism in Northern Ireland is finding new ways to be politically relevant. It is not simply the case that they have given up hope for unionism and have retreated into the private sphere. On the contrary, conservative evangelicals are now beginning to use the new political structures in Northern Ireland to advance their religious goals. This is another important example of evangelical adaptation to political change.

Liberal Evangelicals: Using Experiences of Difference to Redefine Faith

We have focused so far on conservative elements under Northern Ireland's evangelical umbrella. But liberal evangelicals are responding to change in a rather different way.

One of the central tenets of secularization theory is that once people become exposed to new ideas, religious certainties are invariably challenged and this leads to a decline of faith.[46] And of course it is true that in modern societies people encounter more differing viewpoints and cultural practices than ever before and it is increasingly unlikely that religious beliefs will remain unchallenged. However secularization theorists failed to take into account the many different types of religious responses to encountering difference. Indeed, the fact that people can appreciate difference and maintain their faith is crucial to understanding contemporary religion. And evangelicalism, in Northern Ireland as elsewhere, is able to accommodate people who take this more inclusive approach to matters of faith.

In *Evangelical Journeys* we were interested to find similar patterns of experiences amongst evangelicals whose faith became more liberal over time, evangelicals who transformed their faith in a post-modern direction and evangelicals who abandoned their faith altogether. People in these groups all said that travel abroad and time living outside Northern Ireland had prompted them to rethink their faith. Similarly, engagement with popular culture – such as music, film and television – had posed challenges to people's faith and encouraged them to reflect on their beliefs. But what is interesting is that whilst some chose to abandon their faith as a result, many more decided to adapt their faith so that it made sense of their new experiences.

Gillian, for example, a Presbyterian teacher in her 30s, talked about the books of Douglas Copeland – modern American fiction that is full of existential questioning and ideas of redemption – as helping her think differently about her search for meaning in a modern world. Sammy, a Presbyterian youth worker in his

---

Conflict in Northern Ireland (New York: Palgrave, 2008); G. Ganiel, 'Explaining new forms of evangelical activism'.

[46]   P. Berger (ed.), *The Sacred Canopy: Elements of a Sociological Theory of Religion* (New York: Anchor Books, 1967).

40s, describes his early evangelicalism as 'fundamentalist', but his life-long love of rock music led him to Greenbelt, a large Christian music festival in England, where his newfound religious liberalism began to take shape. He cites bands like U2 as helping him think through his spiritual questions, to the point where he came to embrace a more liberal version of evangelicalism. Popular culture – such as music, books and films – allowed people to express creativity, to ask searching questions, to have space to think and to explore alternative Christian ideas and lifestyles. It provided an outlet to interrogate faith and to express difference whilst holding on to core Christian beliefs.

Similarly, where evangelicals encountered new ideas through travel and living outside Northern Ireland, we found that many used their new experiences to redefine, rather than abandon, their religious beliefs.[47] Joan is a student, a Baptist in her 20s from a rural part of Northern Ireland, who says she was led to reconsider her faith after time spent studying at a university in the United States. She describes the ethos of the university as 'feminist-feminist-feminist' and concerned with grassroots political action. When she returned to Northern Ireland, Joan found herself integrating these new insights into her faith. Rather than focusing on feminist rebuttals of faith, Joan started to think about how feminist ideas could improve her church for the better. In these ways we can see that modernity – with all the cultural mixing and cross-pollination of ideas it implies – does not necessarily erode religion so much as change its character for some.

An important question follows from this: viz., does the liberalization of religion lead to its inevitable decline? Casanova argued that strong versions of faith do best in the modern world, whereas more liberal renditions that do not have such clear lines of distinction with secular society invariably become diluted.[48] It remains to be seen if this is the case in Northern Ireland. Based on current evidence, however, I would tend to argue that liberal evangelicalism has helped shore up religion in Northern Ireland. It has provided a religious home for people who may otherwise have abandoned their faith. Furthermore, liberal evangelicalism has played important public roles in the peace process, in social justice work and in civil society.[49] This is a very different kind of evangelicalism to the conservative strand that sees the peace process in Northern Ireland as a sign of an impending apocalypse. But it is clear that it is no less able to adapt creatively to social and political change.

---

[47] See also G. Jordan, *Not of This World? Evangelical Protestants in Northern Ireland* (Belfast: Blackstaff Press, 2001).

[48] J. Casanova, *Public Religions in the Modern World* (Chicago: University of Chicago Press, 1994).

[49] G. Ganiel, 'Emerging from the Evangelical Subculture in Northern Ireland: A case study of the Zero28 and Ikon community,' *International Journal for the Study of the Christian Church*, 6.1 (2006), pp. 38–48.

Transformational Change Within Evangelicalism: The Emerging Church

Another group, this time on the peripheries of evangelicalism, helps us appreciate further why religion is not dead in late modern societies. The post-evangelical movement, sometimes called the 'emerging church', represents a group of people who enjoy the doubt and ambiguity of post-modern thinking and incorporate these ideas into their faith lives.[50] In Northern Ireland post-evangelicalism is a small movement, comprised mostly of highly educated middle-class people in Belfast.[51] Most come from evangelical backgrounds and continue to engage with faith but are very critical of the ways in which their churches have been involved in the conflict in Northern Ireland, have failed to take account of social justice issues and have been prescriptive about life-style issues. They come together in groups such as Ikon, which meets monthly in a pub, to reflect on religious and philosophical questions through readings, music, film and performance art.[52]

For post-evangelicals, doubt is embraced as something positive rather than threatening. But intense questioning exists in conjunction with spiritual seeking. Engaging with the grey areas is what makes their faith relevant. For example, Northern Irish born 'emergent' Peter Rollins says 'none of us know the answer … faith is something 'that you try to reach but never get there.'[53] Peter dislikes the claims that traditional evangelicalism makes to 'truth' but continues to engage with evangelical concepts, debates and churches, offering what he calls a 'friendly critique' of evangelicalism.

Sophie, a teacher in her 50s from Belfast, began her religious life as a teenager in a charismatic evangelical church, where she stayed until her early 40s. She says that, whilst she experienced doubts throughout this time, she chose to 'bury [her] head in the sand'. Eventually, after a series of bad experiences of in-fighting in her church, she left and for many years became disillusioned with religion. In recent years, however, Sophie has started to re-engage with her faith. She meets with like-minded friends in a weekly book group where they explore the 'difficult questions' of faith and doubt. For the first time, Sophie says she 'allowed [herself] to be honest.' Exploring the grey areas has, in fact, deepened Sophie's engagement with her faith. But this is an open-ended belief, encompassing more questions than answers. She says that science fiction helps her appreciate the mysteries of the universe and deepens her search for meaning and for God.

---

[50]   See P. Tickle, *The Great Emergence: How Christianity is Changing and Why* (Grand Rapids: Baker Books, 2008); B. McLaren, *A New Kind of Christianity: The Questions that are Transforming the Faith* (London: Hodder & Stoughton, 2010); J. Caputo, *What would Jesus Deconstruct? The Good News of Postmodernism for the Church* (Grand Rapids: Baker Academic, 2007).

[51]   G. Ganiel, 'Emerging from the evangelical subculture'.

[52]   Ibid.; P. Rollins, *How (Not) to Speak of God* (London: SPCK, 2006).

[53]   In C. Mitchell and G. Ganiel, *Evangelical Journeys*, pp. 153–4.

Post-evangelicals are interesting because they show us how evangelicalism, albeit in this quite avant-garde form, can co-exist with the uncertainties provoked by late- and post-modernity. This provides another important critique of secularization theory which never sufficiently took into account the ways that religion can transform to accommodate post-modern ideas and practices. As such, post-evangelicalism offers some people a means of staying connected with faith, where they may have otherwise left religion completely. Whilst it may not have mass appeal, it has re-energized internal debates within evangelicalism and it has shown another way that faith can respond to the challenges of cultural change.

New Converts

Before concluding, it is worth drawing attention to the fact that evangelicalism in Northern Ireland is also attracting new members. Many of these are 'agnostic' or 'cultural' Protestants who are discovering an active faith.

Some of the stories we heard in *Evangelical Journeys* pointed to events in the Northern Ireland conflict as triggering religious conversion.[54] John for example, a civil servant in his 50s, says that at the outbreak of conflict in 1969 he began to attend Paisley rallies solely to hear a political message but ended up becoming religiously converted. This is an interesting example of how cultural context influences personal religious change and chimes with research in other contexts where using religious symbols or rituals for political reasons stimulates a revival of religion itself.[55]

But, as contemporary Northern Ireland is less and less characterized by violent political conflict, we found few stories of politically triggered religious conversion in the 2000s. Instead, many more stories were rooted in people's family, social and professional lives. It was the death of his father that prompted Paul, a salesman in his 40s, to question 'eternal issues,' including a 'realisation of [his] own death,' which gave him 'a fear of God'.[56] Rachel, a full-time mother in her 30s, described how having children prompted her transition to evangelicalism as she began to worry about their souls. Other people spoke about ill-health, divorce and other family troubles catalysing their religious conversions.

The fact that evangelicalism continues to attract new members, in Northern Ireland and globally, is significant. Sometimes religion can become important to people engaged in political conflicts and to those adapting to new cultural contexts.

---

[54]   C. Mitchell and G. Ganiel, *Evangelical Journeys*.

[55]   For example, on the Serb-Croat conflict, see M. Sells, 'Crosses of blood: sacred space, religion and violence in Bosnia-Hercegovina', *Sociology of Religion*, 64.3 (2003), pp. 309–32.

[56]   On religion helping buffer a fear of death, see P. Wong, 'Meaning of life and meaning of death in successful aging,' in A. Tomer (ed.), *Death Attitudes and the Older Adult* (Philadelphia: Brunner-Routledge, 2000), pp. 23–35.

But daily life can bring just as much stress to people in times of political calm. Indeed it seems that, for many people in times of trouble, religion can provide significant emotional support.[57] And religion does not necessarily die out when a political or personal crisis subsides. In fact, once adopted in a time of stress, religion is just as likely to continue to be significant in the life of an individual going forward.[58] Whilst science has answered many questions for people who live in late modern societies, there are just as many areas of human experience that remain laden with uncertainty and anxiety. And it seems, in this context, that evangelicalism continues to be a significant source of reassurance and support for people who are looking for answers about life's existential questions.

Conclusions

This chapter has outlined a number of different ways in which evangelicals in Northern Ireland are adapting to social and political change. Although the social and political significance of evangelicalism was heightened during the Troubles, as conflict wanes, evangelicals have shown a remarkable capacity to adapt to a new cultural climate.

Conservative evangelicals have shown a surprising ability to update their political narratives, taking into account unionists' vastly reduced power base and the now unpalatable nature of religiously informed opposition to power-sharing. But, rather than shrinking into the background, many conservative evangelicals have re-evaluated their goals, concluding that political loss in Northern Ireland must be divinely ordained, as well as perhaps being a sign that the end times are drawing near. As a result they have a renewed energy for proselytism as well as a revised political agenda, concentrating on moral and lifestyle goals that seem more achievable, such as Northern Ireland's continuing stance against abortion and opposition to the extension of LGBT rights. Similarly, many conservative evangelicals have now softened their attitudes to the Sabbath, alcohol, the role of women and popular culture. And in relaxing these beliefs, evangelicals have been able to ensure that their faith continues to be culturally relevant. Indeed, it is an engagement with modern culture and capacity for adaptation which Smith argues lies behind the continuing strength of American evangelicalism.[59] And this is also the case in Northern Ireland.

But Northern Irish evangelicals are not all conservatives and those with a more liberal predisposition are responding to political and cultural change in rather

---

[57] C. Ellison and L. George, 'Religious involvement, social ties, and social support in a Southeastern community', *Journal for the Scientific Study of Religion*, 33 (1994), pp. 46–61.

[58] C. Mitchell, 'The religious content of ethnic identities', *Sociology*, 40.6 (2006), pp. 1135–52.

[59] C. Smith, *American Evangelicalism*.

different ways. Liberal evangelicals are very much engaged with the secular world and with popular culture and they are constantly exposed to new challenges to their faith. But rather than abandon their religion, many evangelicals revise, edit and adapt their beliefs in the light of their new experiences to arrive at a faith that makes sense for them. Some transform their faith more than others. Some post-evangelicals see ambiguity and doubt as integral to a healthy faith and enjoy faith as a journey of questioning rather than a set of definitive truths. And then there are those who convert into evangelicalism, in many cases returning as adults to the faith of their youth, often provoked by personal troubles and existential questions. In all of these cases we see how evangelicalism continues to thrive in Northern Ireland but in very different ways. Rather than being preserved unchanged, evangelicalism is being appropriated, edited and transformed to make sense of the complexities of life in the late modern world.

So what does this mean for the secularization thesis in Northern Ireland? Certainly the continuing health of evangelicalism must be viewed alongside the increase in numbers of those with 'no religion,' the de-traditionalization of Catholicism and indeed a degree of decline in mainstream Protestantism. But the perseverance and in fact growth of evangelicalism demonstrate that secularization is neither a given, nor a one-way street, in late modern societies. Rather than invariably being challenged by cultural diversity and rationality, believers respond to diversity and change in different ways. Of course some abandon religion altogether. But many others adapt traditional packages of faith, whilst others again edit and transform their beliefs to make sense of the changing world.

Conclusion

The Death and Resurrection of Christianity in Contemporary Britain

David Goodhew

"I congratulate all of you who have come here today because you could be watching the world cup," said London Mayor Boris Johnson from the stage.[1]

Boris Johnson was speaking at the 2010 'Global Day of Prayer', a gathering of thousands of London's Christians in the stadium of West Ham United football club. Johnson's readiness to be associated with an enthusiastically Christian event was in striking contrast to his fellow Conservative, the Prime Minister. David Cameron took pains to avoid associating himself with the 'Global Day of Prayer', fearing such religiosity might be unpopular amongst commentators and amongst the national electorate.[2] The same event caused one politician to fear electoral damage and another to sense electoral value. Cameron and Johnson's contrasting reactions illustrate how Christianity is both declining and growing in contemporary Britain.

A survey of the last 30 years shows that substantial church growth has happened across much of Britain. This growth is strongest in London but is by no means confined to the capital. Such growth crosses the denominations but there are two particular strands of vitality; black, asian and minority ethnic Christianity and new churches. There is significant growth amongst the indigenous British population and amongst established denominations. But there is large-scale church growth amongst black, asian and minority ethnic communities and in the new churches formed during the last 100 years. Such church growth has been happening across the last 30 years and beyond – and shows no signs of slowing down. The notion that all British churches are in inexorable decline is a myth.

However, there is no place for any ecclesiastical triumphalism. Depiction of church growth needs to be coupled with the already widely studied phenomenon of church decline. The key thing to note is that *parts* of the British church have seen serious and long-lasting decline during these same years – but *parts* have grown. British churches are experiencing *both* decline *and* growth. Britain has grown more secular *and* more religious in the last 30 years. It all depends where

---

[1]   http://www.eauk.org/articles/global-day-of-prayer-london.cfm, accessed 22 September 2011.

[2]   David Cameron at Prime Minister's Questions, 7 September 2011, http://www.epolitix.com/policy/education/education-article/newsarticle/epolitixcom-pmqs-briefing-37/, accessed 22 September 2011.

you look. Any portrait of the British church which focuses mainly on decline *or* on growth is unbalanced. This volume has concentrated on congregational growth, not because that is all there is to say but because such growth has been so widely ignored.

Putting together decline and growth amongst British churches shows a church changing very rapidly. In the last 30 years the British church has become much more ethnically diverse. The balance within the church is moving from the older 'mainline' churches towards the new churches. And, as that happens, a partial disestablishment is taking place as the established churches shrink and a new non-conformity grows up. This is 'disestablishment from below', in which the state is not consulted and of which the state is largely unaware. More generally, the British church is shifting from a religion of obligation towards one of consumption, from a religion of 'opting out' to a religion of 'opting in'. In regional terms, London and the South East are becoming more significant, whilst the importance of Wales, Scotland and parts of the north of England has diminished.

What then is the overall picture? The answer is 'confused'! This volume provides significant evidence that current national and regional statistics concerning churches should be treated with caution. In terms of numbers of churches, it is likely that the overall number of congregations in Britain is roughly stable. Those who wring their hands (or dance with joy) at 'thousands of churches closing' are both mistaken and need to recognize that thousands of churches have been opening, too. The number of churches in Britain is static, overall. In terms of numbers of worshippers, more research is needed to pass an overall judgement. Current research shows great variation; some churches are seeing serious decline in attendance, others are seeing significant growth. Figures from the 2011 Census have yet to be properly analysed but they suggest that national levels of affiliation to Christianity have declined markedly since the last census in 2001. It could be that British culture is growing more akin to that of the early Christian centuries in which Christian faith acts as a kind of 'counter-culture', capable of vigorous growth, amidst a wider culture which is essentially non-Christian in tone. Thus we have the paradox that in the recent Census Londoners were the least likely to describe themselves as 'Christian' of any region in Britain, yet London's churches are growing faster than anywhere else in the country.[3] A country or city can, at the same time, grow more secular by one measure and less secular by another.

All this means that the secularization thesis has serious flaws with regard to Britain. The thesis contains truth but is far from the whole truth. In some post-industrial, mainly white cultures – especially where there is an established state church – there has been serious church decline. Thus, the secularization thesis fits parts of the UK, notably parts of Scotland and Wales and parts of England. Even here, however, there are significant signs of church life. But the secularization thesis simply does not work for London, Northern Ireland and for a number of other centres, for people from ethnic minorities and for the newer churches (let alone

---

[3]   www.yougov.polis.cam.ac.uk/archive, accessed 21 September 2011.

many of the non-Christian faiths). For such regions and communities, insights from outside of Britain and Europe are essential for accurate understanding.

The secularization thesis only ever worked in parts of the western world; in America and much of 'the Global South' it is recognized as having limited value. Britain is sometimes seen as culturally and politically straddling the divide between Europe and America. This volume suggests that it increasingly straddles the religious divide between the secularity of, say, Sweden and the robust religiosity of Ghana or China. In religious terms, Britain sits between 'the west' and 'the rest'. In such a context, the insights of Rational Choice Theory (as well as other challenges to secularization theory) deserve consideration.[4] Rational Choice Theory (RCT) is not without its flaws but the exclusion of its voice from most debates in British academia, media and church circles says more about the narrowness of those debates than the validity of RCT. Those churches which have embraced the pluralistic world in which they increasingly work have tended to thrive; those which have presumed still to live in Christendom, where the population is expected to have some residual sense of obligation to believe, have tended to decline. This data fits RCT better than it fits the secularization thesis.

In all discussions, a regional perspective is crucial; growth is far stronger in certain areas of Britain than in others. It is notably strong in London and its environs, along the 'trade routes' of modern Britain and in Northern Ireland. Conversely, decline is strongest in parts of Scotland, Wales and in parts of England which are distant from economic and demographic dynamism. The more multicultural and the more economically buoyant an area, the more likely it is to have growing churches. The absence of such factors is more likely to correlate with decline. This does not mean that all of London's churches are growing nor, for instance, that all of Cumbria's churches are shrinking. However, it is imperative that any assessment of church growth and decline is alert to regional dynamics. It is much harder to grow a church in Kilmarnock than in Kensington.

We should cease thinking in terms of a zero-sum game in which society is *either* becoming more secular *or* more religious. Rather, parts of Britain and parts of society and culture are growing more secular and other parts are growing less secular. A single city may well exhibit both church decline and church growth. Depending on where you look in Britain, both the secularization thesis and RCT have validity. Consequently there is a great need for detailed academic research on the history of church growth and decline. The secularization thesis has cast a baleful shadow in this regard, skewing research to focus on decline. As a result, many vigorous expressions of Christianity fly beneath the radar of contemporary academia. One of the chief aims of this volume is to adjust that radar.

This research has significance for wider society. As the Freedom Centre International (FCI) in Peckham shows, church growth can feed creatively into

---

[4] For a good introduction, see: G. Davie, *The Sociology of Religion* (London: Sage 2007), pp. 67-88.

empowerment and upliftment of communities.[5] But, as the FCI in Peckham also shows, the theological dynamism which fuels such positives also fuels strands which wider society finds less easy to deal with. Just as government, industry and education are having to learn to relate to growing non-Christian communities in Britain, so wider society needs to learn to relate to growing Christian communities.

The most significant ramifications of the research from this volume are for the churches themselves – particularly those that are called (with decreasing accuracy) the 'mainline' denominations. The hegemony of the secularization thesis has instilled in many mainline churches and church leaders an implicit (and sometimes explicit) eschatology of decline – which has led in turn to an ecclesiology of fatalism. The tide of history is assumed to belong to the secular. Hanging on in quiet desperation is the way of much of the English (and British) mainline church. Anyone with experience of churches outside Western Europe may find such a mindset bizarre and, increasingly, it is becoming untenable within the UK as well.

The research in this volume suggests that churches and church leaders can let go of the secularization theory, its eschatology of decline and its ecclesiology of defeat. The research in this volume and wider global experience show that in many places – even in Britain – churches can grow and that decline is not inevitable. The secularization thesis was only ever partly true. Amongst leaders and members of the mainline churches, where growing churches are generally in the minority, there are strong reasons for humility. This study raises the uncomfortable question as to whether mainline leaders and churches can learn from growing congregations beyond the mainline. It is intriguing to ask, for instance, what might happen if Britain's cathedrals could emulate the ecclesiastical entrepreneurialism of Britain's black-led churches.

Whilst many mainline churches and church leaders could let go of the eschatology of decline, other churches and church leaders may need to beware an 'eschatology of victory'. Amy Duffuor's chapter on the way a new church is 'moving out' geographically from the inner city and thereby 'moving up' sociologically is a warning. There is a well-worn path for faith communities from growth to social betterment to eventual decline. The growing churches need to take seriously the question of how they avoid losing their edge, especially as many of their members better themselves socially. More generally, the growth of ethnic minority churches and new churches brings with it additional responsibility. They have, hitherto, tended to interact to a limited degree with wider society and the wider church. Part of the challenge of the coming decades is for such churches to connect deeply with public discourse and to take more of a lead in a new ecumenism which encompasses all Britain's churches and is less dominated by the mainline.

The formation of eschatology is a theological project but one which needs to be informed by sociology and history. It is striking that church growth has happened

---

[5]   For a different example, see: J. Timothy, Pastoral Care and Counselling in the Black Churches in Britain: with Special Reference to those in Leeds (PhD, Leeds, 1990).

predominantly amongst those churches that are unashamed of the core doctrines of Christianity, though often happy to adapt culturally. Analysis of local churches offers building blocks for theological insight. Forming eschatology also requires a nuanced historical perspective. Dominic Erdozain's recent work on modern history, showing how nineteenth century Christians redefined their understanding of sin in a way that fed directly into secularization, is an excellent illustration of why historical perspective matters.[6] Working towards an eschatology that is resistant to both secularization theory and secularization on the ground is an urgent task, but the evidence of this volume suggests that many local churches are ahead of many theologians in this work.

The study of church growth in Britain since 1980 produces remarkable results. Alongside the phenomenon of church decline there has been substantial church growth in Britain since 1980. That growth is focussed in London and amongst black, asian and minority ethnic communities and amongst new churches. But such growth extends across much of Britain and across a range of churches. Recognition of such growth requires a sea-change in academic study (including theology), in wider society and in the churches themselves – which have too often been fixated by decline. There has been resurrection, as well as death, across the British church in the three decades since 1980.

---

[6] D. Erdozain, 'The Secularisation of Sin in the Nineteenth Century', *Journal of Ecclesiastical History*, 62.1 (2011).

Select Bibliography

Aldred, J. *Respect: Understanding Caribbean British Christianity* (Peterborough: Epworth, 2005).

Archbishops' Council, *Mission-Shaped Church: Church Planting and Fresh Expressions of Church in a Changing Context* (London: Church House Publishing, 2004).

Ashworth, J. and Farthing, I. *Churchgoing in the UK; A Research Report from Tearfund on Church Attendance in the UK* (Teddington: Tearfund, 2007).

Bebbington, D. *Evangelicalism in Modern Britain: A History from the 1730s to the 1980s* (London: Unwin Hyman, 1989).

Berger, P. *The Desecularisation of the World: Resurgent Religion and World Politics* (Grand Rapids: Eerdemans, 1999).

Brierley, P. *Pulling out of the Nosedive: A Contemporary Picture of Churchgoing* (London: Christian Research, 2006)

Brown, C. *The Death of Christian Britain* (London: Routledge, 2001).

Bruce, S. *Choice and Religion: a Critique of Rational Choice Theory* (Oxford: OUP, 1999).

Bruce, S. *God is Dead: Secularisation in the West* (Oxford: Blackwell, 2002).

Bruce, S. 'Religion in Rural Wales: Four Restudies', *Contemporary Wales* 23 (2010).

Bullivant, S. 'Sociology and the Study of Atheism', *Journal of Contemporary Religion* 23.3 (2008).

Carnes and A. Karpathakis, T. *New York Glory: Religions in the City* (New York: New York University Press, 2001).

Casanova, J. *Public Religions in the Modern World* (Chicago: University of Chicago Press, 1994).

Chambers, P. *Religion, Secularization and Social Change* (Cardiff: University of Wales Press, 2005).

Davie, G. *Religion in Britain Since 1945: Believing without Belonging* (Oxford: Blackwell, 1994).

Davie, G. *Europe: the Exceptional Case. Parameters of Faith in the Modern World* (London: DLT, 2002).

Davie, G. *The Sociology of Religion* (London: Sage, 2007).

Davison A. and Milbank, A. *For the Parish: a Critique of Fresh Expressions* (London: SCM Press, 2010).

Dobbelaere, K. *Secularisation: An Analysis at Three Levels* (Frankfurt am Main: Peter Lang, 2002).

Erdozain, D. 'The Secularisation of Sin in the Nineteenth Century', *Journal of Ecclesiastical History* 62.1 (2011).

Finke, R. and Stark, R. *The Church of America, 1776-1990: Winners and Losers in our Religious Economy* (New Brunswick, NJ: Rutgers University Press, 2005).

Garnett, J. (et al), *Redefining Christian Britain: Post 1945 Perspectives* (London: SCM, 2006).

Gill, R. *The Empty Church Revisited* (Aldershot: Ashgate, 2003).

Goodhew, D. 'Growth and Decline in South Africa's Churches, 1960-1991', *Journal of Religion in Africa* 30.3 (2000).

Greeley, A. *Religion in Europe at the End of the Second Millennium: A Sociological Profile* (London: Transaction Publishers, 2003).

ter Haar, G. *Halfway to Paradise: African Christians in Europe* (Cardiff: Cardiff Academic Press, 1998).

Hastings, A. *A History of English Christianity, 1920–2000* (London: SCM Press, 2001).

Heelas, P. and Woodhead, L. *The Spiritual Revolution: Why Religion is Giving Way to Spirituality* (Oxford: Blackwell, 2005).

Hirschle, J. 'From Religious to Consumption-Related Routine Activities? Analysing Ireland's Economic Boom and the Decline in Church Attendance', *Journal for the Scientific Study of Religion* 49.4 (2010).

Hornsby-Smith, M.P. *Roman Catholics in England: Studies in Social Structure since the Second World War* (Cambridge: CUP, 1987).

Hornsby-Smith, M. (ed.), *Catholics in England, 1950-2000: Historical and Sociological Perspectives* (London: Geoffrey Chapman, 1999).

Horwood, T. *The Future of the Catholic Church in England* (London: Laicos, 2006).

Hull, J. *Mission-Shaped Church: a Theological Response* (London: SCM, 2006).

Jackson, B. *Hope for the Church : Contemporary Strategies for Growth* (London: Church House Publishing, 2002).

Jackson, B. *The Road to Growth: Towards a Thriving Church* (London: Church House Publishing, 2005).

Jackson, B. and Piggot, A. 'Another Capital Idea: Church Growth and Decline in the Diocese of London 2003-2010' (unpublished report for the Diocese of London, 2011, available on the Diocese of London's website www.london. anglican.org).

Jenkins, P. *The Next Christendom: the Coming of Global Christianity* (Oxford: OUP, 2002).

Kay, W. *Pentecostals in Britain* (Carlisle: Paternoster, 2000).

Kay, W. *Apostolic Networks in Great Britain: New Ways of Being Church* (Milton Keynes: Paternoster, 2007).

Kelley, D. *Why Conservative Churches are Growing: A Study in Sociology of Religion* (Macon: Mercer University Press, 1996).

Kepel, G. *The Revenge of God: the Resurgence of Islam Christianity and Judaism in the Modern World* (Cambridge, Polity Press, 1994).

Livesey, L. *Public Religion and Urban Transformation: Faith in the City* (New York: New York University Press, 2000).

McCleary, R. *The Oxford Handbook of the Economics of Religion* (Oxford: OUP, 2011).

McLeod, H. 'Being a Christian at the end of the Twentieth Century', in H. McLeod, (ed.), *World Christianities, c. 1914–2000, Cambridge History of Christianity* (vol. IX; Cambridge: CUP, 2006).

McLeod, H. *The Religious Crisis of the 1960s* (Oxford: OUP, 2007).

Marler, P.L 'Religious Change in the West: Watch the Women' in K. Aune, (ed.), *Women and Religion in the West: Challenging Secularisation* (Farnham: Ashgate, 2009).

Martin, D. *Tongues of Fire: the Explosion of Pentecostalism in Latin America* (Oxford: Blackwell, 1990).

McClearey, R.M. (ed.) *The Oxford Handbook of the Economics of Religion* (Oxford: OUP, 2011).

Mitchell, C. *Religion, Identity and Politics in Northern Ireland: Boundaries of Belonging and Belief* (Aldershot: Ashgate, 2005).

Mitchell, C. and Ganiel, G. *Evangelical Journeys: Choice and Change in a Northern Ireland Religious Subculture* (Dublin: UCD Press, 2011).

Norris, P. and Inglehart, R. *Sacred and Secular: Religion and Politics Worldwide* (Cambridge: CUP, 2004).

Osgood, H.J. 'African neo-Pentecostal Churches and British Evangelicalism 1985–2005: Balancing Principles and Practicalities', (PhD, School of Oriental and African Studies, University of London, 2006).

Perriman, A. (ed.), *Faith, Health and Prosperity: A Report on 'Word of Faith' and 'Positive Confession' Theologies* (Carlisle: Paternoster, 2003).

Randall, I.M. *The English Baptists of the Twentieth Century* (Didcot: Baptist Historical Society, 2005).

Smith, C.S. *American Evangelicalism: Embattled and Thriving* (Chicago: University of Chicago Press, 1998).

Spencer, A.E.C.W. (ed.), *Digest of Statistics of the Catholic Community of England & Wales, 1958-2005: Volume I* (Tauton: Russell-Spencer, 2007).

Sturge, M. *Look What the Lord has Done! An Exploration of Black Christian Faith in Britain* (Bletchley: Scripture Union, 2005).

Virgin, P. *The Church in the age of Negligence: Ecclesiastical Structure and the Problems of Church Reform, 1700–1840* (Cambridge: Clarke, 1989).

Voas, D. and Crockett, A. 'Religion in Britain: Neither Believing nor Belonging', *Sociology* 39.1 (2005).

Voas, D. 'Religious Decline in Scotland', *Journal for the Scientific Study of Religion* 45.1 (2006).

Walford, R. *The Growth of 'New London' in Suburban Middlesex and the Response of the Church of England* (Lewiston, NY and Lampeter: Edward Mellen Press, 2007).

Ware, K. 'The Orthodox Church in the British Isles', in C. Chaillot (ed.), *A Short History of the Orthodox Church in Western Europe in the Twentieth Century* (Paris: Inter-Orthodox Dialogue, 2006).

Warner, R. *Secularisation and its Discontents* (London: Continuum, 2010).

Warner, R.S. *New Wine in Old Wineskins: Evangelicals and Liberals in a Small Town Church* (Berkeley: University of California Press, 1988).

Woodhead, L. and Catto, R. *Religious Change in Modern Britain* (London: Routledge, 2012).

Index